DATE DUE   W9-AEH-390

HT
148
.S6
L58
1982

Living under
apartheid

DATE			
			JAN '89
		MAR '84	

KVCC   KALAMAZOO VALLEY
COMMUNITY COLLEGE
LIBRARY

55103

ER & TAYLOR CO.

LIVING
UNDER
APARTHEID

The London Research Series in Geography

1 *The land of France 1815–1914*
  Hugh Clout

2 *Living under apartheid*
  David Smith (editor)

3 *London's Green Belt*
  Richard Munton

4 *Urban hospital location*
  Leslie Mayhew

  Nature's ideological landscape
  Kenneth Olwig

  Prehistoric land use in south-east Spain
  John Thornes and Antonio Gilman

HT
148
.S6
L58
1982

LIVING UNDER APARTHEID

Aspects of urbanization and social change
in South Africa

Edited by David M. Smith

Department of Geography, Queen Mary College, London

London
GEORGE ALLEN & UNWIN
Boston   Sydney

KVCC   KALAMAZOO VALLEY
COMMUNITY COLLEGE
LIBRARY

55103

FEB 1 4 1984

© D. M. Smith & Contributors, 1982
This book is copyright under the Berne Convention. No reproduction
without permission. All rights reserved.

George Allen & Unwin (Publishers) Ltd,
40 Museum Street, London WC1A 1LU, UK

George Allen & Unwin (Publishers) Ltd,
Park Lane, Hemel Hempstead, Herts HP2 4TE, UK

Allen & Unwin Inc.,
9 Winchester Terrace, Winchester, Mass 01890, USA

George Allen & Unwin Australia Pty Ltd,
8 Napier Street, North Sydney, NSW 2060, Australia

First published in 1982

British Library Cataloguing in Publication Data

Living under apartheid.
  1. Blacks – South Africa – Segregation
2. Anthropo-geography – South Africa
I. Smith, David M.
323.1'68   DT763

ISBN 0–04–309110–5

Library of Congress Cataloging in Publication Data

Main entry under title:
Living under apartheid
  Bibliography: p.
Includes index.
1. Urban policy – South Africa – Addresses, essays,
lectures. 2. Urbanization – South Africa – Case studies.
3. Blacks – South Africa – Segregation – Case studies.
I. Smith, David Marshall, 1936–
HT148.S6L58   1982   305.8'00968   82–11605
ISBN 0–04–309110–5

Set in 10 on 12 point Bembo by Nene Phototypesetters Ltd, Northampton
and printed in Great Britain by Mackays of Chatham

'These restless broken streets where definitions fail – the houses the outhouses of white suburbs, two-windows-one-door, multiplied in institutional rows; the hovels with tin lean-tos sheltering huge old American cars blowzy with gadgets; the fancy suburban burglar bars on mean windows of tiny cabins; the roaming children, wolverine dogs, hobbled donkeys, fat naked babies, vagabond chickens and drunks weaving, old men staring, authoritative women shouting, boys in rags, tarts in finery, the smell of offal cooking, the neat patches of mealies between shebeen yards stinking of beer and urine, the litter of twice-discarded possessions, first thrown out by the white man and then picked over by the black – is this conglomerate urban or rural? No electricity in the houses, a telephone an almost impossible luxury: is this a suburb or a strange kind of junk yard? The enormous backyard of the whole white city, where categories and functions lose their ordination and logic . . .

. . . a "place"; a position whose contradictions those who impose them don't see, and from which will come a resolution they haven't provided for.'

Nadine Gordimer, *Burger's daughter* (1979).

Preface and acknowledgements

This book originated from a visit to South Africa in 1979. Two months lecturing and travelling enabled me to renew contact with a number of South African scholars with whom I had worked while on the staff of the Universities of Natal and of the Witwatersrand in 1972–3, and to meet others investigating various aspects of apartheid. This time also provided the opportunity to revisit parts of the country and see some of the changes that had taken place during the intervening years. It soon became apparent that certain features of the process of urbanization had become increasingly significant, as responses to apartheid and as a challenge to the power of the state to control the spatial form of development. Principal among these features were spontaneous (or 'squatter') settlement and associated 'informal' kinds of economic activity. The papers brought together in this volume reflect current research into these and other aspects of urbanization in South Africa, in the general context of contemporary social change.

The visit to South Africa in 1979 was sponsored in part by the Students' Union of the University of Cape Town. I am very grateful to Professor R. J. Davies, Head of the Department of Geography, for making the arrangements and for putting so much of his time at my disposal, and to both Ron and Shirley for their warm hospitality during some Cape winter weekends. Other UCT staff who helped me in various ways included Paul Andrew, David Dewar, Neil Dewar and Franco Ferrario. Opportunities to lecture and engage in discussions were also provided by the Universities of the Western Cape, Stellenbosch, the Witwatersrand, Pretoria, Durban and Durban–Westville; I am grateful to the staff in these institutions for the courtesy with which they received a visitor whose highly critical view of apartheid was not always shared. Professor P. Smit of the Human Sciences Research Council was good enough to take me again through part of Bophuthatswana that we had visited together in 1973. Financial assistance provided by the Hayter Fund and the Central Research Fund of the University of London is gratefully acknowledged.

Publication of a collection of papers is dependent on the co-operation of a large number of individual participants. I am extremely grateful to all the contributors for completing their papers to a tight deadline and for responding promptly to editorial queries. John Browett read the entire collection during the tenure of a visiting appointment in the Geography Department, Queen Mary College in autumn 1981 and made many valuable suggestions. Most of the maps and diagrams were drawn in the Cartographic Unit of the Geography Department at Queen Mary College, under the supervision of Lynne Fraser.

I owe a special debt of gratitude to Professor T. J. D. Fair, formerly Director of the Urban and Regional Research Unit, University of the Witwatersrand and now Director of the Institute for Social and Economic Research at the University of Durban–Westville. It was Denis Fair who first aroused my interest in development studies in general and South Africa in particular, while we were colleagues at Southern Illinois University in the late 1960s. I have gained much from his experience and understanding of Southern Africa, most pleasurably during many convivial evenings in Carbondale, Johannesburg and London. My family and I will always be grateful to Denis and Betty for their friendship and hospitality over so many years.

Finally, thanks to Margaret, Michael and Tracey, who have shared my discovery of South Africa from Kruger Park to Crossroads, the Witwatersrand to the Western Cape. We know both the beauty and the tragedy of this country, and are the richer for it. I hope that whatever understanding is conveyed in this book will contribute, however indirectly, to the eventual liberation of a land that means much to us all.

DAVID M. SMITH
Loughton, Essex
Christmas 1981

Contents

Preface and acknowledgements   *page* ix

List of tables   xiv

Introduction
DAVID M. SMITH   1

1 *The evolution of unequal development within South Africa: an overview*
   JOHN BROWETT   10
   The era of colonial conquest   10
   The era of mineral discovery   14
   The era of segregation   17
   The era of apartheid   20
   Conclusion   23

2 *Urbanization and social change under apartheid: some recent*
   developments
   DAVID M. SMITH   24
   Background   25
   The production and reproduction of cheap labour   27
   Employment prospects, social stability and property rights   30
   Spontaneous and planned urban development in the Western Cape   32
   Urbanization in the homelands: the case of Bophuthatswana   38
   Conclusion   44

3 *Apartheid, decentralization and spatial industrial change*
   CHRISTIAN M. ROGERSON   47
   The industrial system of apartheid South Africa   47
   Decentralization and spatial industrial change   53
   Conclusion   62

4 *Migrant labour and frontier commuters: reorganizing South*
   Africa's Black labour supply
   ANTHONY LEMON   64
   The legislative framework   65
   Spatial patterns of migrant labour flow   67
   Changing perspectives of the mining companies   71

Farm labour   *page* 77
Effects of labour migration on the source areas   77
Frontier commuters: a new apartheid concept   82
Directions of government policy   87
Conclusion   88

5 *Urbanization in the homelands*
P. SMIT, J. J. OLIVIER and J. J. BOOYSEN   90
Demographic features of the homelands   91
Urbanization in 'white' South Africa compared to the homelands   93
Consequences of homeland urbanization   101
Conclusion   104

6 *The informal sector of the apartheid city: the pavement people of*
   Johannesburg
K. S. O. BEAVON and C. M. ROGERSON   106
Informal activity as a response to structural unemployment   107
The urban informal sector under apartheid: a case study of street
trading in Johannesburg   111
Conclusion   122

7 *Urbanization, unemployment and petty commodity production*
   and trading: comparative cases in Cape Town
D. DEWAR and V. WATSON   124
Introduction   124
An empirical study   127
The policy response   138

8 *Informal housing and informal employment: case studies in the*
   Durban Metropolitan Region
GAVIN MAASDORP   143
Legislative impediments and official policies   143
The Durban Metropolitan Region   144
Surveys in informal settlements   147
The informal sector   154
Conclusion   160

9 *Segregation and interpersonal relationships: a case study of*
   domestic service in Durban
ELEANOR PRESTON–WHYTE   164
The racial ecology of Durban   165
The nature of domestic service   167
Conclusions   182

10 *Council housing for low-income Indian families in Durban:*
    objectives, strategies and effects
    PETER CORBETT   183
    Policy objectives for Indian housing in Durban   184
    Policy strategies for Indian housing in Durban   187
    Conclusion   196

11 *Government dispensation, capitalist imperative or liberal*
    philanthropy? Responses to the Black housing crisis in
    South Africa
    J. P. LEA   198
    The Black housing question   199
    The post-Soweto reforms   203
    Conclusion   215

12 *The geography of urban social control: Group Areas and the*
    1976 and 1980 civil unrest in Cape Town
    JOHN WESTERN   217
    Spatial planning for social control: theory   218
    Patterns of riot, spatial and aspatial   221
    The effectiveness of spatial planning in practice   226

    Conclusion
    DAVID M. SMITH   230

    Bibliography   236

    Contributors   250

    Index   253

List of tables

2.1 Distribution of population and income by race, 1977   *page* 27
2.2 Selected economic and social indicators by race   27
4.1 *De jure* and *de facto* homeland population in relation to migrant
     labour   68
4.2 Foreign migrant labour in South Africa, 1973–80   69
4.3 White–Black mine wage differentials and Black wage increases   71
4.4 Sources of South African mine labour, June 1979   72
4.5 Residence and workplace of frontier commuters, 1976   83
5.1 The rural–urban distribution of population in 'white' South
     Africa and the homelands in 1980   91
5.2 Increases and decreases in homeland population, 1970–80   92
5.3 Total Black homeland population, 1980   97
5.4 Number of houses built and expenditure on housing for Blacks
     in 'white' areas and in the homelands from 1967/8 to 1976/7   98
5.5 Estimated number of commuters from homelands, 1979   103
6.1 Numbers of fixed stands in the restricted area of Johannesburg   119
6.2 Characteristics of hawking in central Johannesburg   120
7.1 Comparison of sample areas   128
7.2 Petty production and trading: some international comparisons   132
7.3 Distribution of petty production and trading according to
     activity in Cape Town sample areas   134
7.4 Petty production and trading in Cape Town: weekly turnovers,
     expenditures, profits and capital investments   135
7.5 Percentage of petty producers and traders generating under
     R50 profit weekly   136
7.6 Average number employed per business   137
8.1 Percentage distribution of migrants by reason for migrating,
     Clermont   149
8.2 Percentage distribution of temporary urban dwellers by sex
     and factors influencing date of return migration, Clermont   151
8.3 Comparison of major perceived needs – African and Indian
     squatters   154
8.4 Comparison of housing aspirations – African and Indian squatters   154
8.5 Percentage distribution of operators in the informal sector in
     Clermont by category, sex and origin   157
10.1 Poverty in Chatsworth, April 1977: percentages of sample   190
10.2 Monthly income of applicants for Indian housing, March 1981   193
10.3 Monthly rentals for different types of dwelling at Phoenix by
     income category, March 1981   194
11.1 Chief donors to the Urban Foundation of South Africa,
     October 1978   207

Introduction

DAVID M. SMITH

Few countries attract such sustained interest as South Africa. The racial discrimination formalized in the policy of apartheid is a focus of constant media attention, both in its own right and in association with other events ranging from sports boycotts to riots. The nature of South African society offers a continuing challenge to social science, revealing a complexity that narrow interpretations confined to race or class conflict fail fully to comprehend. South Africa has a special fascination for the geographer and others concerned with spatial analysis, for apartheid comprises a state-directed reorganization of the spatial structure of society, economy and polity on a scale with few if any contemporary parallels. Indeed, it would not be too much of an exaggeration to describe apartheid as the most ambitious contemporary exercise in applied geography.

Despite many predictions to the contrary, the general framework of the policy of apartheid, introduced when the Nationalists first came to power in 1948, has now survived for a third of a century. It has proved to be resilient and flexible, and largely successful in its own terms. The whites still rule, capital flows in and continues to profit, social stability has been maintained for the most part and South Africa retains its self-styled status as a bastion of what it considers to be the 'free world'. Indeed, the prosperity of an economy still highly sensitive to the price of gold, together with the prospects of some rapprochement with the USA under President Reagan's administration, gives the Nationalist regime an appearance of greater strength than at any time since the Sharpeville massacre of 1960.

But the impressions of stability and strength themselves obscure the inevitability of change and its potential threat to the political and economic *status quo*. Apartheid is ridden with tensions and contradictions, the resolution or at least control of which may be possible in the short run, but which in the long run must surely transform South African society in some fundamental way – for better or worse. Quite significant changes are already taking place. The administration of Prime Minister P. W. Botha has set in motion developments which are seen in some quarters as strengthening the rigid control of the cheap (black) labour economy which is central to apartheid, but which are convincing enough as 'liberal' relaxations of racial domination to have provoked a marked right-wing backlash in the 1981 general election. These changes have important implications for the lives of the blacks, as they seek work and shelter within new legal or administrative structures.

Other changes are taking place with less deliberation and central direction. For blacks the key to survival or relative prosperity is some kind of foothold in the economy of white-controlled metropolitan areas. However much the government may resent it, or even deny the fact itself, the process of urbanization is taking on a momentum of its own, with spontaneous settlements spreading on the edge of most major towns and cities. As new urban forms emerge, they become part of the reality promoting or constraining further economic, political and social change. It is in this sense that the black population is helping to create its own future, both because of and in spite of apartheid, in the everyday struggle for material existence.

Before proceeding further, some comments on terminology are required. The very nature of South Africa's apartheid system requires the application of a racial nomenclature. Officially there are four groups, the Asians (largely of Indian descent), the Blacks (formerly officially termed the Bantu, or the indigenous African people), the Coloureds (of mixed blood) and the whites. The Asians, Blacks and Coloureds are sometimes referred to together as 'blacks', to express a collective identity and avoid the possibly perjurative term 'non-whites'. This usage of black is indicated throughout the book by lower-case 'b' as opposed to the capital letter to indicate the Black or African population.

As a matter of convenience it is frequently necessary to refer to certain parts of South Africa as 'white'. They are deemed to be so in apartheid legislation, e.g. 'white' areas or 'white' cities. We employ quotation marks to indicate this usage, recognizing that they are 'white' *de jure* even if not *de facto* (by virtue of the number of blacks who also live there) or by right in any moral sense.

A difficulty in adopting the accepted terminology is the possibility of indirectly bestowing legitimacy on the social reality that has generated them, namely apartheid itself. This is exemplified with particular effect by the term 'homeland' used to denote the former tribal reserves now set aside under apartheid for the African population in the form of independent nation states. In a footnote in Chapter 3 (p. 51), Rogerson quotes the journalist and author John Kane-Berman's acute appreciation of the danger of adopting the term homeland. To paraphrase, this is to concede a terminological victory to the ideologues of apartheid, for to say that a certain area is the homeland of the Zulus, for example, is to imply that the rest of South Africa is not; thus insidiously the term homeland gains general currency and helps to shape political thought. The same could be said for the expressions 'separate development' and 'multi-nationalism' that are adopted in government circles to dignify the splitting up of national territory under apartheid. Rogerson's solution to the problem of the term homeland is to adopt the alternative of 'Bantustan' with its derisory overtones. Elsewhere in this book, however, we do use the term homeland as the generally understood shorthand for a facet of apartheid the true meaning of which we seek to clarify in our analysis.

This collection of papers is an attempt to provide an up-to-date account of how the process of change is affecting certain aspects of the lives of black people. The primary focus is on urbanization as a crucial feature in the spatial organization of South Africa's society and economy, and on its implications for housing and employment. Particular emphasis is placed on the emergence of what is usually referred to as informal sector activity, as a source of shelter and work for blacks. It will be shown that South Africa reveals features of underdeveloped countries on a scale not generally appreciated; some contribution may thus be made to the broader field of underdevelopment and development studies.

The papers brought together here are all based on recent research. The contributors include both South African scholars and others who have chosen to specialize on various facets of South African society. Most are geographers by both training and present professional identity, but few have been constrained by a narrow disciplinary perspective. There are two economists and one anthropologist, as well as three whose affiliation is now with urban and regional planning. (Biographical notes on the contributors will be found on pp. 250–2.)

The primary objective of the collection is to set down some facts and interpret them within what should, for the most part, be familiar methods of analysis. We have tried to avoid using the case of South Africa for exercises in pretentious theorization or moralizing polemics; the tone of the collection is thus largely empirical and non–judgemental, with matters of conceptualization and social evaluation left implicit for the most part. The choice of contributors and topics has been governed·more by the interest of the research findings available than by an attempt on the part of the editor to provide a comprehensive and tightly integrated coverage of all aspects of life affected by the process of urbanization. However, it is hoped that the picture provided is coherent if not complete. The brief summaries of the papers that follow are offered as an aid to readers seeking the threads of continuity that bind the individual contributions together.

In the first chapter John Browett offers an overview of the emergence of unequal development in South Africa, in time and in space. This provides an historical context for subsequent chapters, as well as background information for readers less familiar with South African affairs. The account recognizes four periods of development. The first – the era of colonial conquest – saw the white settlers force the indigenous people into a subservient position so that, supplemented by imported workers, they would satisfy the needs of the whites for cheap labour. The second was the era of mineral discovery, which greatly changed the space economy and stimulated demand for labour on an unprecedented scale. Then came the era of segregation, under which spatial separation of the races began to be enshrined in legislation to prevent the permanent settlement of large numbers of Black workers in 'white' cities. Finally, the era of apartheid has seen the earlier

trends consolidated as crucial elements in the state's policy of racial domination in the interests of the effective functioning of the capitalist mode of
production. Browett stresses the complex interrelationship of economic,
political, social and cultural considerations, woven together over a long
period of time, to produce the contemporary reality of life in South Africa.

The second chapter seeks to relate some contemporary features of urbanization to the wider process of social change. The aim is to bring together
some observations on race, class, geographical space and the role of the state,
in a broad interpretation of certain recent developments. The general principles of spatial reorganization under the policy of apartheid are explained in
the context of the operation of the cheap labour economy. Problems of
labour supply in the major 'white' cities are shown to be closely associated
with provision of housing and to the question of property rights for blacks in
'white' South Africa. The Western Cape is then taken as a case study of
housing opportunities for blacks in what apartheid theory deems to be
'white' territory, and reveals something of the scale of spontaneous settlement as exemplified by Crossroads. While residential choice for Africans is
severely constrained, the rearrangement of Coloured space under apartheid
makes provision for the emergence of a home-owning middle class. African
aspirations of this kind are expected to be satisfied outside 'white' South
Africa in their homeland. A brief examination of part of what is supposedly
the independent state of Bophuthatswana provides a contrast with the
Western Cape, to show the significance of the homelands in the grand design
of apartheid as it is currently emerging.

In Chapter 3 Christian Rogerson looks at spatial aspects of industrial
change, with particular emphasis on the government's decentralization
policy. The state played a prominent role in the development of manufacturing in South Africa, acting as both catalyst and direct participant. State
involvement is also central to the 'exclusionary' nature of industrialization,
whereby the black majority are reduced largely to the status of cheap labour.
The African labour reserves, reconstituted as quasi-independent homelands
or Bantustans, have been the focus of state decentralization strategy, with
attempts to stimulate industry in growth points within them or in so-called
border areas just outside the homelands. The aim has ostensibly been to
promote economic development within the homelands, but of greater
significance is the wish to slow down the spatial concentration of Black
population drawn to the 'white' cities by industrial employment prospects.
Despite increasing pressure from the state, the volume of new employment
generated in decentralized locations has not been substantial, and is miniscule
compared with the growth of the African population of working age. As in
other countries, large-scale decentralization of industry beyond the major
metropolitan core into an uninviting periphery flies in the face of the
agglomerative tendencies of a modern capitalist economy; in South Africa
only the prospect of especially cheap labour in certain locations can be

expected to encourage decentralization. Nevertheless some impact of decentralization policy is reflected in recent changes in the geography of manufacturing. This includes a loss of jobs which would otherwise have been created
in the core areas – a perverse outcome of state policy which has actually
exacerbated the Black unemployment problem.

The fourth chapter completes the broad examination of national trends, by
looking specifically at Black labour supply. Anthony Lemon distinguishes
between migrant labour and what he terms 'frontier commuters' living in
homelands but travelling to work each day in 'white' South Africa. The
system of migrant labour has existed for a long time in South Africa and continues to be important today, albeit under changing conditions. A substitution of domestic (i.e. homeland) labour for foreign sources is taking place,
accompanied by attempts on the part of the mining companies to secure
a more contented and stable workforce. The detrimental effect of the
migratory labour systems on the source areas is identified. The rapid increase
in frontier commuters in recent years, associated with the building of townships in the homelands where they adjoin major 'white' cities, represents an
important new development in the spatial organization of labour supply
under apartheid.

In the next chapter P. Smit, J. J. Olivier and J. J. Booysen review the
process of urbanization within the Black (African) homelands, drawing on
preliminary results of the 1980 census. Compared with 'white' South Africa,
urbanization in the homelands is a recent phenomena. The rapid growth of
urban population in the homelands reflects the strength of what the authors
refer to as the political–centrifugal forces making for population dispersal to
the periphery (to prevent Blacks from swamping the cities), as opposed to
the economic–centripetal forces promoting concentration in the core. The
expanding urban areas of the homelands, whether formal townships or
spontaneous settlements, comprise for the most part physical extensions of
the major metropolitan areas of 'white' South Africa, displaced beyond what
the government views as national boundaries between white territory and
the African nation states (present or future). It is therefore misleading to con-
ceive of an autonomous urbanization process within the homelands. Economic interdependence inevitably binds the homeland to 'white' South Africa
and renders inseparable the urban areas of these two types of territory.
Despite the dominance of political–ideological forces over the urbanization
of the Black population in recent decades, the authors see economic forces to
an increasing extent gaining the upper hand. This interpretation reinforces
the significance of policy developments with respect to the status of Blacks in
'white' urban areas.

With the next chapter attention shifts to the more local and personal
impacts of apartheid on the way in which the struggle for a living is engaged.
Keith Beavon and Christian Rogerson take the case of the 'pavement people'
of Johannesburg to reveal something of the operation of the informal sector

of the economy, which provides work for some of the blacks. Informal sector activity has a long history in South African cities, and reflects the structural unemployment, endemic to the apartheid society, which greatly limits employment opportunities for blacks in the 'white' cities. Beavon and Rogerson report the results of a survey of street hawkers in Johannesburg, showing how the organization and conduct of this type of activity reflects legal constraints as well as economic forces. Street trading represents but one of a multitude of coping strategies whereby blacks are able to survive, with difficulty, in the so-called City of Gold and elsewhere in urban South Africa.

Next (Ch. 7), David Dewar and Vanessa Watson review the constraints on Black (African) residence in the Western Cape, and draw on their recently completed study of petty commodity production and trading to show the scale and characteristics of this type of activity in sample areas of the Cape Town metropolis. They point out that the informal sector provides earning opportunities for the poor Coloured as well as African, but that its development is severely restricted by legislative and administrative measures. Petty commodity production and trading thus makes a less significant contribution to the relief of unemployment and poverty in South Africa than is typical of the Third World generally. Dewar and Watson review recent government policy aimed at stimulating small business activity in South Africa, and argue that, on the basis of their investigation in Cape Town, the new Small Business Development Corporation is unlikely to be of much assistance to the mass of petty commodity producers and traders at the bottom end of the business size continuum.

Then comes the first of three chapters on various aspects of life in Durban. In Chapter 8 Gavin Maasdorp summarizes the results of surveys of the informal sector within selected areas of spontaneous settlement. Most of the attention is given to the African area of Clérmont, with detailed information on various characteristics of informal housing and economic activities. Some reference is also made to two areas of Indian informal settlement. The findings of such studies enable comparisons to be made with the situation elsewhere in the Third World, to reveal some of the special features of these phenomena in South Africa. While the scale of spontaneous activity is presently smaller than in other Third World countries, by the end of the century well over a million Africans could be living this way in the Durban Metropolitan Region alone. Maasdorp sees the legislative rigidities of apartheid as a major obstacle to the adoption of more enlightened policies that would take advantage of the potential for self-improvement offered by informal housing and economic activity.

Employment of Blacks in domestic service in white households is a major feature of the economic structure of South African cities. In Chapter 9 Eleanor Preston-Whyte provides a case study of the lives of female domestic servants in Durban. Domestic servants either live in quarters on the properties of their employers, or travel to work daily from Black (African) townships or from hostels within 'white' areas. Whether the servant is resident or non-resident has an important bearing on the kind of life that the woman in question lives, not only with respect to the time and effort involved in getting to work in the case of the non-resident but also in the organization of interpersonal relations during leisure time. These differences are exemplified by a detailed examination of the spatial and social distribution of leisure time on the part of two women, representative respectively of resident and non-resident domestic servants. This research highlights the impact of residential segregation on the lives of those employed in domestic service. It also draws attention to the ingenuity of certain Black social and cultural responses to their situation. In particular it shows that, despite the inconvenience of a township residential location compared with living on the premises of the employer, township life provides non-resident domestic servants with some independence, freedom and group solidarity denied to resident domestic servants.

The next contribution, the third on Durban, reveals something of the problems of housing policy for low-income Indians. Peter Corbett reminds us that state intervention under capitalism is conventionally interpreted by economists as a means of enhancing the utility of poor families in circumstances where the housing provided under free market conditions is not of a high enough standard. However, he argues that in Durban the objectives of housing policy have not been entirely or predominantly to create welfare benefits for low-income (Indian) families; rather, the achievement of residential segregation for the benefit of the whites has been a major influence. The operation of the Group Areas Act has led to the forced removal of a large number of Indians from their former residential areas in the inner parts of Durban to new housing estates on the edge of the city. The findings of a survey undertaken in Chatsworth, the first of the peripheral estates built for Indians, suggest that the process of rehousing Indians has actually increased the proportion of families living in poverty, by obliging them to occupy dwellings which are more expensive than the price or rentals that they would otherwise choose to pay. It also identifies the problems of long-distance commuting to city centre jobs and of sub-letting accompanied by overcrowding to spread the cost of housing. The author, who is a member of Durban City Council, suggests that housing policy could be improved if the council would give Indians greater freedom of choice and subsidize housing of a minimum acceptable standard.

Continuing to address housing problems, the next chapter offers a broader analysis and critique of the role of the state and of major business interests. John Lea looks at the development of housing policy for Blacks (Africans) since the Soweto riots of 1976. Two changes that might be regarded as evidence of a growing enlightenment on the part of state authorities are the granting of limited tenure rights for certain Blacks living in 'white' areas, and a recognition that self-help housing might assist in providing shelter in circumstances where formal state provision is failing to keep up with need. However, Lea argues that these developments simply assist in maintaining the *status quo*. The housing question is isolated from its broader societal and political context, and treated as a physical planning problem rather than as an outcome of structural inequality. Lea is insistent that the intervention of capital, in the form of major national and international corporations, is motivated by self-interest and not by a desire to see fundamental social change. Thus the activities of the Urban Foundation set up to channel private-sector resources into projects to improve the quality of life of urban Blacks is seen as an adjustment on the part of capital to threats of social instability. An important dilemma recognized by Lea is that developments accomplishing some short-term improvements in housing conditions for Blacks may strengthen the *status quo* and hence frustrate the long-term structural change on which real moves towards equality depend. This is precisely the problem faced by all those who, in the liberal tradition, seek to promote measures with some immediate material benefit for the black population, but within the constraints of apartheid policy.

The final paper looks at one of the more dramatic outcomes of life under apartheid for blacks – civil disorder. John Western examines the geography of riots in Cape Town in 1976 and 1980. He argues that the residential rearrangement and racial segregation accomplished under the Group Areas Act assists in containing unrest by keeping it largely in peripheral areas and away from the centre of the 'white' city. The spatial separation of the Coloureds from the Blacks (Africans), which in apartheid theory reduces conflict, also serves to reduce the scope for alliance among these two groups. Thus the built environment under apartheid has a direct role in the social control of the dominated people, as well as its more obvious effects on their daily lives.

Taken together, these papers provide new information on various aspects of life under the changing conditions of apartheid society. They should also reveal something of the interdependence of employment and housing opportunities for blacks, in the distinctive circumstances moulding the process of urbanization in South Africa. The crucial role of geographical space in the policy of apartheid requires no further reinforcement. But what this collection should also show is that a spatial perspective has an important part to play in the necessarily multi-disciplinary endeavour of attempting to comprehend what Drury (1967) has aptly referred to as 'a very strange society' in a process of change.

One final editorial observation is required. The chapters which follow represent the work of 15 different scholars, who reflect differences not only in academic perspectives but also in ideology. Just as no attempt has been made to force the papers into a single, consistent interpretation, nothing has been done to obscure the ideological position that inevitably exists, however implicitly, in any pieces of social analysis. In a situation as sensitive as South

Africa, where most of the contributors live, it would be quite wrong to try to impose a common ideology; we all have our own moral position, with idealism tempered to a greater or lesser extent by life experience. The visiting scholar from overseas may be no less prone to the compromises required by everyday life under apartheid than is the South African citizen or permanent resident. But there is another more strictly academic reason for preserving ideological heterogeneity: it is an intrinsic part of scholarship itself and, as such, a contribution to social process. Perhaps nowhere else in the world is the way in which scholars actually view society more interrelated with the dynamics of society itself than it is in South Africa.

Note on currency
The South African Rand (R) exchanges at about R1.80 to £1.00 at the beginning of 1982. One Rand is roughly equivalent to one US dollar.

1 *The evolution of unequal development within South Africa: an overview*

JOHN BROWETT

This chapter presents a brief overview of the evolution of unequal development within South Africa since the first permanent settlement of white people in 1652. The purpose is to establish a context in which the remainder of this volume can be set, and also to assist those readers who may benefit from some background on the dominant trends and pervasive themes which have shaped, and are continuing to shape, the lives of people in South Africa. As such, what follows is a broad empirical account of the emergence and perpetuation of those forces underlying the more dramatic and dynamic changes in the economy, polity and society of South Africa.

Within this over-arching framework attention is focused upon the relationships between unequal development, the imperatives of capitalism and the racist ideologies of, first, the colonial segregationist and then the Afrikaner apartheid state. Special emphasis is given to the unfolding of, and the interaction between, race- and class-based inequalities and their manifestation in space in general and in the urbanization process in particular. To this end four time periods, with their somewhat arbitrary terminal dates, are identified: the era of colonial conquest (1652–1870), the era of mineral discovery (1870–1910), the era of segregation (1910–48) and the era of apartheid (1948 onwards).

The era of colonial conquest

In 1652 the Dutch East India Company established a victualling and supply station at Cape Town for its passing ships. For a long time, however, the Cape was assigned a restricted role in order that its trade and manufactures would not prove detrimental to the company's interests at large. Consequently, in comparison with the pace of subsequent colonial conquest, territorial advance was of a limited and spasmodic nature, the company attempting on several occasions to prevent contact between whites and aboriginal people through the demarcation of frontier boundary lines. Nonetheless the settlement grew in two ways (Fair & Browett 1979, pp. 262–3). First, the arrival of Dutch free burgers, French Huguenots and Germans and the importation of slaves led to an expansion of Cape Town and also growth of wine and grain production in the south-west Cape. Secondly, frontier expansion into the drier lands to the east was accomplished by semi-subsistent nomadic pastoralists (the Trekboers).

The impact of this territorial expansion upon the aboriginal people of the Western Cape was a disaster. They were exterminated in frontier skirmishes and decimated by diseases contracted from the white settlers. With the loss of their land and cattle, those who somehow managed to survive either retreated northwards into the Karoo desert (mainly the Khoi San) or were incorporated, as servants, into the Boer economy (mainly the Khoi Khoi). It was during the course of this conflict that there can be traced the emergence of the Afrikaner *volk*, a people 'struggling to survive in a stern environment and accustomed from birth to treating non-white people as slaves, as serfs, or enemies' (Katzen 1969, p. 229).

It was after the ultimate establishment of British political control over the Cape in 1806, however, that territorial aggrandizement and the partitioning of the expropriated land through defined and defended boundary lines proceeded apace. The next 60 years witnessed a considerable expansion of the land controlled and organized, if only nominally in some cases, by white people – land taken largely from the Bantu-speaking Nguni and Sotho people. In the Eastern Cape this was accompanied by increasing conflict, initially over access to land and water, between white and Nguni people (mainly Xhosa), who had been slowly migrating south and westwards between the Drakensberg range and the Indian Ocean. In response to the Xhosa presence, the British colonial government sought the close settlement of European immigrants in the border areas (the 1820 settlers around Grahamstown and the German legionnaires around King William's Town and East London – see Fig. 1.1), and the further extension of the frontier to approximately the present-day western border of the Transkei. However, in many respects the paramount government consideration was to obtain labour.

The intermittently fought 'Kaffir Wars' (1835–79) were not so much land wars as about labour supply. They did not lead to the extermination of the Xhosa, but rather to the confiscation of their means of independent livelihood (land and cattle) as a way of securing, as cheaply as possible, their labour. In this process the role of missionaries and traders was of crucial significance in persuading Blacks, after physical subjugation, to enter into wage labour on 'white' farms or in 'white' urban areas. At the same time a policy of 'civilization by mingling' was adopted (as had been attempted earlier for the Khoi Khoi) whereby Blacks, scattered in settlement locations throughout the rural areas of what is now the Ciskei, were to be exposed to the diffusion of 'westernization'. Nevertheless Black subsistence production proved to be remarkably resilient, so that complaints of labour shortages

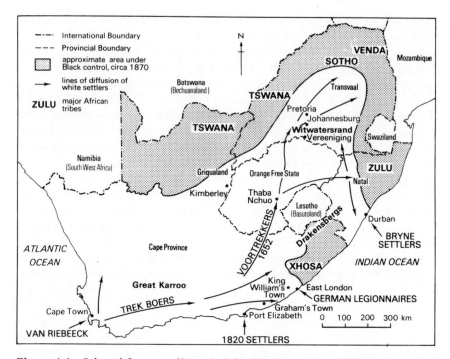

Figure 1.1   Selected features of historical development in South Africa.

were constantly recorded, especially from white farmers in the Western Cape in the years after the abolition of slavery.

It was from an area immediately to the west of this zone of conflict that in 1836 there began the Great Trek, a substantial migration of the Boer farming community northwards to those areas beyond the sphere of British colonial influence (Fig. 1.1). The departure of the Voortrekkers was founded on grievances – the abolition of slavery, the repeal of the 1809 pass laws (which sought to ensure a Khoi Khoi labour supply by controlling their movement) and disenchantment with the imposition of the alien value systems inherent in British colonial government. They left not to found a new society but to preserve an existing one that was under threat. They trekked to areas where land would be more freely available, the natives less populous and the government less demanding. Within five years their ox wagons had travelled to and through a large part of the interior where they established, after the defeat of the Sotho and Zulu people whom they encountered, independent republics in Natal, the Orange Free State and in the Transvaal. In the course of this conquest the Voortrekkers 'appropriated large areas of tribal land, much of it sparsely populated, on the grassland plateau, but certainly did not dispose of the Africans who, on the one hand, filtered back to the former lands as dependants of the white or who, on the other, engulfed the Boers in a vast horseshoe of tribal territory too mountainous, too arid, or too malarial for easy white occupation' (Fair & Browett 1979, pp. 266–7).

The life of the Republic of Natal was of a limited duration, however. With its early annexation as the colony of Natal by the British government and the subsequent arrival of British (the Byrne) settlers, the majority of the Voortrekkers left. The Natal colonial government, unlike that of the Cape, chose not to institute a policy of civilization by mingling, but instead established native reserves to act as labour reservoirs. Although much of Zululand was still independent, by 1870 over 300 000 Blacks were confined in a little more than 800 000 ha in the colony (Fair 1953, p. 42). In addition Blacks were forced to enter the cash economy to obtain money either to pay the hut taxes that were imposed or to purchase clothes which had to be worn while in the 'white' urban areas. As in the Cape, however, labour was not forthcoming on a sufficient scale, at the wages and conditions being offered. So it was that indentured Indian labourers were imported to work in the sugar plantations which the white settlers established in the coastal regions to the north and south of Durban. This response to labour shortage was similar to that made earlier in the only other area of substantial commercial arable agriculture at this time – the importation of slaves from the East Indies and Africa to the South-West Cape.

In the independent Boer areas of the Orange Free State and the South African Republic (Transvaal) the Voortrekkers practised a rural-based, semi-subsistence and relatively self-sufficient existence on farms of 2500 ha or more to which they had laid claim. In both republics some Blacks were incorporated into the Boer economy as servants, as squatter tenants or via a system known as farming on the half (a quasi-feudal arrangement). It was, moreover, an incorporation in which inequality between races was legally enshrined (in contrast to the Cape), through the proclamation in 1852 of the 'Fundamental Law' according to which 'the people will admit of no equality of persons of colour with white inhabitants, neither in church nor state' (Becker 1878, p. 41). Earlier it had been decreed that official permission was required before Blacks would be allowed to settle near towns, thus initiating the pervasive idea that they are the preserves of white people (Welsh 1971, p. 186). In general, however, there was no systematic or comprehensive Black land or labour policy in the Transvaal, although a few scattered settlement locations were proclaimed for Black occupation. In contrast, in the Orange Free State the Griqua and Sotho lands were gradually acquired, either by purchase or conquest, so that the land at ThabaNchuo (now part of Bophuthatswana) is the only tribal land that remains in Black hands.

In the space of a little over two centuries from the time of van Riebeeck's landing at Cape Town, white people's influence and settlement, albeit in varying degrees, had thus been extended throughout the greater part of what was to become the Union of South Africa. Colonial conquest resulted in the loss by the aboriginal people of their exclusive use and control over much of the land that they previously inhabited and, subsequently, in the founding of British colonies and independent Boer republics. However, unlike the situation in North America and Australasia, the white settlers did not exterminate the indigenous peoples but rather incorporated them, in a subordinate position, as and when their labour was required in the 'white' economy.

The era of mineral discovery

This era commenced with the discovery of diamonds near Kimberley in 1867. It was dominated by the exploitation of the gold reserves along the Witwatersrand in the Transvaal from 1886 onwards, by the associated inflow of overseas investment (mainly British) and by the construction of the railway network called into being to connect the mines and ports. It closed with the attainment of political union, the decline in the relative importance of mining in the national economy and the emergence of a threat to the hegemony of imperial capital. At the same time this era also witnessed a consolidation of trends previously identified. The themes of consolidation and change are examined in turn below.

Continued territorial aggrandizement by white people was responsible for consolidation of settlement and for the outward expansion of the borders of the South African Republic in all directions except to the south. This involved the incorporation of Griqualand, the Northern Cape and the Transkei into the Cape Colony and of Zululand into Natal, and the proclamation of British protectorate, over Basutoland (Lesotho), Bechuanaland (Botswana) and Swaziland. It also led to the formation of the British South African Company by Cecil Rhodes, to extend the sphere of British influence into what became Southern Rhodesia (now Zimbabwe). Consolidation could also be detected in the patterns of economic activity – in the continued expansion of the commercial arable areas of the South-West Cape and the coastal regions of Natal, in the underdevelopment of Black economy and society and in the preservation of much of the extensive livestock economy in the 'white' rural areas. Finally, throughout this era repeated attempts were made to subvert and destroy the indigenous economy in order to obtain more Black labour. In the face of increasing labour shortages on the mines and farms, poll taxes were levied, hut taxes extended and individual land tenure introduced (the Glen Grey Scheme) in an attempt to force more Blacks into the wage-labour economy through the dissolution of their traditional social structure. The institutionalization of white supremacy and, as a corollary, the suppression of Blacks, was continued and then confirmed as one consequence of the accommodation reached between Boer and British elites in the Act of Union in 1910.

Despite all this evidence of continuity the dominant feature of these 40 years was that of rapid and radical change. This was accentuated by the fact that the new activities (diamond, gold and coal mining and railway construction) did not unfold slowly from within the previous economic structure, neither were they located in close proximity to pre-existing centres of economic activity. As a result the new order tended to dominate but not displace the old; rather it was grafted or superimposed on top of it and, in some cases, in spite of it. The mining centres could be regarded as foreign bodies of intensive localized activity, inserted by outside forces into a vast expanse of land which was either devoid of other human activity or at least gave the appearance of being so. Indeed, in the face of increasing demands made by the new urban population of the interior for agricultural produce, little response was forthcoming from the Boers who, having existed for so long with little in the way of markets or commerce, were either unwilling or unable to respond sufficiently to these demands (Goodfellow 1931, p. 133).

To a very large degree the mining centres were tied to the world economy, from which they derived their skilled labour, machinery, technology and capital and whither the dividends, profits and precious stones and metal were sent. However, although the externally organized and controlled activities did not effect a rapid structural transformation of the Boer economy, their introduction did very quickly lead to a struggle for political power in the South African Republic (Transvaal) as the owners of mining capital and, to a lesser extent, railway interests sought to gain an ascendancy in the political arena. This struggle was to result in armed conflict (the Anglo–Boer war of 1899–1902), a period of reconstruction and then political union.

The discovery of gold and diamonds was also responsible for prodigious population growth at the mining centres and for its stimulation at the ports, especially Durban, that had been settled earlier. By 1871 the white population at Kimberley outnumbered all the whites that had taken part in the Great Trek (De Kiewiet 1941, p. 81). The urban population of the Transvaal increased from an estimated 4000 persons in 1870 to over 600 000 in 1911; largely a reflection of the growth of the Pretoria–Witwatersrand urban region, which in 1911 contained over half a million people (almost 35 per cent of the urban population of South Africa), and of the growth of Johannesburg which had replaced Cape Town as the largest urban centre in the country. Such was the dominance of the urban structure by the mines and the ports that by 1911 the major diamond and gold mining centres comprised 37 per cent of the total urban population, and four ports (Cape Town, Durban, Port Elizabeth and East London) accounted for a further 23 per cent (Browett 1975, p. 136).

The population increase at the mining centres was achieved not so much by a relocation of the rural population living in the sparsely populated hinterlands of these foreign inliers as by two migration streams. On the one hand, there was the arrival of large numbers of European immigrants (uitlanders). Their impact upon population growth in the Transvaal was dramatic, especially in the two years following the Anglo-Boer war: in 1890 there were only 14 334 alien (white) residents, comprising 12 per cent of the total white population, whereas 21 years later there were 124 490 (almost 30 per cent of the white population) living there who had been born outside of South Africa (Browett 1975, p. 110). On the other hand, there was the long distance temporary migration of Black males to the mines and urban centres. Henceforth, as a result of this migration, 'the native problem was urban and industrial as well and no longer simply rural. The first step was taken towards the later detribalised and landless urban proletariat of South African industrial towns' (De Kiewiet 1941, p. 91). By 1911, Blacks comprised a little over 55 per cent of the South African urban population.

The *uitlanders* were able to demand and obtain high wages in the mines, not only because of the scarcity of their skilled labour but also because of the bargaining strength that they could wield through the artisan trade unions which they formed. In contrast, unskilled cheap Black labour was obtained by inducing Blacks, by means of 'extra-economic coercion' or otherwise, to accept low-wage, short-term employment contracts. To the measures mentioned earlier can be added the enforcement of Location and Vagrancy Laws and the adverse effects suffered by peasant agricultural output as a result of droughts in the 1890s, the rinderpest epidemic of 1896–7 (which resulted in large cattle losses) and the direct and indirect effects of government policies which aided white agriculture and discriminated against the marketing of the surplus production of Black farmers.

In spite of all these attempts to push Black labour to the mines, the dangerous work conditions and the prison-like accommodation could hardly be expected to prove an attractive pull factor. At Kimberley the Black workers were housed in compounds, ostensibly for security reasons to prevent the smuggling and sale of stolen diamonds. It was this system which was also adopted on the Witwatersrand (where the same security reasons did not apply) because of its cheapness and effectiveness in controlling labour, in reducing desertions and in preventing the emergence of Black trade unions.

One response to the almost constant shortage of labour was the search for migrant workers outside of South Africa. This was even extended as far as China, and for a short time (until their repatriation in 1910) indentured Chinese labourers were brought in to work on the mines in the wake of disruptions caused to the established sources of migrant labour in the aftermath of the Anglo-Boer war. However, of much greater significance was the signing of the Mozambique Convention in 1909, and the establishment by the Chamber of Mines (gold) and De Beers (diamonds) of the Witwatersrand Native Association (WINELA). According to the former, Portugal, in return for gold, was to supply up to 100 000 Blacks from Mozambique to work in the gold mines. According to the latter, Black labour was to be sought from elsewhere in southern Africa (mainly Botswana, Lesotho and Swaziland) and central Africa (especially Malawi), in a combined operation to avoid competition for labour which would push up Black wages.

This, then, was an era of exceptional change of pace and direction in the economy, polity and society of South Africa. The dominant new elements were the mines, the ports and the space-bridging railway network which connected the two. Their introduction and expansion brought about a fundamental change in labour relations both through the emergence of the *uitlanders* as a labour aristocracy and, more importantly, through the depen-dence of mining capital upon the exploitation of Black labour. These were the relationships that were to define the economic bases for the succeeding periods of economic growth in the 20th century. Thereafter, as De Kiewiet (1941, p. 234) has remarked, racial segregation in industrial employment, urban residence and landownership becomes the leading principle of govern-ment policy.

The era of segregation

This era can be characterized by six dominant features. First, there was a rela-tively steady growth of mining along the Witwatersrand and the discovery of new reserves there and elsewhere (most spectacularly in the northern Orange Free State). Secondly, manufacturing activity was promoted by the state through a diversion of part of the profits of imperial mining capital towards this sector via the tax system. This was especially so after 1924 when an alliance (the Pact government) was formed between the white working class movement (the Labour Party) and Afrikaner Nationalists. The policies adopted included both direct ownership (e.g. in iron and steel, in electricity and the activities of the Industrial Development Corporation) and the encouragement of import substitution industry (e.g. motor vehicle as-sembly) through the imposition of protective tariffs and quotas. The contribution of the manufacturing sector to gross domestic production increased from 3.8 per cent in 1911 to 16.3 per cent in 1948, while that of agriculture declined from 20.8 per cent to 15.2 per cent and mining from 28.4 per cent to 10.3 per cent.

Thirdly, white agriculture was promoted through the construction of branch railway lines to provide access to markets, by favourable railway rating policies and by the stabilization of relatively high farm prices through the establishment of agricultural marketing boards (see Richards 1935). Fourthly, this era witnessed the proletarianization of the white, particularly the Afrikaner (Boer), labour force. Landless Boers *(bywoners)* were pushed off the land by the re-organization of agricultural production to serve the expanding markets. Such was the drift of the 'poor whites' to the urban areas (the second Great Trek) that if account is taken of natural increase, then the loss by migration from the rural areas between 1936 and 1951 was of the order of 250000 whites, or approximately 40 per cent of the white rural population in 1936 (Brookfield 1957, p. 232).

Fifthly, the voting power of these 'poor whites', in combination with the demands of the white miners, confirmed the establishment of a white labour aristocracy. In the 1922 Witwatersrand revolt banners proclaimed, 'Workers of the World Unite for a White South Africa'. Thus it was that, to secure and entrench white privilege, from the 1920s onwards, the state enacted colour-bar and job reservation legislation and adopted a 'civilized labour policy', especially on the railways, under which preference was given to the employment of 'poor whites' in unskilled jobs which paid a 'civilized' wage.

The sixth and final characteristic identified as being of particular significance in this era is that of the search to find ways, other than increasing wages, of ensuring an adequate but not excess supply of cheap Black labour for the mines and farms. As before, the major means of ensuring this supply (other than the use of prison labour) was the promotion of a Black migrant labour force. In addition to the labour from Mozambique and the efforts of WINELA to provide labour from outside of South Africa, four main tactics were employed. First, the Native Recruiting Organization, established in 1912, sought to regulate, channel and control the flow to the mines and sugar plantations of Black labour from within South Africa. Secondly, attempts were made to prevent effective labour organization amongst Blacks. Although the Industrial and Commercial Workers Union (a multi-racial organization) flourished for a time in the 1920s, an attempted strike by Black mine workers in 1946 was brutally repressed by government forces. Thirdly, the independent means of existence of Blacks in their tribal lands was undermined by government neglect and the enforced decline of peasant commercial output (Bundy 1978). Congestion, landlessness and crop failure were all welcomed as stimulants to the labour supply; concomitantly income produced in the reserves remained unchanged so that income per capita actually fell (South Africa 1955, p. 99). Finally, territorial segregation – the most powerful tactic of all and the dominant distinguishing theme of this era – was invoked to serve the interests of both racism and capitalism.

The move to extend the principles of territorial segregation was launched as a two-pronged attack. One prong was legislation passed to restrict black settlement. The Immigrants Regulation Act of 1913 prohibited the movement of Indians across provincial borders and placed restrictions upon land-ownership by them outside of Natal. Similarly, Black landownership was confined first to only 7 per cent of South Africa's land area (the Scheduled Areas of the Natives Land Act 1913) and then to 13 per cent (the reserves) with the addition of the Released Areas (land 'released' from the restricted provision of the 1913 Act by the Natives Trust and Land Act 1936). One of the intentions of these acts was to foreclose the option of choice for Blacks living in 'white' rural areas and so force them to seek temporary wage-employment in the 'white' economy.

The second prong was legislation against the permanent residence of Blacks in 'white' urban areas and against the presence there of economically inactive Blacks. According to the Stallard Commission of 1922, 'non-whites should only be permitted within municipal areas in so far and for so long as their presence is demanded by the wants of the White population' (Transvaal 1922, p. 47). This was necessary for, 'If the Native is to be regarded as a permanent element in municipal areas there can be no justification for basing his exclusion from the franchise on grounds of colour. The Native should be allowed to enter the urban areas . . . when he is willing to enter and minister to the needs of the white man, and should depart therefrom when he ceases so to minister.' The following year (1923) these principles were enshrined in the Natives (Urban Areas) Act. Under this, Blacks were regarded as temporary urban residents and as such were to be repatriated to the reserves if not economically active, to be entitled to no freehold tenure if not gainfully employed, and to be physically, socially and economically separated from the white population (Welsh 1971, pp. 187–9). So the reserves were to be not only labour reservoirs and the means of cheaply reproducing the Black labour force, but were also a dumping ground for surplus Blacks no longer required by the white economy in the urban areas.

At first the combined effects of all these policies led to spectacular results. In spite of the greater efficiency of Black labour and the levying of taxes on them, Black wage rates in the mining industry (which set the standard for Black labour in other sectors of the economy) were lower in 1914 than in 1896, while between 1914 and 1930 they remained static (Browett 1975, p. 202). On the Witwatersrand the masculinity rate was 432 males per hundred females, whereas in the reserves it was between 55 and 65 (South Africa 1946, p. 46). Towards the end of this era, however, the segregationist policies (and hence also the migrant labour system and the cheap labour policies) and the attempts to confine Black domicile to the reserves by policies of urban containment were starting to break down. In large part this can be attributed to specific developments in the reserves and in the urban areas.

In the reserves there was an increase in the number of landless Blacks. At the same time, the decline in the level of output meant that the reserves in general were not able to bear the costs of the reproduction of the labour force. In the face of the dissolution of the pre-capitalist modes of production, widespread material deprivation, malnutrition, high infant mortality and the disorganization of tribal life, the failure of the reserves and their residents to perform the social security functions required of them to support the migrant labour system and to serve as the reserve army of labour posed a serious threat to the segregationist policy. This could be underpinned only by reserving increasingly larger tracts of land for exclusive Black settlement.

In the urban areas there emerged an even greater threat to the policy of territorial segregation. This was manifest both in the growing permanence of part of the urban Black population and in the increasing flow of Blacks to the urban areas. On the one hand, there existed a group of permanent urban

Black dwellers who no longer retained any family ties or land in the reserves and who were no longer able to accept inclusion in the traditional, and mainly rural, tribal economy and society. On the other hand, the flow of Blacks to the urban areas proceeded apace so that by 1946 they had displaced whites as the largest racial group in the urban areas – a change which, in part, can be attributed to the growth in demand for Black labour on the part of manufacturing, especially after 1939.

The type of manufacturing activity which rose to prominence in this era favoured a location in the Southern Transvaal (to provide inputs to the gold mines or to have access to the large urban market) and at the ports (to take advantage of the break-of-bulk functions), and by so doing confirmed the dominance of these regions. Indeed, the urban oligarchy of core regions (the Southern Transvaal, Port Elizabeth, the Western Cape and Durban–Pine-town) increased their contribution to the national net value of output in secondary industry from 73.7 per cent in 1915–6 to 82.4 per cent in 1945–6 (McCrystal 1969, pp. 150–1). As cause and effect of this piling up of economic activity in core areas, streams of Black migrants from the reserves and the 'white' rural areas moved to these zones of industrial concentration, particularly to what could be regarded as the economic heartland of the Southern Transvaal. By 1951 44 per cent of the urban population was Black.

Although the Native Laws (Fagan) Commission was prepared to accept the reality of a permanent and expanding Black population in the urban areas, it was not acceptable to the white labour aristocracy, to mining capital and to the Afrikaner *volk*. Their combined opposition brought to power an Afrikaner Nationalist government, undiluted by the coalitions with English-orientated parties that had marked previous governments. With the defeat of Smuts and his United Party by the National Party in 1948, and the unbroken rule of this party from then onwards, political ideologies changed. The era of segregation came to an end and that of apartheid began.

The era of apartheid

The distinctive characteristic of the apartheid era is the introduction of tighter, more systematic, more comprehensive and strictly enforced control by the state over Blacks in their movement to urban areas and in their em-ployment and residential opportunities. The principal policy instrument is the creation of quasi-independent so-called homelands, based on the former tribal reserves (see Fig. 2.1). The essence of Prime Minister Verwoerd's grand apartheid vision was that 'whilst we have a multi-racial population, we have no intention of developing into a single multi-racial community' Eiselen (1959, p. 3). In general, the policy measures adopted were neither original nor revolutionary when seen in the context of earlier coercive and discriminatory legislation or of the norms and mores of white South African society. What distinguishes the apartheid legislation is that the previous *ad hoc* segregationist measures were amended, supplemented and combined within a political ideology that has been pursued with a single-mindedness of purpose. Thus, for example, Niddrie (1968, p. 150) observed that 'The decade which followed upon the Nationalist Party victory was rather one of increasingly restrictive legislation, designed for the most part to meet the prejudices of a rural white electorate long indoctrinated for this moment of sweet triumph'.

So it was that the Afrikaner state acted to allay the fears of whites of being crowded out and swamped by increasing numbers of blacks, especially in the urban areas. Nonetheless, whereas in 1936 whites outnumbered Indians in Durban and Coloureds in Cape Town, by 1960 the tables had been turned (Fair 1969, pp. 337–8). Indeed, by 1960 whites were in a minority in every South African city (Sabbagh 1968, p. 16), while in the rural areas over 5000 farms were vacated by their white occupants between 1945 and 1959 (South Africa 1959, p. 19) – a trend that continues to this day. At the same time the apartheid policies of the Afrikaner state were also functional to the capitalist mode of production for they ensured a continued supply of cheap black labour (Wolpe 1972).

In an attempt to serve the interests of both Afrikanerdom and capitalism, a number of measures were undertaken to preserve white supremacy, privilege and power and to maintain the exploitation of black labour as a lever of capital accumulation. Three inter-related themes may be identified: the containment of urban Blacks, regional decentralization and the suppression of dissent.

In the apartheid era the containment of the urban Black population has become more effective. This is particularly so in the principal metropolitan region (the 'P–W–V' – a cruciform area which stretches from Pretoria in the north to Vereeniging in the south and from Carletonville to Nigel along the Witwatersrand), where vigorous attempts have been made to curtail the employment of additional Black labour, and in metropolitan Cape Town – officially a white and Coloured labour preference area in which Black employment is severely restricted. Efflux from the 'white' and reserve or homeland rural areas is controlled through the establishment of Labour Bureaux, to which all Blacks have to go to obtain permission to enter 'white' urban areas for more than three days. Concurrently, influx control has become more effective through the classification of all individuals according to race and control of the movement of those classified as Bantu (Blacks) through a reference book. This so-called pass is to be produced on demand to prove that the holder is entitled to be present in any 'Proclaimed Area' which, after 1952, encompassed all urban areas in the country. All others (i.e. idle, non-productive Blacks and those surplus to white needs) are to be 'endorsed out' to the homelands – a process which continues as the government imposes fines on firms employing 'illegal' Black labour and seeks to remove 'illegal'

Black residents from the squatter and spontaneous settlements outside the major urban areas (e.g. Cape Town – see Ch. 2).

Furthermore, as amendments have been made to earlier urban area legislation, and homeland citizenship forced upon certain urban Blacks, so the qualification conditions to be met for Black families to remain permanently in urban areas (the so-called Section 10 rights) have become increasingly hard to attain. Concomitantly, as the construction of family accommodation for urban Blacks has slowed down or halted, so emphasis has been placed more upon the housing of migrant labourers in single-sex, prison-like hostels. However, even for those blacks who are able to claim legal entitlement to remain in 'white' urban areas, choice of home location is extremely limited in that residential areas are segregated along racial lines under the several Group Areas Acts. The enforcement of these Acts has provided an opportunity to move blacks out of inner area settlements. Examples are the displacement of Indian traders from their central city locations, particularly in Durban, of Coloureds from District Six in Cape Town to the Cape Flats and beyond, and of Blacks from Sophiatown in Johannesburg to the southwestern townships known as Soweto.

Urban containment has been linked with a second theme – the deliberate and conscious attempt to encourage industrial decentralization (see Ch. 3), to the overcrowded and poverty-stricken reserves–Bantustans–homelands along the lines first suggested by the Tomlinson Commission. Tomlinson had warned that unless the concentration of economic activity was reduced in the urban areas, 'no other result can be expected than that the relative share of the Bantu in the composition of the urban population will increase' (South Africa 1955, p. 29). To date, however, the efforts to promote the dispersal of manufacturing activity to the border areas (i.e. the 'white' areas bordering the homelands) and more recently to growth point sites within the 10 ethnically defined and fragmented homelands have not proved successful in offering a counter-magnet to Pretoria–Witwatersrand–Vereeniging and the other urban areas, despite the waiving there of the minimal wage and work conditions that apply to Black labour elsewhere. Rather, the settlement of Blacks in homeland townships in close proximity to 'white' urban areas (KwaMashu for Durban, Ga-Rankuwa and Mabopane for Pretoria, and Mdantsane for East London) has resulted in the rapid growth of a daily or weekly 'international' commuting labour force (see Ch. 4). In contrast, in homelands more distant from the major centres of economic activity (e.g. Venda and Transkei) the temporarily oscillating migrant labourer still predominates, particularly since the recent decline in the number of Black migrants from outside South Africa who are working on the mines.

Other roles that the homelands have played have, however, been more decisive. They provide a dumping ground in resettlement camps (e.g. Limehill, Dimbaza and Sada) for over a quarter of a million Blacks forcibly removed from 'Black spots' (isolated and small-sized reserves) and, with the cancellation of the remaining Black labour tenancy contracts on white farms, from the 'white' rural areas in general. It has been estimated that, between 1960 and 1980, 1.75 million Blacks were relocated in the homelands from the 'white' rural areas (*Guardian* 15 Sept. 1981). Moreover, the homelands provide one means of deflecting some Black dissent by co-opting certain Black elites as 'quisling' leaders of homelands granted 'independence' (to date, Transkei, Bophuthatswana, Venda and Ciskei).

Of much greater significance in containing and emasculating opposition to the policies of apartheid has been the third and final theme – that of suppression. In the apartheid era the final disenfranchisement of blacks has been accomplished. Protests have been brutally and ruthlessly repressed with armed force, as at Sharpeville in 1960 and Soweto in 1976. Many organizations have been declared illegal, for example, the African National Congress and the Pan African Congress. Dissent has also been silenced by people being held in detention without trial or 'banned', i.e. confined to one place, forbidden to attend gatherings of people, and not allowed to be quoted. Such events are part of everyday life for the black population of South Africa and also the experience of numerous white opponents of apartheid.

Conclusion

This chapter has sought to highlight the emergence of those forces underlying unequal development within South Africa. The presentation of an overview of how certain pervasive aspects of the economy, society and polity are woven together will serve as a backdrop against which to set the remaining chapters, which deal in greater detail with recent changes in the structure and organization of urban life in South Africa. The account given above has, of necessity, been selective in terms of the issues raised and of the interpretation given to the impact of racial oppression and capitalism upon the lives of South African people, particularly Blacks. Yet it has attempted also to give some indication of the complexity of the issues surrounding the current debates on South Africa, debates which could well have a wider significance, for South Africa may not only be the polecat of the world but also a microcosm of it.

2 Urbanization and social change under apartheid: some recent developments

DAVID M. SMITH

Urbanization under apartheid takes peculiar forms. The 'townships' evoked by Nadine Gordimer's description at the beginning of this book, and epitomized by the millionaire 'city' of Soweto, assail conventional conceptions of the urban condition: 'These restless broken streets where definitions fail . . . The enormous backyard of the whole white city, where categories and functions lose their ordination and logic'. For the whites there are the familiar suburbs of single-family homes, distinguished from those of Western Europe and North America only by details of house design and garden flora, by the density of swimming pools, tennis courts and Mercedes in the more affluent areas, and by the adjoining huts built for domestic servants. For most of the Blacks there are slots in the monotonous single-storey rows set down with the characteristic regularity of state-constructed labour storage projects – harsh, repressive forms relieved only by individual human endeavour manifest in a newly painted front door, an attempt to lay a lawn, and, occasionally, an extension or rebuilding imitative of what would be found in a modest white suburb. For workers living without their families, there are the hostels built by the state or by private employers, barely distinguishable from barracks or prison.

By the criteria of sanitary standards and orderly design that tend to predominate in state housing provision, the townships are a great improvement on what they replaced. This was, for the most part, massive shanty accretions around and within the 'white' towns and cities – the so-called squatter settlements typical of Third World urbanization elsewhere. Such settlements are generally regarded with misgivings by state authorities, which see them as threats to the existing social order (if not to the health and security of their inhabitants). Thus it was that in South Africa, when the National Party came to power, the squatter settlements became an early target for slum clearance or urban redevelopment policy. A decade ago township construction had almost eliminated the shanties. But spontaneous settlement has now re-emerged as a major feature of urbanization in South Africa, viewed with distaste by the government, vigorously debated within academia, and becoming international news as places like Cape Town's

'Crossroads' escape (or otherwise) the bulldozer. Today something over a million South Africans live in shantytown shacks.

In this chapter special attention is given to spontaneous settlement and to housing as property, in the general context of urbanization in contemporary South Africa. What is offered is a broad brush-stroke exercise to reveal something of the general dynamics of the South African economy–society–polity, with some detail sketched in for two contrasting areas selected as case studies (the Western Cape and part of Bophuthatswana). Subsequent chapters fill out the canvas and provide more finely drawn pictures of particular aspects of life in the major urban areas. The analysis presented here seeks to highlight certain crucial features of social change, as reflected in the peculiarities of urbanization in South Africa. Specifically the aim is to clarify something of the complex relationship between race and class, played out in the differentiated residential space created as the South African state pursues its distinctive purpose.

Background

The dual imperatives of the South African state are the preservation of white privilege and the perpetuation of capitalism. Pursuit of these objectives and the resolution of possible conflict between them involves both the racial identity encouraged by apartheid ideology and the class affiliation that is fundamental to capitalism. The most common analysis of South African affairs stresses racial discrimination, which is viewed not only as an afront to 'human rights' but also as holding back a process of economic development capable of bringing prosperity to all. An alternative view is that 'the present relationship between apartheid and the structural imperatives of the economy is one of minor readjustment rather than fundamental conflict' (Ehrensaft 1976, p. 86): apartheid is thus, for the most part, functional to capitalism. Yet as capitalism consolidates its grip as the dominant mode of production it creates class alignments that could eventually transcend race, and thus undermine the very basis of the racist society which is supportive of capitalism.

Apartheid is an explicitly spatial planning strategy implemented by the state. At the national level apartheid involves the splitting up of the Republic of South Africa into 10 homelands (or Bantustans) for the exercise of political 'rights' by the Black African majority, with the rest of the republic (almost 87 per cent of the land area) preserved for the whites (Fig. 2.1). The homelands form a discontinuous crescent about the economic heartland of South Africa centred on Johannesburg. The division among 10 tribal groups, together with the spatial fragmentation of most of the individual homelands, reflects the white government's strategy of divide and rule. The grand design is for the homelands eventually to become independent of South Africa; four

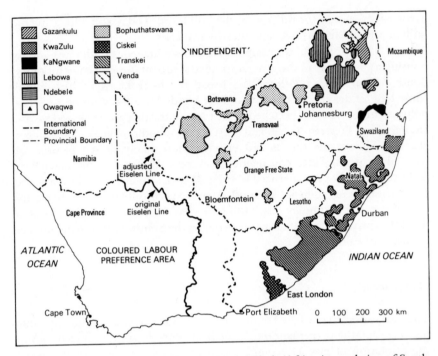

Figure 2.1 Homelands or Bantustans for the Black (African) population of South Africa, and the Coloured labour preference area of Cape Province west of the Eiselen line. (Note: the homelands are shown according to 1975 consolidation proposals; maps elsewhere in this volume may adopt different definitions with slightly different boundaries.)

of them have already been granted this status. The official government view is that the homeland concept recognizes and helps to preserve the distinctive ethnic and cultural identity of the African tribal groups. A more plausible interpretation is that this plan actually serves the interest of white domination and exploitation of Black labour. The homelands perform an important function in the maintenance of the Africans as a cheap and disenfranchised labour force for (predominantly white) South African capital and for foreign investors. But with the 'independence' of these territories they take on a broader and more explicit role in furthering the basic objectives of the South African state. This will be explained later in the chapter, as certain aspects of the process of urbanization in part of one of the homelands (Bophuthatswana) are examined.

But before proceeding, a reminder of some of the facts of inequality in South Africa is in order. Table 2.1 compares the distribution of population and income among the four officially recognized race groups, emphasizing the privileged position of the whites and the disadvantage of the Africans or Blacks. The extreme disparities in income distribution by race revealed here

Table 2.1 Distribution of population and income by race, 1977.

Race group	Population		Income
	no.	%	%
African	19 370 000	71.9	26
White	4 373 000	16.2	64
Coloured	3 438 000	9.1	7
Asian	765 000	2.8	3
total	26 946 000	100.0	100

Source: estimates based on Gordon et al. (1979, pp. 49, 161).

have changed little in recent South African history (Smith 1977, p. 250). Table 2.2 indicates the extent of racial differentiation with respect to selected economic and social conditions. As well as underlining the favourable status of the whites compared with the Africans, these figures show something of the relative deprivation of the Coloured people. This should be borne in mind in the examination of the situation of the Coloureds in the Western Cape, to which this discussion will direct itself in due course.

Table 2.2 Selected economic and social indicators by race.

	Race group				Ratio
Indicator	African	White	Coloured	Asian	w : Af.
average monthly wages in manufacturing (R) 1980	237	979	273	307	4.13
average monthly wages in mining (R) 1979	146	880	384	432	6.03
infant deaths (per 1000 live births) 1970–5[1]	nd	16.6	89.3	28.0	nd
tuberculosis cases (per 100 000 popn) 1979	779.9	13.5	185.0	15.0	57.77
expenditure on school pupils (R per capita) 1978–9	71	724	225	357	10.20
maximum social pensions (R per month) 1980	33.00	109.00	62.00		3.30
prisoners (daily average per 100 000 popn) 1978–9	450.6	97.1	847.2	68.1	4.64

Sources: Gordon (1981); except [1] – from Gordon (1980).
nd no data.

The production and reproduction of cheap labour

We may now return to the operation of apartheid as a system of cheap labour production, and to the role of the homelands in this process. There are three kinds of labour represented in the African population, other than those working within the homelands themselves. The first and most numerous are those workers permanently resident in what apartheid ideology deems to be 'white' South Africa. These are mostly inhabitants of the townships attached to the 'white' cities, but also include agricultural workers living on white farms. If the actual *(de facto)* population of the African homelands is compared with the *(de jure)* population that would exist if all members of the tribal group in question lived in their respective homeland, the difference comes to about half the total African population (see Ch. 4, Table 4.1). This is accounted for by those living in 'white' areas.

The second kind of African labour is the migrant worker, employed in 'white' South Africa and resident there except for the (usually) annual return to the homeland for short spells between contracts. This system originated to serve the gold mines of the Witwatersrand but has subsequently expanded so that today 60 per cent of all economically active African men in 'white' areas are migrants (Lukes 1979, p. 586). The Witwatersrand remains the major focal point for streams of migrants from the homelands (see Ch. 4, Fig. 4.2), as well as from beyond South Africa's borders.

The third type of labour comprises those 'frontier commuters' who live with their families in the homelands and travel on (usually) a daily basis across what apartheid ideology depicts as national borders, into 'white' South Africa. The major flows are from that part of Bophuthatswana which comes closest to the city of Pretoria (and to which further reference will be made later in this chapter), and from parts of KwaZulu which adjoin the city of Durban (see Ch. 4, Fig. 4.3).

Of these three kinds of African labour, the South African authorities have a strong preference for the migrant and the frontier commuter. There are two reasons for this. The first is that the presence of millions of Africans as permanent residents of 'white' cities undermines the credibility of the notion that their proper place is actually in the homelands; renders implausible the claim that homeland citizenship gives them a meaningful franchise; and raises the awkward question of African property rights in 'white' South Africa (to which we shall return). The second is that the attribution of both migrants and commuters to homeland (i.e. foreign) residence reinforces existing means of reducing the costs of production and reproduction of labour to be borne by capital or the state in 'white' South Africa.

The role of what were formerly the African reserves and are now the homelands, in the process of cheap labour production, has been clarified by Harold Wolpe. Two stages are recognized: 'In the earlier period of capitalism (approximately 1870 to the 1930s), the rate of surplus value and hence the rate of capital accumulation depended above all upon the maintenance of the pre-capitalist relations of production in the Reserve economy which provided a portion of the means of reproduction of the migrant labour force' (Wolpe 1972, p. 432). Interaction between the two modes of production gradually broke down the pre-capitalist social relations in the reserves, how-ever, in the development towards a dominant capitalist mode. In the current (second) stage: 'Apartheid, including separate development, can best be understood as the *mechanism specific to South Africa* in the period of secondary industrialization, of maintaining a high rate of capitalist exploitation through a system which guarantees a cheap and controlled labour-force, under circumstances in which the conditions of reproduction (the redistributive African economy in the Reserves) of that labour-force is rapidly disintegrat-ing' (Wolpe 1972, p. 433).

The specific means by which cheap labour is produced are as follows. In the first stage: 'The extended family in the Reserves is able to, and does, fulfil "social security" functions necessary for the reproduction of the migrant work force. By caring for the very young and very old, the sick, the migrant labourer in periods of "rest", by educating the young, etc., the Reserve families relieve the capitalist sector and its State from the need to expend resources on these necessary functions' (Wolpe 1972, p. 435). In the contem-porary period this implicit subsidy still happens to some extent, but apar-theid makes the system more sophisticated: 'the practice and policy of Separate Development must be seen as the attempt to retain, in a modified form, the structure of the "traditional" societies, not, as in the past, for the purpose of ensuring an economic supplement to the wages of the migrant labour force, but for the purpose of reproducing and exercising control over a cheap African industrial labour force in or near the "homelands", not by means of preserving the pre-capitalist mode of production but by the political, social, economic and ideological enforcement of low levels of subsistence' (Wolpe 1972, p. 450).

Wolpe (1974) has subsequently elaborated these arguments in the context of the circuit of capital, into which some of the product of the reserves is shown to be drawn in the form of labour as a commodity. Further support for this perspective comes from other Marxian economists, most notably Williams (1975) and Legassick (1974a, 1977). It is also adopted by some liberal observers: 'Inescapably, the logic of apartheid is that on the one hand the Bantustans will remain labour reservoirs from which employers in the Republic will be able to draw at will, while on the other they will provide disposal areas where the unemployed, the old, the sick, and the disabled can be sent when the central economy no longer has use for them' (Kane–Berman 1979a, pp. 251, 246–7). This depository role is illustrated by the fact that from 1968 to mid-1975, 171 259 Blacks from 'white' areas were resettled in the various homelands (Smit & Booysen 1977, p. 20). In 1977 alone the number was 22 552, including 716 classed as 'idle' and 28 as 'undesirable' (Minister of Plural Relations, quoted in Gordon *et al.* 1979, pp. 324–5).

That all this leads to cheap labour is beyond dispute. Kane–Berman (1979a, p. 162) reports that 'some of the mining houses have made the point that if the migratory labour system were to be abolished, it would cost five times as much to house black workers and their families on the mines as it presently costs to house the men in compounds without their families'. The ideal labour unit for the capitalist is the single hostel resident. The basic inconvenience is the human embodiment of labour, which not even the ingenuity of the South African state can overcome. A Nationalist MP (quoted in Adam 1971, p. 96, citing Horwitz, *Political economy*, p. 412) once put the problem with impeccable clarity as follows: 'They are only supplying a commodity, the commodity of labour . . . it is labour we are importing and not labourers as individuals'. Apartheid comes as close as possible to the literal dehumanization of labour. Or, as Williams (1975, pp. 24–5) explains in the context of the mines: 'The workers in the gold sector are important only in so far as they produce surplus-value for the capitalists, their wives and daughters are important only in so far as they manage to maintain, in their allotted "reserves", the living labour power from which capital derives its surplus-value'.

Employment prospects, social stability and property rights

A static view of the current situation in South Africa might suggest that, apart from the occasional riot, prison death and public scandal, apartheid provides a rather effective means of reducing the majority of the population to the status of cheap, disenfranchised and docile labour. But the supply of Black African labour is growing so rapidly as to threaten the stability of the system. Fair and Bowett (1979, p. 280), quoting a government source, state that 'During 1973–5 the annual average of new work-seekers from the homelands numbered 100 000. Of these 28.4 per cent found employment inside the homelands; 36.8 per cent in white areas, including metropolitan centres, bordering on homelands; and 34.8 per cent were migrant workers in towns, mines and on farms or remained unemployed'. Thus something like 70 000 additional Africans a year cannot be provided with jobs in the homelands. On top of this, a similar number of new African job-seekers are generated within 'white' South Africa by natural increase. Kane-Berman (*Guardian* 16 Oct. 1979) cites estimates of Black unemployment approaching 2 million (against government figures of almost half a million); four out of every 10 Blacks could be jobless by the year 2000, unless the current rate of economic growth is speeded up dramatically.

Whether employed or not, the concentration of Black labour in and around the major cities creates a strategic threat to the whites, as well as a political inconvenience. Hence the efforts being made to decentralize industry (see next chapter): ostensibly to provide jobs in the homelands but in reality being a logical refinement of the process of exploitation of cheap labour: 'The *Bantustans*, pools of unfree labour, are to have manufacturing industry situated adjacent to them in so-called "border areas". In this way the traditional structures continue to reduce "welfare" and "social control" costs to the South African state, the benefits of migrancy are retained, and large concentrations of Africans in major industrial centres are avoided. The State, with its wide powers over wage determination, has authorized low wages to the workforce in such areas' (Legassick 1977, p. 195). But the 'border areas' are not very attractive to industry, unless close to a 'white' city. The section of Bophuthatswana close to Pretoria reveals one area of substantial industrial development just inside a homeland; its impact is part of the story to be developed later in this chapter.

Whatever prosperity the South African economy may generate for Africans, it will continue to be highly selective. Geographically it will be confined to the major cities, and to such peripheral growth points or border areas as capital finds attractive under state dispersal policy. It is unlikely to penetrate far into the predominantly rural homelands, where severe poverty will remain the norm. And even within the cities, those Africans able to ascend from the ranks of wage labourers will be very few, unless measures are taken to facilitate this process.

The development of a black 'middle class' is widely viewed as being in the interests of the perpetuation of a white-dominated capitalist system in South Africa. There is, indeed, evidence that it is becoming deliberate state policy to promote the selective recruitment of Africans (as well as Coloureds and Indians) into a trans-racial bourgeoisie. Property ownership has long been recognized as a source of political stability, and as supportive of the preservation of capitalism. But to allow Africans to own land and housing in 'white' areas conflicts with the idea that they have permanent residence rights only within their homeland. The significance of this contradiction is now becoming apparent, as more Africans aspire to property ownership in the metropolitan industrial areas. Kane-Berman (1979a, p. 156) quotes a *Memorandum to the prime minister* from the Transvaal Chamber of Mines (dated 29 July 1976): 'The emergence of a "middle class" with Western-type materialistic needs and ambitions has already occurred in these areas. The mature family-oriented urban black already places the stability of his household uppermost, and is more interested in his pay-packet than in politics'. He also helps to build up the domestic market for manufactured goods, so restricted by low African wages – an important consideration in future economic growth and capital accumulation.

The Soweto riots of June 1976 revealed the frustration of urban Africans. The response, at the Businessmen's Conference on the 'Quality of Life in Urban Communities' held at the end of November 1976, further emphasized the significance attached to the encouragement of African property ownership. One outcome was the establishment of the Urban Foundation, an aim of which was to try to come to grips with the problem of African housing in the cities (see Ch. 11). Kane-Berman (1979a, pp. 191–2) quotes Mr Justice Steyn, executive director of the Urban Foundation, referring at the Annual

General Meeting of the United Building Society to 'enormous benefits which would flow from making land-tenure and home-ownership available for all blacks who aspire thereto', including 'social stability arising from security of tenure and pride of ownership; the opportunity of providing capital formation by blacks; the consolidation of the concept of private ownership of land and the confirmation of private enterprise values among blacks'. The chairman of the society added, 'It is important that this privilege (home ownership) be granted to blacks without delay and that we create a stable middle-class participating in the capitalist system'.

Responding to African middle class aspirations is an important element in Prime Minister P. W. Botha's strategy for restructuring apartheid. As Patrick Lourence puts it (*Guardian* 24 Sept. 1979): 'Linked to these changes is a new urgency about encouraging the growth of a black middle class with the clear motive of increasing the conservatism of the black bourgeoisie by making it a junior partner in the white financial establishment'. Thus, a policy of divide and rule by race and tribal affiliation is being augmented by divide and rule by class stratification.

The remainder of this chapter explores some of the implications of the opportunities for property ownership (in the form of housing) open to different race groups in two different parts of South Africa where the process of urbanization is subject to different forces and controls. The first case is that of the Western Cape centred on the city of Cape Town, where both the Africans and Coloureds have resorted to spontaneous settlement. The experiences of these two groups highlights their different status in this part of the country – officially a 'Coloured labour preference area' (see Fig. 2.1) – where African residence is even more precarious than elsewhere in 'white' South Africa. In the second case, part of the quasi-independent homeland of Bophuthatswana is taken to illustrate the opportunities for African property ownership and selective Black upward mobility, which are in stark contrast to the situation of Blacks in the Western Cape.

Spontaneous and planned urban development in the Western Cape

Spontaneous settlement has a long history in the Cape Town area. It has re-emerged as a phenomenon of major proportions in recent years, with a public housing programme unable to keep pace with the demands of natural population increase on the part of both Africans and Coloureds, in-migration of Africans and Group Areas evictions (which have displaced about 50 000 Coloured people). Under the Prevention of Illegal Squatting Act 1951 all persons living in wood and iron or substandard structures are defined as squatters and are acting illegally. However, the local authorities in the Cape have surveyed and numbered all shacks erected before 1975, their existence thus being legitimized until their occupants can be rehoused. The local authority may put in communal water points and rudimentary lighting, and remove sewage, for which payment is exacted from the residents. Squatter settlements not officially recognized may be removed. Squatting provides homes for both African and Coloured families in various parts of the Cape Town metropolitan area and its fringes (Fig. 2.2). For Africans, it is

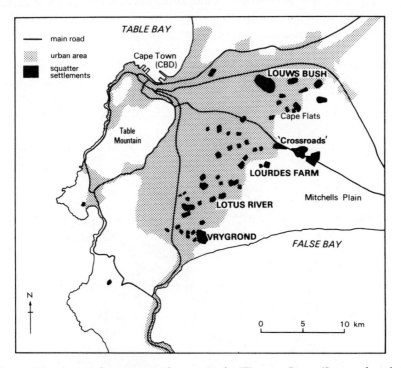

Figure 2.2   Areas of squatter settlement in the Western Cape. (Source: based on Dewar & Ellis 1979, p. 59.)

a way of avoiding the harsh township environment, or the single-sex hostel in the case of men who wish to live with their families and are prevented from doing so by the laws regulating African residence rights (which are particularly stringent in the Cape). For the Coloureds, squatting is a way out of the overcrowded public housing areas for those unable to buy their way into the private housing sector.

In 1976 there were approximately 120 000 people living in 22 400 structures in squatter areas in Greater Cape Town (Nash 1976, pp. 6–7). Another source gives a figure of 120 000 Coloureds, which may possibly be as high as 180 000, with some 30 000 of the over 90 000 illegal African residents of the area also squatting (Ellis *et al.* 1977, p. 6). Andrew and Japha (1978) refer to about 130 000 people living in shanties among the 300–400 000 people estimated to be without adequate accommodation in 1977 (out of a total Western Cape population approaching 2 million, metropolitan Cape Town has 1.1 million).

The housing problem in general, and squatting in particular, is a matter of much current attention in the political arena. This is reflected in the strength of recent academic interest (e.g. Granelli & Levitan 1977, Dewar & Ellis 1979). Urbanization in South Africa is being seen (belatedly) to exhibit Third World characteristics, but with distinctive features arising from the implementation of apartheid.

The settlement known as Crossroads has attracted world-wide interest and a brief account will help to highlight some general features of the squatter phenomenon in South Africa. Crossroads is occupied by Africans, and adjoins the township of Nyanga (Fig. 2.3). Andrew and Western (1978,

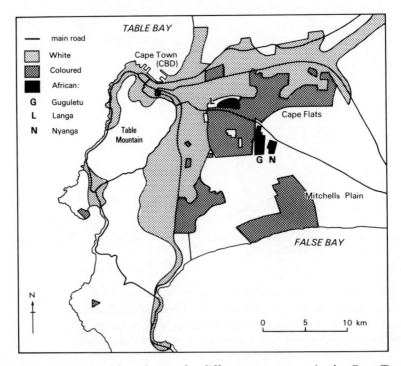

Figure 2.3 Major residential areas for different race groups in the Cape Town Metropolitan Area. (Source: based on Western 1981, p. 280, following Ellis *et al.* 1977.)

p. 1) cite a population of approximately 20 000 in 3038 shanties or structures; Kane-Berman puts it at 24 000 (*Guardian* 4 Oct. 1979), and *The Economist* (21 June 1980) at 60 000. As with most spontaneous settlements, its superficial chaos hides internal order: 'The settlement with greater physical unsightliness may possess in fact the greater social cohesion, especially because it is a settlement of families and because it has to create itself and its institutions by community participation' (Andrew & Western 1978, p. 19); the comparison is with Nyanga. This view conforms to the 'slums-of-hope' (as opposed to 'despair') interpretation of spontaneous settlements, popularized by Mangin and Turner (1969).

A survey of a random sample of the Crossroads population in December 1977 (Maree & Cornell 1978) reveals some significant features of the occupants. There were 6.2 residents per house, 3.0 of them children. Half the heads of households (usually men) were legally qualified to be in the Cape Town area, but only 9.3 per cent of spouses or wives were. Of heads of households in the labour force, 81 per cent worked in the formal wage sector, 11.2 per cent were in the informal sector, and only 6 per cent were unemployed. Heads of households in the formal sector averaged R24.3 per week in earnings; in the informal sector it was R28.3 (both were well below poverty-level income). Only 2 per cent of heads of households had come to Crossroads direct from outside the Cape Town region (17 per cent for spouses); average residence in the region was 18.2 years (11.7 for spouses). One-third of families interviewed had their previous squatter houses demolished; for about 10 per cent this had happened at least three times! Thus, far from being a shiftless mass of unemployed illegal immigrants, as the government tends to portray them, the people of Crossroads were found for the most part to be a stable element of the workforce necessary to the city economy. To them, squatting was simply preferable to living as a split family or (if qualified) to township family life.

Personal field inquiries confirm the reputed safety, order and relative cleanliness of Crossroads. There is evidence of a vibrant informal sector, with dozens of small businesses growing up, including the making of tin trunks, clothing and rugs; retailing includes food, furniture sales and general stores; other activities include welding, transport services and a travel agent. There is a school, numerous churches are active, and various voluntary organizations provide services not supplied by the state. At the time of writing (1981) the future of Crossroads is uncertain. In 1979 the Minister of Community Development, Dr Piet Koornhof, reprieved the settlement from impending destruction and announced the building of a new township for the residents, near Nyanga (*Argus* 10 Aug. 1979). This was regarded as an enlightened break with previous policy of resolving matters with the bulldozer, as it was believed that most of the people would be allowed to stay in the Cape area. However, Kane-Berman (*Guardian* 4 Oct. 1979) reported one of Koornhof's Deputy Ministers – Dr George Morrison – as saying that only a quarter of the people will be rehoused, and that 3600 families or 18000 people will be removed to the Transkei or Ciskei homeland. Dr Morrison is quoted as describing Crossroads residents as engaged in 'scrounging' and undermining the jobs of legitimate work-seekers. However inaccurate this may be, it appears that many of those facing removal had lost their jobs as a result of an increase to R500 in the penalty for employers of Africans who lack the proper pass-law qualifications. Whatever the final resolution (see Ch. 6 for more recent developments), any precipitous use of the bulldozer will be opposed by those who argue the positive side of the spontaneous settlement phenomenon, as a self-help solution to low-income housing.

A consideration which tends not to surface in debate is that do-it-yourself housebuilding may have advantages for capital as well as for squatter settlement residents themselves. If workers can demonstrate that they are able and willing to erect their own homes in their own time and with their own labour and resources, there may be a possibility of relieving employers of the obligation to pay for housing through wages (or the construction of compound dormitories). Part of the real cost of production and reproduction of labour would, in effect, be passed on to the worker. Some of the strength of individual initiative and community self-help associated with spontaneous settlements (applauded in itself by free-enterprise ethics) would thereby be tapped by capital, in the same way that the pre-capitalist mode in the reserves relieved capital of some of its costs, in the Wolpe (1972) argument outlined above. In a sense, the African spontaneous settlements simply bring part of the homeland labour reserves to the edge of the 'white' city in the Western Cape, thus offering the convenience of a pool of labour that can be hired (legally or otherwise) and fired on the basis of short-term fluctuations in demand. Thus there could be a conflict between the orderly urban development sought by the national government and the possibility of reducing the real cost of labour in these special circumstances.

Let us now turn to the housing opportunities open to the Coloured population of the Western Cape. While the Africans are (officially) confined to the three townships of Langa, Nyanga and Guguletu, the map of Group Areas (Fig. 2.3) indicating residential space allocated to specific race groups reveals large areas open to Coloureds. The Coloureds comprise a majority of the population of Cape Town (roughly three-quarters of the total of 1.1 million), and this threat to white supremacy has resulted in the massive relocation of Coloureds in a southeasterly direction, to leave the central part of the city and its northern and western suburbs in the hands of the whites (see Ch. 12 for further discussion). Integral to this process is a planned structure to facilitate upward mobility in housing for Coloureds, including private ownership, in sharp contrast to the constraints on the Africans.

Two phases may be recognized in the imposition of the spatial order of apartheid on the Coloured population of the Western Cape. The first phase involved relocation from their traditional residential areas (Fig. 2.4) to vast uninviting estates in the Cape Flats (Western 1978) – an area of harsh (sandy, windswept) environment away from the main employment centres of the city (Fig. 2.3). These are the districts of 'subeconomic' or subsidized

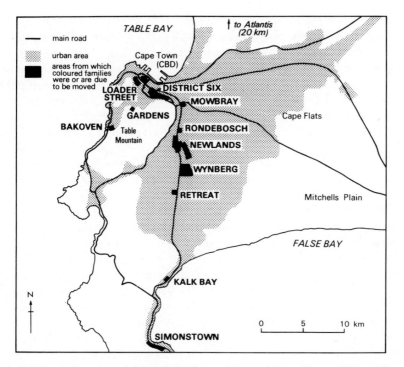

Figure 2.4 Relocation of the Coloured population of Cape Town. (Source: based on Andrew & Japha 1978, p. 43.)

housing, which is all that most Coloureds can afford. The Group Areas Act, as implemented in Cape Town, has affected about 12 500 families, 11 814 of them Coloured (Andrew & Japha 1978, pp. 42–3). The most widely publicized activities in Cape Town under the Group Areas Act concern the destruction of the so-called District Six, former heart of the inner-city Coloured community. Elsewhere, old Coloured residential areas with small houses of some architectural distinction have been renovated or 'Chelseafied' as fashionable districts for whites (e.g. Wynberg). The Group Areas Act has thus accomplished a transfer of property with particular locational advantage from Coloureds to whites.

The first phase of relocation reduced opportunities for home ownership on the part of the Coloureds. The Cape Flats townships were built very largely as rental accommodation for low-income people, with only small enclosures of better quality private housing available for middle class Coloureds. But in the peculiar circumstances of segregated residential space there is under-supply, to the extent that a Coloured person may pay substantially more for a house in his group area than a white would pay for the same house in a 'white' area. So, to encourage home ownership, a new city is being built at Mitchells Plain (Fig. 2.3). It is largely for private ownership, at favourable terms which include deposits as low as R100. Its major disadvantages are shortage of local jobs, distance from the Cape Town central business district (CBD) and remoteness from main transport routes until new rail and road links are built. Even further out, to the north of Cape Town, a second new city (Atlantis) is under construction, with a mixture of private and public housing. Mitchells Plain is designed for 250 000 people, Atlantis for some 500 000 (Dewar & Ellis 1979, p. 63). These two cities represent a second stage in the forcing of the Coloureds into the regional periphery, where they pose less of a threat to public order than they would if congregated around Cape Town's central area. The importance of this strategic consideration is underlined by the civil disorder that has on occasions broken out among the Coloureds, most recently in 1980 (see Ch. 12).

The construction of the new city at Mitchells Plain must be understood principally as an attempt to create a stable, property-owning middle class among the Coloureds. Its location on the shores of False Bay makes for an attractive environment and the quality of urban design is high. There is nothing covert about the government's intentions: a publicity brochure produced by the Information Service of South Africa refers to the creation of an 'instant' Coloured middle class at Mitchells Plain – a statement which reflects as much wish-fulfilment as reality. A leaflet reminds prospective residents that 'Where your children grow up determines their future' and proclaims, '*There's room for you now!*'. Unstated, of course, is the proviso: if you are classified as Coloured. Where there is room for you in South Africa's urban fabric depends on your race group, the need for your labour, and how it fits into the grand design of national residential space under apartheid. For Coloureds with the cash, there is somewhere in the Western Cape. For the mass of poor Coloureds, and for the Africans, the only choice is township life or squatter settlements.

Looking more broadly at the spatial arrangement of the Coloureds within the Western Cape, the Cape Flats townships, Mitchells Plain and Atlantis will form *de facto* homelands for the Coloureds. They could provide a territorial basis for a revival of the Coloured franchise (lost when the Nationalists came to power) in some future federal state, without losing white control of the city of Cape Town. Some form of franchise for the Coloured population as a whole would be a logical extension of the development of a property-owning class, whereby the present government seeks to achieve the compliance of the Coloureds in the continuing domination and exploitation of the African majority.

Urbanization in the homelands: the case of Bophuthatswana

We may now turn to the situation facing the Africans in their allotted 'race' space. The pace and characteristics of the urbanization process in the homelands has attracted much recent interest within South Africa (Smit & Booysen 1977, Smit 1979; see Ch. 5). Attention has been drawn to the rapid rise in the number of Africans living in urban areas within the homelands, as well as to such demographic features as the distortion of age and sex structure arising from the presence of disproportionate numbers of dependants (young and old) and the absence of many males of working age (Smit 1976). The intention here is to focus on some specific features of urban development in part of Bophuthatswana, so as to highlight the difference in opportunities and constraints placed upon African people in the process of settlement formation in a homeland, when compared with the situation in the 'white' Western Cape described above. We will observe that, as in the case of the Coloureds, there is room somewhere for African home ownership, within the carefully contrived spatial structure of apartheid. And we shall argue that this is itself an integral feature of the state strategy for continued exploitation of African labour under the capitalist mode of production.

Bophuthatswana has a *de facto* population of about 1.2 million (all but 300 000 of whom are Tswana). It was the second of the homelands to be granted 'independence' (after the Transkei). In apartheid theory, Bophuthatswana is as independent of South Africa as is Swaziland or Lesotho, indeed as independent as is South Africa itself or any other sovereign nation state. The questionable legitimacy of such a claim is underlined by the fact that the South African government retains responsibility for homeland 'defence'. Bophuthatswana, like the Transkei, has been refused membership of the United Nations, and is almost universally regarded as an artificial puppet state of South Africa. However, Bophuthatswana's 'independence' is not total illusion, simply a clever sleight of hand whereby a real change in the territory's political status updates its traditional role within South Africa's system of racial domination and cheap labour supply.

Despite the drawing of an 'international' border and such trappings of statehood as a legislative assembly, coat of arms and flag, Bophuthatswana remains an integral part of the South African capitalist system. This is clearly revealed in the section closest to Pretoria (Fig. 2.5). The homeland comes within 20 km of the 'white' city, and it is just across the border that the major dormitories for African workers were built at Mabopane and Ga-Rankuwa during the period before 'independence'. Thus workers who would previously have been housed in townships on the edge of Pretoria in 'white' South Africa (e.g. Atteridgeville and Mamelodi) became foreign residents for whom the question of the franchise in 'white' South Africa is no longer relevant. The vast majority of those living in the new townships just inside Bophuthatswana travel daily to jobs in Pretoria. In all, about 150 000 Tswana people commute to work in 'white' South Africa, in addition to 50 000 migrant workers (Leistner 1977, p. 143), and the bulk of this movement is between that part of Bophuthatswana shown in Figure 2.5 and the greater Pretoria area. (These figures are themselves overshadowed by the half

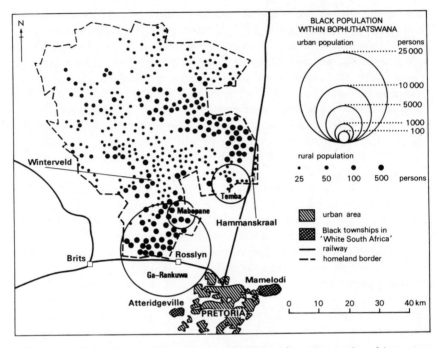

Figure 2.5 Part of Bophuthatswana, north of Pretoria. (Source: based in part on a map in Moolman 1977; Pretoria area from *Southern Transvaal land use map*, Urban and Regional Research Unit, University of the Witwatersrand, 1973; population distribution in Bophuthatswana from a map in Smit 1977.)

million or so Tswana living and working in 'white' South Africa on a continuous basis, resident in Soweto as well as the townships of Pretoria and other 'white' cities.)

While the movement of labour from the homeland to Pretoria still predominates, capital can itself seek labour by moving to the border or to locations within Bophuthatswana. Rosslyn was established in 1960 as South Africa's first border industrial area, and by 1975 had attracted about 130 South African and multinational firms with an investment of R110 million (including R33 million from the South African government's Industrial Development Corporation). The major growth point within Bophuthatswana is at Babelegi, where R105 million (R40 million of it from the South African government) has been invested since 1970, to create 10 000 jobs. These two industrial satellites thus add significantly to Pretoria's industrial base and employment opportunities.

As in the Western Cape, Africans are attracted to places where jobs may be available. In 'white' South Africa, the spatial search for employment on the part of Africans is tightly constrained by influx control measures such as the pass laws, but this is not so within the homelands. Large numbers of people

have moved into that part of Bophuthatswana where employment opportunities appear to be greatest. The result has been a massive growth of spontaneous settlements, enveloping the formal townships. Smit (1979, p. 8) cites
official 1976 estimates of 350 000 squatters in the Winterveld, Klippan and
Oskraal areas around Ga-Rankuwa, Mabopane and Temba (Fig. 2.5). If, as
seems likely, the inhabitants of these settlements now approach half a
million, this would be roughly two-fifths of the entire Bophuthatswana
population. Elsewhere in the Third World, these settlements would appear
as accretions around Pretoria itself; in South Africa this feature of the urbanization process is displaced, to surface beyond the homeland border.

The process of urban development in the homeland area north of Pretoria
reveals something of the opportunities for property ownership on the part of
Africans living there. Because the rigid controls on African property rights in
'white' South Africa do not apply in the homelands, freedom exists to own
land and to build or improve a house – for those with the money. Both the
townships and the squatter settlements in the area of Bophuthatswana
referred to above provide ample evidence of the emergence of a small yet
significant middle class, with homes markedly better than the standard
township type and which, in some cases, would not be out of place in a well-
to-do white suburb. There is also evidence of an emergent capitalist class,
ranging from owners of small shops and bars to proprietors of supermarkets
and manufacturing establishments; the severe constraints on African business
enterprise that exist in 'white' South Africa no longer apply. It is from this
increasingly affluent, property-owning elite that the political *status quo* can
expect to find support in Bophuthatswana.

However, the emergence of a property-owning bourgeoisie in Bophuthatswana is complicated by the problem of tribal affiliation, illustrated
vividly by process of urbanization in the Winterveld area (for further particu-
lars see Ch. 11). Africans acquired freehold land here as far back as 1938,
when plots were released as smallholdings (SAIP 1980, p. 23). As increasing
numbers of people moved to Winterveld, existing landowners facilitated
spontaneous settlement by renting plots to squatters, thereby becoming
wealthy enough themselves to improve their own homes. Many of the
landowners, like the squatters, were non-Tswana, and when Bophuthatswana became 'independent' in 1977 members of other tribal groups found
themselves no longer welcome. Steps were taken to remove non-Tswana:
for example many Ndebele were resettled in their own homeland. The result
has been that landowners and some well-to-do businessmen have left
Bophuthatswana, and those of non-Tswana origin who remain may feel
insecure. Thus the tribal affiliation which is emphasized in apartheid ideology and its homeland policy to some extent frustrates the emergence of an
indigenous middle class within Bophuthatswana. Yet this middle class may
be crucial to the stability of the homelands in their reconstituted form.

The new role of the homelands as cheap labour reserves has a number of different features. It is greatly to the advantage of capital to have a pool of potential workers so close to Pretoria, eager to get a foothold in the 'white' economy, and often building their own homes without state assistance. Those in employment spend their earnings largely in white-owned shops in Pretoria, so much of the multiplier effect is retained there rather than benefiting the homeland. The costs associated with the production and reproduction of this labour force, and the various economic and social problems associated with spontaneous settlement, can be externalized in a literal spatial sense. As an 'independent' political entity, Bophuthatswana can be portrayed as a separate nation with normal state responsibilities for the welfare of its 'citizens' or residents. This is reflected in the following observations, from Smit (1977, pp. 190–1, 198):

> The rapid natural increase in population has far-reaching implications for the Bophuthatswana government, especially in regard to creating employment and providing social services such as education and hospitalisation. In addition it becomes difficult to raise the general standard of living.
>
> . . . an effort has been made, especially since 1968, to resettle elderly blacks in the homelands . . . The presence of such a large percentage of elderly people in Bophuthatswana increases both the dependency burden and the demand for social services.
>
> An independent Bophuthatswana government will undoubtedly be faced with the increasing problems associated with urbanisation. As in the rest of Africa the population will steadily move to the urban areas, resulting in problems such as squatting, unemployment and an increasing drain on services . . . One of the major challenges facing the Bophuthatswana government is effective administration of the expanding urban settlements.

These perceptions of the problems facing *the Bophuthatswana government* are a clear indication of how the prevailing ideology of apartheid legitimizes what is, in effect, the subsidy of 'white' South African business by the 'state' of Bophuthatswana. The general implications for the homelands are recognized elsewhere by Smit (1979, p. 13), who points out that the South African government currently meets much of the cost of housing in the townships. He goes on:

> It is obvious that homeland governments will have difficulty in providing housing on this heavily subsidised basis after independence. Drastic increases in rent and service fees may, however, have important political implications for homeland governments. Twenty-four per cent of KwaZulu's budget expenditure was allocated to the establishment and development of towns in the 1975/76 financial year. Such expenditure

along with allocations to education and social services leaves very little for other development projects.

The first obligation is to meet costs associated with the production and reproduction of labour in towns which are, in the case of KwaZulu, mainly African suburbs of Durban. The labour requirements of the white capitalist economy of South Africa come before the developmental needs of the home-lands, the independence of which simply makes the regressive transfer of costs easier to legitimize. The South African state need now step in with financial assistance, dignified as 'foreign aid', only to the extent that the labour reproduction function is threatened. And it must be recognized that, with a growing surplus of African labour, there is little incentive to invest in programmes to reduce infant mortality or starvation.

The political status of Bophuthatswana involves acceptance of the concept of separate development, under a homeland government explicitly support-ive of capitalism. The stance of Bophuthatswana's Chief Minister, in whom executive power is vested, is summarized by Leistner (1977, p. 137):

> Chief Mangope misses no opportunity to affirm his deep belief in the individual's right to dignity, justice and freedom . . . This is not just a vague general posture but reflects his basic philosophy which, amongst others, logically leads him to advocate a market economy characterized by freedom and equal opportunities for all rather than a socialist order dominated by the dictates of a small elite.

The irony of such a statement in South Africa no doubt eludes him. A 'politi-cal backgrounder' entitled *The independence of Bophuthatswana*, published by the Department of Information at the South African Embassy in London quotes (with evident approval) Mangope's opposition to one man one vote in South Africa, his dedication to free enterprise, his preference for poverty rather than accepting help from communist countries, and his categorical assertion that Bophuthatswana would not become a 'socialist welfare state'. Such leadership assures Bophuthatswana's future in South Africa's grand design.

In addition to its updated labour-reserve role, Bophuthatswana forms an essential component of South Africa's geo-strategical survival strategy. This has been likened by Wilson (1979) to an onion, with successive protective rings or layers around the central core of 'white' South Africa. The first ring comprises the non-independent homeland, over which the South African government still exercises a substantial degree of control. The second ring is that of the homelands granted 'independence', including Bophuthatswana, where the government is of a complexion that suits South Africa's purpose. The third ring represents the former High Commission Territories of Botswana, Lesotho and Swaziland, which are integral to the South African economy. There is an outer layer of Namibia, Malawi, Zimbabwe, Mozambique, Angola, Zambia and Tanzania, already partially peeled off the onion. Preservation of the core is crucially dependent on the prevention of further peeling, or, to change the analogy, on tying as much as possible of Southern Africa into a web of economic interdependency so that potentially hostile states (such as Zimbabwe) will see their own interests advanced by stable relationships with a prosperous (white and capitalist) South Africa.

Conclusion

We began by asserting that urbanization takes some peculiar forms under apartheid. Fair and Davies (1976) have recognized a process of 'constrained urbanization', with South Africa's influx control measures holding at bay some of the forces promoting the rapid growth of cities elsewhere in Africa and other parts of the underdeveloped world. The massive spontaneous settlements observed in Bophuthatswana represent a spatial displacement of the familiar Third World phenomenon. The existence of settlements such as Crossroads within 'white' South Africa suggest that containment is breaking down, as harsh necessity drives increasing numbers of Africans to seek some foothold, however precarious and illegal, in those places perceived to offer some prospect of escape from poverty. While these local labour reserves may provide short-run advantages to capital, they are perceived by the state as a threat to social order. The response takes the form of revisions of public policy with respect to urbanization, settlement planning and the control of labour supply. The dialectics of action and reaction, on the part of people and the state, drive on the process of social change.

Some of the immediate problems facing the state have recently been addressed by the reports of two government inquiries (the Wiehahn and Riekert Commissions) set up to consider various aspects of the legislation governing labour affairs. Among other things it is proposed to use the Labour Bureaux to perform the major function of labour supply control hitherto accomplished (with much irritation and dubious efficiency) by the infamous pass laws. The objective is to facilitate labour mobility within the core of 'white' South Africa, while tightening up on influx from the homelands. Wilson (1979) sees this as fortifying the boundary between the core and first layer of his onion, so that the homelands can be used more effectively to externalize the problems of unemployment.

Within the core there are proposals to improve the lot of the urban African, especially with respect to property rights. Ways of facilitating home ownership are to be found (see Ch. 11), so as to encourage family life and social stability. But such apparently laudable objectives founder on the fundamental contradictions of a system which seeks self-preservation through the creation of a property-owning middle class among a poor proletariat deemed to be foreign citizens. Some of the perverse outcomes are revealed in a report by the Black Sash (1980). They point out that neither the East Rand nor West Rand Administrative Board has initiated any schemes for low-cost housing; the WRAB's cheapest house for purchase costs R6600 while in the ERAB an immediate deposit of R1600 is required. Only the wealthy can afford this; for the rest there is the nine-year long waiting list for a rented house in Soweto and, in the meantime, the single-sex hostel, the illicit shared dwelling, or the shanty. Black Sash (1980) conclude their report as follows:

> Apart from any questions of justice and morality could anything be more dangerous? The present visible alliance between Government and big business in the 'total strategy' which is seen to be causing immediate personal disaster to thousands of individuals can only result in the black/white political conflict becoming irrevocably identified with the Marxist/Capitalist economic conflict.
>
> Any so-called free enterprise system which totally denies all freedom to the majority of the people cannot possibly survive. Those who believe that the benefits of capitalism and free enterprise can be spread through the whole population and can bring about justice must prove it and do so *now*. Tomorrow will be too late.

But it may already be too late. The racial cleavages nourished by apartheid ideology are even now giving way to a class polarization, promoted by the actual operation of South African capitalism. The emergence of a black (African, Coloured and Indian) bourgeoisie may well be in the short-run interests of the whites, but the longer-term implication is that privilege cannot be exclusive to whites. And, as the growing recruitment of Africans into skilled occupations undermines the status of the white working class as a labour aristocracy, repressive exploitation will cease to be exclusively the fate of blacks. Apartheid may remain functional to capitalism for some time to come, but the state is likely to find it increasingly difficult to handle the tensions generated by the interplay between the traditional inter-racial antagonisms and the emerging trans-racial class alignments. For all its protective rings, the onion is rotting at the core. But within it are the seeds of a new society, the nature of which will eventually be determined by the struggle of those currently consigned to the squatter camps or the townships: 'a "place"; a position whose contradictions those who impose them don't see, and from which will come a resolution they haven't provided for'.

Acknowledgements

This chapter is a revised version of a paper originally prepared for a workshop held in the Research School of Pacific Studies of the Australian National University, Canberra, in August 1980. The author is grateful to John Lea and John Browett for helpful comments on earlier versions of the chapter. Quotations from *Burger's daughter* are included by permission of Nadine Gordimer and Jonathan Cape Ltd.

3 Apartheid, decentralization and spatial industrial change

CHRISTIAN M. ROGERSON

An understanding of the industrial system of South Africa is central to an appreciation of the functioning and contemporary dynamics of apartheid. The policies and programmes which fall under the rubrics of apartheid or separate development represent, as Wolpe (1972, p. 427) argues, 'the attempt by the capitalist class to meet the expanding demand for cheap African labour in the era of industrial manufacturing capital'. The lives of at least one generation of black South Africans have been conditioned by the making of this apartheid industrial system.

It is the intention in this chapter to address two dimensions of South African industrialization. First, the evolution and salient characteristics of the industrial system of South Africa are set forth. Secondly, the impress of apartheid upon spatial change in the industrial system is investigated. Particular attention centres on the effects of the implementation of the Environment Planning Act, the cornerstone of legislation in South Africa's programme for industrial decentralization.

The industrial system of apartheid South Africa

The Republic of South Africa, a 'semi-peripheral' country in terms of the capitalist world economy (Frank 1979, Wallerstein 1979), possesses the most highly industrialized economy on the African continent. In 1976 manufacturing engaged some 1.36 million workers (South Africa 1978) and contributed almost a quarter of the Gross Domestic Product. The tempo of growth is greatest within heavy industry, reflecting the increasing integration, sophistication and potential self-generating capacity of South African manufacturing. Historically there occurred in South Africa 'a much greater degree of genuine diversification than has been possible for most countries seeking to develop secondary industry' (Milkman 1977–8, p. 71). At the root of this substantive and relatively sophisticated industrial base are three interrelated factors: (a) the actions of the South African state, (b) the role of foreign capital and technology, and (c) the exploitation of large supplies of cheap black labour. The most distinctive facet of South Africa's industrialization is the exclusion of the overwhelming majority of the country's black populace from the fruits of manufacturing progress and their concomitant relegation to the position of a source of low-cost labour.

The role of the state   Historically the state has assumed a pivotal role in the industrialization of South Africa. In the 1920s and 1930s state power was used to resolve the conflicts between agricultural, mining and industrial capital such as to foster a 'national' alliance against foreign capital (Legassick & Hemson 1976, Bozzoli 1978). There was constituted in South Africa a 'national bourgeoisie sufficiently strong to uphold a "national interest" *vis-à-vis* the metropolitan countries' (Arrighi & Saul 1973, p. 55). This permitted the retention and accumulation within South Africa of capital which in other peripheral states simply drained off to the core countries. Because of the reluctance of private capital to invest in basic industry, the South African state intervened extensively in the economy channelling retained surplus (diverted from mining) into the creation and later sustenance of an industrial base. In this fashion 'South Africa, a country which experienced imperial conquest of a far-reaching and violent nature, "broke out" of the vicious cycle of underdevelopment and embarked on a path of comparatively independent capitalist development' (Bozzoli 1978, p. 41).

The major tools applied by the state to catalyze industry were direct investment through the establishment of parastatal corporations and the introduction of a panoply of import controls to stimulate import-substitution industrialization (Seidman & Seidman 1977). The initial state ventures were in iron and steel in the late 1920s and energy in the 1930s. The numbers of parastatal corporations multiplied, particularly after the National Party achieved power in 1948 (Phillips 1974). State investment in manufacturing expanded both absolutely and as a percentage of total manufacturing investment; by 1974, the state contributed 45.6 per cent of total investment and 29.6 per cent of industrial investment. Through the operations of parastatal corporations such as ARMSCOR (military equipment), ISCOR (iron and steel), ESCOM (electricity), SENTRACHEM (chemicals), SASOL (the production of oil from coal) and NATREF (oil refining) the state enjoys a high degree of control over the commanding heights of the economy (Weiss 1975, Rogerson 1981). Moreover, the degree of state ownership and control over South African manufacturing is extended further by participation since 1948 in a host of 'private' enterprise concerns, especially those controlled by Afrikaner capital (Ehrensaft 1976).

In addition to the stimulus of direct investment in key economic sectors the state further encouraged South African industrialization through a series of indirect supports, most importantly through the imposition of import controls and extensive tax incentives. The post-war expansion of manufacturing owes a great deal to a commercial policy which assured substantial protection to domestic manufacturers for a growing range of goods and preferences for the import of required capital goods and materials (Seidman &

Seidman 1977). The general pattern of industrial expansion was of major growth until the 1950s in 'light' and comparatively 'labour-intensive' industrial activities, such as metals and engineering, textiles, clothing, food and drink, and footwear. But in the aftermath of the Sharpeville massacre and of threats of international sanctions against South Africa, the state increasingly pursued the development of more capital-intensive strategic sectors of manufacturing. The major industrial 'growth poles' of the 1960s and 1970s have therefore been motor-cars and auto accessories, chemicals, pulp and paper, military hardware, capital goods equipment, and electronic and computer manufactures (Legassick 1974a). The motor-vehicle industry illustrates the catalytic role of the state in South Africa's industrialization: initially this was based upon the local assembly of imported components, but by introducing high taxation on cars with a high percentage of imported components, the state has encouraged the local evolution of backward linkage manufactures (Grundy 1981). This pattern of industrial development is currently being repeated in the newly introduced sector of television manufacture (Rogerson 1978).

Foreign capital and technology Foreign capital began to move into South African manufacturing only after 1945. British capital dominated inflows until the 1960s, after which United States and EEC investment became considerably greater (Seidman & Makgetla 1978, 1980). It is difficult to evaluate the importance of foreign capital in South African industry quantitatively, especially with the emergence of monopoly capital and the growing interpenetration of foreign with local private and state capital. Nevertheless a recent investigation estimated that approximately 28 per cent of manufacturing employment in South Africa is in foreign-controlled enterprises (Rogerson forthcoming). A study of the leading 100 industrial companies quoted on the Johannesburg Stock Exchange revealed that 17 were majority-owned by overseas investors and that foreign holdings were registered in a further 29 firms (Savage 1978). Such data may still understate the full involvement of foreign capital in South African manufacturing. Suffice it to note that foreign firms dominate motor-cars, oil, tyres, electrical equipment, computers and pharmaceuticals as well as being strongly represented in such areas as food and chemicals. Schollhammer's (1974) investigation of the determinants of the international locational strategies of multinational corporations shows that the particular form of racial domination that lies at the heart of South African society is of no particular concern to international capital except insofar as it presents certain operational difficulties. Indeed, it is commonly argued that the interests of the South African state and of international capital coincide concerning apartheid, in that the burdens of underdevelopment are borne entirely by blacks whose exploitation enriches both South African whites as a group and the foreign concerns (Seidman & Seidman 1977, Seidman & Makgetla 1978, 1980; Milkman 1979, Seidman 1979).

The benefits of foreign capital to South Africa have been not so much quantitative as of a qualitative nature. As Legassick (1977, p. 189) notes: 'South African industrialization has depended on the employment of more and more capital-intensive and "modern" methods in a succession of industrial sectors. And, in each case, it has been foreign capital which has financed the purchasing of the required machinery; and it has been foreign firms which have imported the expertise to initiate the handling of such machines'. Yet, notwithstanding the benefits of foreign technology in strengthening South Africa's industrial base, there exists another dimension to the country's traditional reliance upon imported technologies – the implications for employment.

The industrial system of South Africa is locked into the world economy, through linkages of finance, trade and, most importantly, technology. The patterns of these linkages determine the local techniques of production, types of product manufactured, marketing practices and so forth, which in turn determine overall levels of industrial production. For South Africa these linkages facilitate capital accumulation and increases in output, but without a corresponding impact upon levels of employment (Erwin 1978). That South African industry applies predominantly capital-intensive techniques is highlighted by a recent survey showing that 71 per cent of firms use manufacturing technologies embodying at least 90 per cent of foreign technology (Nattrass & Brown 1977), the overwhelming bulk of which originates in the USA or Western Europe where labour is often in short supply and relatively expensive. With production technologies and the types of products manufactured determined largely by foreign capital, South Africa has followed an increasingly capital-intensive trajectory of industrialization, which is contributing little to solving the country's massive unemployment problems (Maree 1978). Moreover, South Africa suffers an added potential employment loss, typical of semi-peripheral countries in the world economy (cf. Taylor & Thrift 1981), as a result of the drain of repatriated profits and surplus to the 'core' capitalist countries (Samoff 1978, Milkman 1979). The full contemporary significance of this arrested industrial employment growth is apparent only in the light of South Africa's reservoir of cheap Black labour.

*Cheap Black labour** ★   South Africa's rapid industrialization has been underpinned by the creation of a system in which the Black majority participates only as a source of cheap labour (Seidman & Seidman 1977). The origins of this system, its elaboration or 'modernization' to the conditions of an industrializing society and the lineaments of the present-day apartheid political economy are treated elsewhere (e.g. Legassick 1975, 1977; Magu-

★ Black is capitalized from this point on in the chapter, as the discussion focuses on the African population; however, blacks in general (including Coloureds and Asians) serve as sources of cheap labour [Ed.].

bane 1979). In relation to the present discussion it is important to recognize that the forms of integration, or incorporation, of South Africa's Blacks into the capitalist world economy 'have been consistently shaped by White political power and manifested in a system of racial differentiation' (Legassick 1975, p. 232). The combined apartheid apparatus of segregationist legislation, the industrial colour-bar, the perpetuation of migratory labour and, latterly, of programmes for establishing so-called 'independent' Bantustans or homelands† serves to insure that the mass of Blacks are forced into a reservoir of low-skilled labour from which avenues of escape are few.

The much publicized 'improvements' to South Africa's labour legislation, as incorporated in the recommendations of the Wiehahn (South Africa 1979c) and Riekert (South Africa 1979a) Commissions of Inquiry, offer only cosmetic efforts toward de-racialization. By granting limited rights the new legislation provides a means of co-opting the small but increasingly skilled group of urban Blacks at the expense of further tightening apartheid controls on the majority of Blacks (see Shafer 1979, *South African Labour Bulletin* 1979a, b; Hindson 1980). The proposals of Wiehahn and Riekert together constitute a broad attempt by the state to restructure capitalist social relations in order to make them more effective and to secure capitalist domination and exploitation of Black labour under the changed circumstances of class struggle which now characterize South Africa (Davies 1979, Hindson 1980). The recommendations of these two commissions represent no attack upon the essential structures of the cheap labour economy. The rural Bantustans are today the form in which the 'industrial reserve army' exists in South Africa (Legassick & Wolpe 1976). From these areas, industry augments its labour needs in times of expansion; to these areas workers return after completing the period of selling their labour in one of the metropolitan–industrial complexes of 'white' South Africa. The 'cheapness' of Black labour for South African industry is assured as the social costs of reproducing that labour – of caring for children, the unemployed, the aged and the non-working dependants – are transferred on to the Bantustan governments (see Ch. 2).

† The term 'Bantustan' is preferred in this chapter to the official designations of homeland or Black state. Many Black South Africans, particularly those born in the 'white' area, deny that these poverty-stricken and mostly geographically fragmented territories, constituting 14 per cent of the area of South Africa, are their homelands. Moreover, they disavow also the notion that the South African government has the right to confer 'independence' on them, thus stripping them of claims to citizenship in the wealthier 86 per cent of the country. As pointed out by Kane-Berman '. . . to use the term "homeland" is to concede a terminological victory to the ideologues of separate development. Although this may seem a small point at first, it . . . in fact (goes) to the heart of (South African) politics. For when government says that the homeland of the Zulus is KwaZulu or that of the Tswanas Bophuthatswana, what it really means is that *only* these areas are their "homeland" and that the rest of South Africa is not. Thus, *insidiously* with the term "homeland" gaining general currency, does language help to shape political thought' (Kane-Berman 1979b, p. 41).

The imperatives of exclusionary industrialization Upon the advantages afforded by this system of cheap labour, the South African state, supported by foreign capital in the post World War II period, has constructed a modern and relatively independent industrial system. The industrial transformation of South Africa occurred in a time-span of just over 50 years during which living conditions for most Blacks improved only marginally, if at all (Legassick & Hemson 1976, Seidman & Seidman 1977). Herein rests the key structural feature of contemporary South African manufacturing, viz. its *exclusionary* character. This feature derives, in part, from the particular phase in the capitalist world economy during which South African industrial growth has taken place, a phase in which the linkages of South Africa to the core countries result in a limited employment impact in terms of an expanded industrial capacity. More important, however, is that the structures of racial domination in South Africa forged white workers into a classic labour aristocracy. Creating this relatively high-income group of whites, at the expense of the Black majority, allowed a market for early South African manufacturers. But as industry expanded, the sharp market limitations imposed by the country's exclusionary path of industrialization and by the impoverishment of the Black masses had to be faced (Seidman & Seidman 1977, Rogerson 1981).

Seeking to resolve this contradiction, the South African state is currently pursuing simultaneously several economic strategies (Ehrensaft 1976, Milkman 1979):

(a) *The growth of a military–industrial complex.* One partial solution to the constraints imposed by the narrowness of the domestic market is found in expanded state expenditures on defence. Nevertheless the emergence of a military–industrial complex (Seidman & Makgetla 1978) in South Africa provides only a temporary relief. It does nothing to alleviate the long-term structural problems facing South African manufacturing.

(b) *'Sub-imperial' expansion.* The exigencies of searching for new outlets for domestic manufactures accentuates South Africa's 'sub-imperial' role in Africa and of its outward reach into surrounding countries, particularly Botswana, Lesotho, Namibia and Swaziland (Rogerson 1981). The much discussed programmes for a 'constellation' of Southern African states (Herbst 1980), and for a zone of regional economic co-operation, centre around the exchange of the labour and raw materials of the surrounding states for the manufactures of South Africa.

(c) *Export subsidization.* A third strategy is that of using export revenues to subsidize export industries, increasing their scale of production to the point at which South Africa's cheap labour costs yield competitive advantages, in the context of what Fröbel *et al.* (1980) style as the 'new international division of labour'. Together with this programme, the state seeks also to take advantage of the leverage afforded by world

demand for South Africa's mineral resources and to force tariff concessions from core countries upon the entry of South African manufactures.

(d) *New high technology industries.* One final response centres on the use of
state capital to develop new advanced technology exports in selected
industrial sectors (e.g. uranium enrichment) that can be internationally
competitive with the manufactures of core states.

In summary, the shaping of the apartheid industrial system is a product of
the actions of the state, the contributions of foreign capital and technology
and, most importantly, of the exploitation of cheap Black labour within the
framework of South Africa's 'labour-coercive' economy (Legassick 1977,
p. 190). Paralleling the country's industrial transformation, South Africa
increasingly has assumed the role of a sub-imperial power within Southern
Africa. Moreover, the continuing importation of foreign capital and technology strengthens the capacity of the minority-ruled white military–
industrial complex to confront the struggles of South Africa's Blacks to
secure their liberation from the apartheid system (Seidman & Makgetla
1978).

As part of the strategy for arresting the progress of Black liberation in
South Africa the state operationalized the Bantustan programme for establishing a series of formally independent ethnic nations (Southall 1980). In
attempting to provide these fledgling nations with at least a facade of
economic viability, the policies of decentralization and spatial industrial
change assumed a new importance. It is to an examination of the history of
these policies and of their current status that attention now turns.

Decentralization and spatial industrial change

A persistent theme in the economic geography of South Africa since 1948 has
been the efforts by the state to restructure spatial patterns of manufacturing
in accord with the changing imperatives of apartheid. In particular the state
has sought to arrest and reverse the geographical concentration of industry in
the four major metropolitan complexes – the Pretoria–Witwatersrand–
Vereeniging (P–W–V) region, Western Cape, Durban–Pinetown and Port
Elizabeth–Uitenhage – which by 1960 contained almost 80 per cent of all
manufacturing employment. The programmes for industrial decentralization, which were introduced progressively after 1948, became incorporated
as a key component in apartheid, forming part of the mythology of the state
attempting to help 'develop the Bantu peoples' (Gottschalk 1977). If Blacks
were not to be accorded social, political or residential rights in 'white' areas,
it followed naturally that industry should be encouraged to move toward or
into the Black areas of South Africa. The requirements of separate development guided the objectives and directions of the programme of decentral-

ization: 'The major goal was to accomplish a regional redistribution of economic activity in South Africa, so that 9 or 10 million Bantu expected to be born during the half century up to the year 2000 should settle in their own areas rather than in or around the concentrations of White Communities in the Republic' (Lombard 1974, p. 463).

Industrial decentralization   A brief survey of the origins of South Africa's programme of industrial decentralization must begin in 1955 with the Report of the Tomlinson Commission. The report, which is generally acknowledged as laying down the spatial blueprint for apartheid, advocated the entry and investment of white industrial entrepreneurs into the Black areas (today the Bantustans). Government responded, however, by emphasizing that the establishment of industries within the Bantustans could be undertaken only by Black capital. Thus in 1960 began promotion of the alternative policy for the decentralization of industries into the border areas or selected 'white' towns which adjoin the Bantustans (Bell 1973).

The shifting geography of government-sponsored decentralization efforts may be charted through the construction of a simple location preference matrix (Keeble 1977) for South Africa (Fig. 3.1). The initial thrust of policy was in favour of locations such as Rosslyn and Hammarsdale, small centres

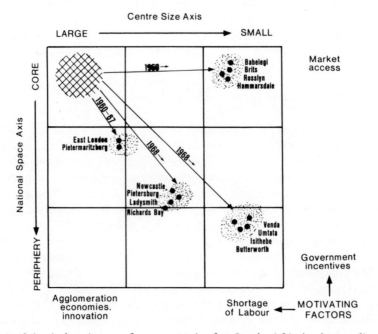

Figure 3.1   A location preference matrix for South Africa's decentralization programme.

adjoining existing metropolitan complexes. The accent of policy then shifted toward places such as East London and Pietermaritzburg, more distant from the major national cores yet relatively high-order centres in the national urban system. From 1968 onwards the focus of decentralization veered away from these earlier locations. At the heart of the programme were now a suite of new growth points, for example Newcastle, Pietersburg and Ladysmith, important country towns in the urban hierarchy but at some distance from existing concentrations of industrial production. In addition to these border area growth points, the initial decision disallowing white investment in the Bantustans was reversed and from 1968 government launched a programme for industrial expansion within the Bantustans. Again, this policy was to be focused around the promotion of a set of growth points. With the exception of the highly core-orientated Bophuthatswana growth point of Babelegi (50 km north of Pretoria) the remaining Bantustan growth points are all small centres located in the outermost periphery of national economic space. Throughout the 1970s this group of 20 growth points (see Fig. 3.2) formed the centrepiece of South Africa's decentralization efforts. Of this group, 12 centres (East London, Berlin, Phalaborwa, Pietersburg, Newcastle, Richard's Bay, Brits, Rustenburg, Potgietersrus, King William's Town,

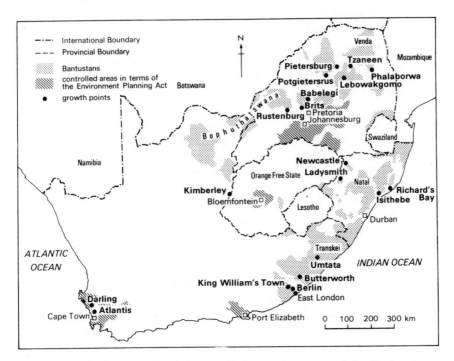

Figure 3.2 Growth points and controlled areas in terms of the Environment Planning Act.

Ladysmith and Tzaneen) fall under the rubric of border area localities, five growth points (Babelegi, Lebowakgomo, Isithebe, Butterworth and Umtata) are located in the Bantustans, and the remaining three growth points (Kimberley, Atlantis and Darling) represent extensions of the decentralization programme to South Africa's Coloured population, with the goal of deflecting future employment and population growth away from metropolitan Cape Town (see Chs 2 & 12).

Over a period of two decades, therefore, there occurred a progressive spatial shift in decentralization policy away from large and core-oriented centres in favour of small centres in the geographical periphery. The changing spatial thrust of policy accords with the central objective of the whole programme, to stem the continuing growth of Black employment and populations in the 'white' metropolitan areas.

In seeking to counter the continuing attractions for industrialists of the agglomeration economies and the high innovative capacity of the major core regions, in the early 1960s the government introduced a suite of incentives to steer firms towards border areas. No attempts were made at this time to hector industry into relocating from existing industrial complexes, nor were any constraints placed upon expansion in these areas. Nevertheless the direction of policy underwent substantial change as the early results of the border area programme proved disappointing. Although some industrial expansion was stimulated at locations such as Rosslyn and Hammarsdale, only glacial progress was recorded at those border areas in the periphery. At the close of the 1960s the spatial industrial system reflected the paramountcy of the forces of economic polarization over those of dispersal (Rogerson 1975).

It was against such a backdrop that the Environment Planning Act (née The Physical Planning and Utilization of Resources Act No. 88) was introduced in 1967. The Act represented the first statutory controls in South Africa designed to accelerate the programme of industrial decentralization. The accordance of the Act with the political economy of apartheid is revealed clearly by its provisions, inter alia, controlling the establishment and extension of factories in certain proscribed areas of South Africa. Section 3 of the Act requires that ministerial permission be granted before any new industrial developments or extensions can occur. The key aspect of the legislation is the definition of the term 'factory extension', which refers exclusively to any increase in the number of a firm's Black employees. In terms of this stipulation the employment of white, Coloured or Asian labour was not affected. Firms in the controlled or proscribed areas (see Fig. 3.2) were limited to the size of their Black work force as of 19 January 1968. The impress of the Act was felt most notably in the metropolitan areas of the Transvaal, Western Cape, Port Elizabeth–Uitenhage and Bloemfontein. The Durban–Pinetown region and more broadly the whole of Natal was not controlled in terms of this legislation. In addition to these prohibitions on the employment of Black labour, proclamation R 6 as applied to the Act further limited industrial growth in the controlled areas through constraining the zoning of new industrial land. This last provision was applied with great force, particularly in the P–W–V region (South Africa 1979c).

The introduction of the Environment Planning Act and specifically of the provisions surrounding the employment of additional Black labour generated considerable consternation, confusion and protest among industrialists in the affected areas (Ratcliffe 1979). Amid a Stock Market slump, the government appointed an interdepartmental committee of inquiry into the whole programme of decentralization. The resultant white paper (South Africa 1971) recommended that enterprises classified as locality-bound be permitted to settle and expand freely in the controlled areas. But enterprises categorized as non-locality-bound were to maintain a future ratio of Black to white employees not exceeding 2.5:1, a figure later reduced to 2:1. Additional Black labour would not be granted to this latter group of firms in terms of the Section 3 legislation. Thus refashioned, the legislation now directly threatened the employment expansion of Black-labour-intensive industries in the metropolitan areas generally and in the P–W–V region in particular.

The Environment Planning Act formed the cornerstone of government efforts since 1967 to deflect industrial growth in South Africa into the border area and Bantustan growth points. To provide a further impetus for the movement of industry into these areas, government used its powers over wage determination and sanctioned the payment of lower wages and the existence of poorer working conditions (in respect of holidays, sick leave and length of working week) in these areas (Gottschalk 1977). Indeed, from 1970 onwards all minimal wage legislation for Black workers inside the Bantustans was terminated. Not unexpectedly, the so-called independence of, successively, Transkei, Bophuthatswana and Venda, had no impact in terms of improving wage and industrial working conditions in these particular Bantustans. Seen in the above context whatever the consequences of the Environment Planning Act for spatial change in the South African industrial system, they appeared to offer meagre benefits for the ordinary Black worker.

Spatial industrial change since 1967   The industrial employment map of South Africa (Fig. 3.3) highlights the concentration of manufacturing. Over 1 million of the total 1.3 million workforce are in the four major metropolitan areas, the P–W–V region alone accounting for almost 600 000 jobs. By contrast the 20 decentralized growth points contained a total of approximately 110 000 manufacturing jobs. The map presents evidence also of the first fruits of the programme for Bantustan industrial development. Most successful of these locations is Babelegi in Bophuthatswana, where there are currently nearly 90 enterprises providing 10 000 job opportunities (Palmer 1980). But in total all the Bantustans record only 20–25 000 manufacturing

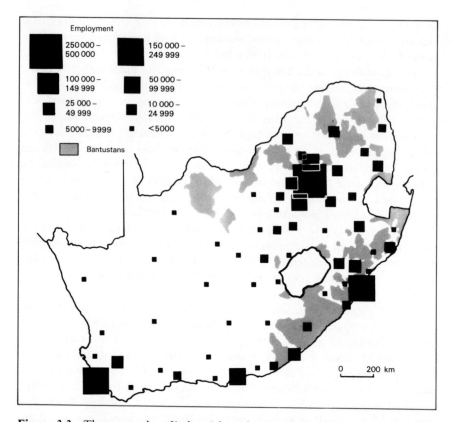

Figure 3.3   The geography of industrial employment in South Africa, 1976. (Note: analysis of the latest *Census of manufacturing* can be undertaken only in the broadest terms in view of the reshuffling of statistical units which makes impossible a comparative analysis with the earlier 1967 census on a magisterial district basis. In addition, as the census was undertaken in the year of Transkei's 'independence', no statistics for that Bantustan are made available. In the construction of Fig. 3.3 and in subsequent analysis of the 1967 and 1976 census, an estimate of manufacturing employment in the Transkei for 1976 from the South African Institute of Race Relations was used. Source: South Africa 1980b.)

jobs, compared with the estimated average new job requirements of these areas of 105 000 per annum. Irrespective of the inevitably high *percentage* growth rates for industrial employment recorded in many of the Bantustans (and much quoted by apologists for apartheid), the conclusion remains inescapable that the *absolute* volume of industrial development occurring in these areas in no way threatens the position of the Bantustans as continuing reservoirs of cheap Black labour for the core regions of South Africa. Nor, it might be added, was the programme for industrializing these impoverished rural areas ever intended to challenge this central function of the Bantustans in the political economy of apartheid (Rogerson & Pirie 1979). The continu-ing development of industry in the Bantustans must be understood as com-plementary to rather than in any way competitive with South African manufacturing (Southall 1980, Rogerson 1981).

Spatial industrial change between 1967 and 1976 was analysed in terms of the patterns of absolute change and patterns of relative change, the latter revealed through the application of the standard technique of shift analysis pioneered by Perloff *et al.* (1960). The patterns of absolute employment change between 1967 and 1976 are presented on Figure 3.4. Notwithstanding

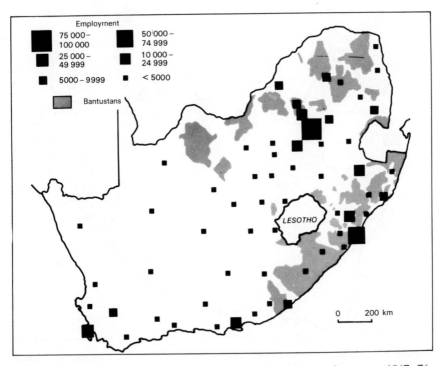

Figure 3.4 Absolute changes (increases) in industrial employment, 1967–76. (Source: South Africa 1980b.)

the constraints of the Environment Planning Act, the major centres of employment generation continued to be the leading metropolitan areas of South Africa; a net employment gain in industry of 140 000, 55 000 and 42 000 was recorded respectively for the P–W–V, Durban–Pinetown and Western Cape regions. The results of applications made under the Environ-ment Planning Act for extensions and new establishments during the period 1968–78 (Dewar 1980) show only a 10 per cent rate of refusal for applications for additional Black labour. This finding, however, masks the considerable differentiation in the application of the Act both in terms of different metropolitan areas and different industrial sectors. Geographically, the greatest number and rate of refusals occurs with firms located in the P–W–V region. Sectorally, Section 3 has been most strictly applied to the expansion of the Black-labour-intensive clothing industry (Rogerson & Kobben 1982).

The uneven spatial impress of the legislation is revealed also by Figure 3.5,

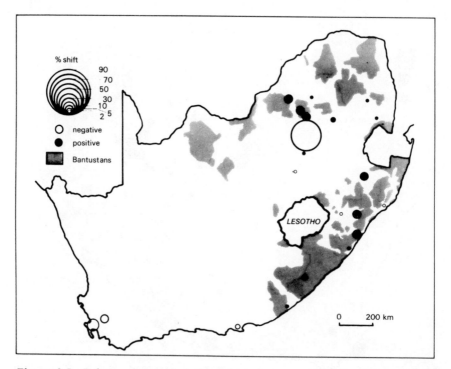

Figure 3.5 Relative changes in industrial employment, 1967–76. (Source: South Africa 1980b.)

which presents the results of a shift analysis of regional industrial employment change in South Africa between 1967 and 1976. The map shows the spatial patterns of positive and negative shifts, indexing relative employment changes in the industrial space economy since the introduction of the Environment Planning Act. The most dramatic finding is that over 80 per cent of the negative employment shifts are accounted for by three regions, namely, the Witwatersrand, Western Cape and Port Elizabeth–Uitenhage. The Witwatersrand alone accounts for over half of all the negative shifts, much of which is explicable in terms of the stringent application of the Section 3 legislation to the region's clothing and textiles trades (Rogerson & Kobben 1982). It is striking that the three metropolitan areas experiencing the largest relative employment losses during this period were all controlled in terms of the Environment Planning Act. By contrast, the Durban–Pinetown region, unaffected by the Section 3 legislation, recorded a net positive employment shift during this same period. The geographical pattern of the positive shifts in employment points to the influence of the decentralization programme in partially remoulding the South African spatial industrial mosaic. With the exception of the Durban Metropolitan Region, all the major positive employment shifts were recorded at locations where decentralization incentives were in operation, notably at Rosslyn, Babelegi, Hammarsdale, Brits, Ladysmith and Rustenburg. The most recent study of employment creation in the decentralized areas places the rate of new job creation as between 7000 and 8000 jobs per year (Decentralization Consultants of South Africa 1980). The majority of such jobs, it must be recalled, are at severely depressed wage levels and accompanied often by staggeringly poor conditions of service (Gottschalk 1977).

Against these small increments in industrial employment which are being generated at several decentralized locations, including the Bantustans, must be balanced the net employment loss experienced in metropolitan areas as a consequence of the restrictions imposed by the Environment Planning Act. The direct impact of the Act is reflected partly in the annual statistics of the refusals for employment of additional Black workers in terms of Section 3; between 1968 and 1978 these refusals affected over 100 000 jobs. Additional losses follow directly from government powers in rejecting applications for the proclamation of new industrial townships. The Minister of Labour triumphantly reported to white voters that such powers had prevented the employment of, at least, another 220 000 Black workers in the industrial metropolitan areas (Gottschalk 1977). Much harder to quantify but of equal potential importance are those employment losses that derive indirectly from the imposition of this legislation. These include, inter alia, losses of firms forced to close down or which failed to expand as a consequence of the Act. Evidence from an examination of the effects of the Act upon clothing and textiles manufacture revealed that in 1977 and 1978 alone 4000 jobs were lost in the Transvaal through factories being forced into closure (Rogerson & Kobben 1982). Finally, consideration must be accorded also to the incalculable employment losses that resulted from the Black-white employment labour ratios stimulating substitution of capital for labour in the metropolitan areas. The only substantive attempt so far to draw up a balance between the employment gains and losses resulting from decentralization concluded that for every one job created in the decentralized areas, nine potential jobs were lost in South Africa's metropolitan areas (Gottschalk 1977).

In the light of the foregoing, it is clear that the Environment Planning Act has destroyed a significantly higher number of employment opportunities for Blacks than it has nurtured. Contrary to government propaganda of the supposed beneficial effects of the strategy for Blacks, the major impact of the industrial decentralization programme has been to further contribute to raising levels of Black unemployment and poverty in South Africa.

Conclusion

The exclusion of the Black majority from the substantive benefits of manufacturing growth is the most outstanding feature of South Africa's semi-peripheral pattern of industrialization. Under the policies and programmes of apartheid, the institutions of the country's cheap labour economy have been progressively modernized and expanded to meet the circumstances of an industrializing economy. Supported by foreign capital and foreign technology, the South African state has forged the most integrated and sophisticated industrial system in Africa.

The consequences of excluding Blacks, except as a source of low-cost labour, find expression in the several contemporary strategies which seek to overcome the restrictions of the domestic market and open new markets for the products of South African industry. Not the least of these strategies is that which involves restoring the respectability of South Africa in the eyes of international opinion. This goal is sought by introducing a suite of policies and legislation which, superficially at least, afford the appearance of change. For example, the much discussed proposals contained in the Wiehahn and Riekert Commissions' reports foster an illusion of major changes in apartheid industrial legislation. But nowhere do these reports challenge the underlying institutionalized structure of white privilege and exploitation of Blacks (Seidman & Makgetla 1980) which lies at the heart of the apartheid industrial system.

The illusion of change is similarly apparent in the programmes for spatial industrial change in South Africa. Again, this sort of change is not one that threatens to recast the central function of Bantustans as cheap labour reservoirs. The programme of industrial decentralization is often portrayed as progressive, bringing positive benefits in the form of new employment opportunities for South African Blacks. Nevertheless the strategy is one which first and foremost buttresses apartheid, seeking to contain the numbers of Blacks in the 'white' areas of South Africa. The proclaimed benefits of new job opportunities mask the poverty wage levels and poor working conditions in areas where the labour of a recently impoverished peasantry is tapped without imposing on capital the social welfare costs that accompany permanent urbanization. Furthermore, it is argued that the employment creating effect of decentralization for Blacks is a myth; rather, the chief effect of the implementation of the Environment Planning Act has been to contribute towards further raising levels of Black unemployment.

The considerable publicity and propaganda which surrounds the issues of 'developing' the Bantustans and 'improving' labour legislation affecting Blacks obscures a subtle yet potentially important change which is presently taking effect in the South African industrial landscape. Engineered by the provisions of the Environment Planning Act there is emerging a 'new spatial division of labour' (Massey 1979) in South Africa. The pattern in the metropolitan areas is one of the continuing concentration of high-order business functions alongside a progressively capital-intensive form of manufacturing production. To the border area and Bantustan growth points are being sloughed off certain low-wage and Black-labour-intensive industrial activities. Recent announcements of plans to establish new 'regional development axes' (Gordon 1981), growth areas situated between white areas and Bantustans, appear a further step towards such a new spatial division of labour in South African manufacturing. Nevertheless, as long as the objective of stemming Black influx into white areas remains the pivot of the whole programme for spatial industrial change, so long must Blacks suffer the continuing burdens of mounting unemployment, poverty-in-employment and miserable work environments under apartheid.

Acknowledgements

An earlier version of this chapter was prepared as a paper for the International Geographical Union Commission on Industrial Systems. Mr P. Stickler is thanked for the preparation of the diagrams.

4 *Migrant labour and frontier commuters: reorganizing South Africa's Black labour supply*

ANTHONY LEMON

Migrant labourers in the Southern African context may be defined as those who oscillate between home and workplace over a greater distance than can be travelled on a daily commuting basis (Wilson 1976, p. 2). Such workers are by no means unique to South Africa. Migrant labour has been a natural response to labour demand in economic core areas and poverty of opportunity in peripheries in many parts of the world. In Western Europe where migrant labour is essentially a post-war phenomenon, a high degree of labour stabilization and family reunion has already occurred (King 1976, Salt & Clout 1976, Lemon 1980). But in South Africa, despite a century of migrant labour, the system remains intact. It is indeed the keystone of apartheid: the means whereby social and political separation may be made compatible with economic interdependence in a modern sector which is still rapidly expanding. It is the institutionalization and legal entrenchment of the migrant labour system, on racial lines, which is distinctively South African. This may be viewed, from the earliest times, in terms of two conflicting needs: for Black labour and continued white dominance.

No attempt is made here to deal with all dimensions of migrant labour in South Africa. Historical detail is minimized, apart from a summary of the 20th-century legislative framework. Attention is not focused on the motivation and behaviour patterns of migrants, nor on the nature of their urban experience: the reader must look elsewhere for the perspectives of anthropology and sociology. The emphasis is upon recent developments, especially in relation to the policies of government and employers, and on the economic, demographic and political context in which they are being pursued. In other words we are asking how the conflicting needs already mentioned are being met in changing circumstances. The growth of 'frontier commuting', or daily travel from homeland towns across what apartheid deems to be international borders to 'white' South Africa, is a major element in the changing geography of labour supply in the 1970s, and as such forms a necessary part of this study.

The legislative framework

The origins of migrant labour legislation might be traced back as far as 1849, when tribesmen on the eastern frontier of the Cape Province, their livelihood already all but ruined by war and drought, were forced to choose between assigned 'locations' and service on colonial farms. Indirect measures such as taxation and the erosion of hitherto accepted systems by which Africans farmed white-owned land forced Africans to work for the white man in the ensuing decades. The construction of branch railway lines to white farms, which circumvented or entirely missed most African reserves, left the emerging peasant farmers of Fingoland and elsewhere at an impossible disadvantage in terms of market access: thus a potential threat to Black labour supplies was removed (Bundy 1972, pp. 376–7).

Early labour flows to white farms were dwarfed by those which followed the discovery of diamonds at Kimberley in 1867 and gold on the Witwatersrand in 1886. By 1899 nearly 100 000 Africans were employed on the gold mines alone, drawn from every tribe south of the Zambezi and many farther north. It was inevitable that early African recruitment should be based on a migratory system: the initial contrast between subsistence and modern economies, traditional and Western cultures, was too great to envisage an immediate transition. Many early 20th-century policy makers believed that the Black man in urban areas was just a temporary phenomenon because the diamond and gold mining operations were expected to be of short duration (Smit 1979, p. 6).

The closed compounds in Kimberley, built to prevent illicit diamond buying, set the pattern for the decades that followed on the mines. In the towns, Blacks settled in backyards or on any vacant lot, a situation which gave rise to white demands for segregation. This was introduced in the Natives (Urban Areas) Act 1923, which also provided for stricter control over the influx of Blacks into urban areas. This Act embodied the view that the towns were the white man's creation: Africans should be allowed to enter them only in so far as their labour was needed. This principle of impermanence, enunciated by the Transvaal Local Government Commission (Transvaal 1922, para. 42), remains part of the official attitude to urban Africans today. It has had far-reaching implications for the provision of services, property ownership, participation in administration, and the morphology of Black townships (Smit & Booysen 1977, p. 5).

Influx controls were also applied to Black women from 1930, but the pace of industrial development nevertheless attracted increasing numbers to the towns and controls were reinforced in 1937. From 1923 until 1937 housing was provided almost exclusively for migrant labourers, but thereafter attempts were made to provide for Black families legally in the towns.

In the 1940s when industrialists began to stress the value of semi-skilled Africans in manufacturing employment, the government appeared slowly to be recognizing the need for reform of urban African policy. Wartime industrial expansion was accompanied by greatly increased labour demands. The Van Eck Commission considered further African urbanization a necessary prerequisite for the raising of rural incomes (South Africa 1941, p. 248), an enlightened and perceptive view which applies even more forcefully today. The Smit Committee (South Africa 1943, para. 8) and the Social and Economic Planning Council (South Africa 1946, para. 11) condemned the migrant labour system, the latter emphasizing the need to develop a permanent labour force. Smuts (1942, p. 10) himself observed that 'You might as well try to sweep the ocean back with a broom' as to stop African urbanization, yet his government was responsible for the Natives (Urban Areas) Consolidation Act 1945. Under Section 10 of this Act, which remains in force (as amended), an African may claim permanent residence in an urban area only if he has resided there continuously since birth, has lawfully resided there continuously for 15 years, or has worked there for the same employer for 10 years. Section 10 was, however, only applicable in areas specifically proclaimed at the request of the local authority.

Subsequent measures considerably tightened up the 1945 legislation, partly in response to the increasing concern voiced by white farmers about the loss of Black labour to the mines in the 1930s and early 1940s, and increasingly to the towns later in the 1940s (Morris 1977, p. 5). The Prevention of Illegal Squatting Act 1951 was aimed at peri-urban squatting by Africans seeking or already in employment in adjacent towns. Previously if an African farm worker squatted immediately outside urban limits, he was legally outside the jurisdiction of the local authority and not subject to influx control.

The Native Laws Amendment Act 1952 is described by Morris (1977, p. 36) as 'the most important piece of legislation in the post-war era'; it laid the basis for all state intervention to control the distribution of labour between town and country, and between towns, from 1952 onwards. The Act introduced the principle of efflux control and the practice of canalizing labour through Labour Bureaux. Henceforth permission to go to 'prescribed' (mainly urban) areas had to be obtained from the nearest Labour Bureau in the rural area where an African lived. Similar controls also applied between prescribed areas, and were related to labour demand. Influx controls were also tightened; Section 10 became automatically applicable in all urban areas, unless specifically excluded. Furthermore, the loophole created by Section 13 of the 1945 Act which had exempted mine Africans from Section 10 proclamations was removed by the 1952 Act which stated that an African working in the mines was governed by Section 10 from the moment he ceased to work on the mines.

The pass laws were simplified by the Natives (Abolition of Passes and Co-ordination of Documents) Act 1952, which introduced a more effective system of registration and identification, to be implemented uniformly in all provinces. This was made possible by the passing two years before of the Population Registration Act 1950, under which all South Africans were classified as members of one or other population group.

Dependants of those who qualify under Section 10 of the 1945 Act were originally entitled to permanent residence in the same area. Since 1964, however, women have been refused entry unless they qualify independently of their husbands.

Finally, reference must be made to the Coloured labour preference area in the Western Cape. The policy of giving preference to Coloured over Black labour in this region began to operate in 1962 and was extended to a further 22 magisterial districts in 1971 (Fig. 2.1, p. 26). Within the affected area, it has to be shown that Coloured labour is unavailable and that suitable accommodation has been provided before permission is granted for the 'importation' of Black labour. The current effects of this legislation in Cape Town have recently been investigated by Bekker and Coetzee (1980); some of the implications for Africans are indicated in Chapter 2 of the present volume.

Spatial patterns of migrant labour flow

The formerly clear-cut distinction between internal labour movements (from homelands to 'white' areas) and international migration has been somewhat blurred by the granting of 'independence' to Transkei (1976), Bophuthatswana (1977), Venda (1979) and Ciskei (1981). In this chapter these and other 'national states', as the South African government now prefers to call the homelands, will be treated as domestic sources of migrant labour. The role of the 'independent' homelands as suppliers of labour is in no way diminished by changed political status (see Ch. 2): indeed Transkei has recently increased dramatically as a source of mine labour (172 575 migrant miners in 1980) for reasons considered below. All homelands show high levels of employment dependency: in none was more than 40 per cent of the de jure male population aged between 15 and 64 actually resident in the homeland in 1970. An estimated 1 770 000 people were 'continuously absent' (Lombard & Van der Merwe 1972, p. 31), including those with Section 10 rights in urban areas and those living permanently (or until 'resettled') on white farms, with or without their families. According to Nattrass (1976, pp. 66–8) there were 1 295 000 male migrants, equivalent to 59 per cent of the African male labour force in the modern sector, in 1970; for every five economically active men living in the homelands, six were absent.

Detailed 1980 census results were not available at the time of writing and precise comparison with the above figures is not possible; no results at all were available from the separate Transkeian and Bophuthatswanan censuses. The 1978 population estimates (Table 4.1) indicate the high proportions of each ethnic group (the basis of the de jure population) absent from their homelands. Migrant labour figures for all homelands rose steadily from 866 300 (1970) to 1 038 700 in 1976, after which these statistics have, curiously,

Table 4.1 *De jure* and *de facto* homeland population in relation to migrant labour.

Homeland	De jure population 1978 (estimate)	De facto population 1978 (estimate)	(2) as a percentage of (1)	Migrant labourers 1976
Bophuthatswana	2 219 600	1 273 000	57.3	51 100[1]
Ciskei	1 023 200	554 000	54.1	24 900
Gazankulu	858 900	353 800	41.2	72 500
KaNgwane	622 300	219 700	35.3	7 700
KwaZulu	5 304 500	2 898 100	54.6	273 400
Lebowa	2 121 200	1 470 000	69.3	196 900
Qwaqwa	1 791 700	95 100	5.3	11 000
Transkei	4 142 800	2 483 700	60.0	343 300[1]
Venda	473 200	357 600	75.6	57 900
total	18 557 400	9 705 800	52.3	1 038 700

Source: BENSO (1980).

[1] Official figures (disclosed to the House of Assembly by the Minister of Co-operation and Development 1 March 1981) give 549 704 Transkeians working in South Africa (172 575 in mining) and 613 409 people from Bophuthatswana. These totals clearly include *de jure* citizens, economically active in 'white' South Africa but continually absent from their official homelands.

ceased to be published. If migrant labourers are added to the *de facto* population, it is apparent that nearly 8 million other *de jure* homeland citizens – over 40 per cent – are 'continuously absent'. Assuming the activity rate of the *de facto* homeland population to be the same as that for the Black population as a whole (32.06 per cent in October 1977, excluding Transkei and Bophuthatswana), the migrant labour force represents some 32 per cent of the total homeland labour force. In practice, the economically active population in the homelands, which has been subject to both influx control and re-settlement of non-productive dependants from 'white' urban and rural areas, will be a much smaller proportion. Given the age and sex selectivity of migrant labour, it is clear that well over half the younger men were absent from the homelands, as Nattrass concluded in 1970.

The extent of foreign migrant labour has declined sharply in the 1970s (Table 4.2). This is closely related to changes in mining recruitment policies, which are discussed below. The drastic reduction of migration from Malawi and Mozambique, and the appearance of Zimbabwe as a supplier in the closing years of UDI, are the principal changes. Recruitment from Malawi was suspended in April 1974 pending investigation of an air crash in which 74 Malawian miners were killed, and its resumption is relatively recent, but numbers are unlikely even to approach the 1973 level again. Recruitment from Rhodesia began only in December 1974, following an agreement intended partially to replace the shortfall after the loss of Malawian miners, but the number of Zimbabwean migrant labourers has also fallen since 1977.

Spatial patterns of migrant labour in South Africa have been examined by Board (1976). The Southern Transvaal draws from the whole country, but chiefly from the north and east where the African population is greatest. The Orange Free State goldfields have a more restricted catchment area, but are nevertheless national rather than provincial in scope. Africans in the Western Cape travel to work from all parts of the Eastern Cape, but particularly Transkei and Ciskei. East London's migrant labour hinterland is mainly local, reflecting its proximity to Ciskei and Transkei, and Durban draws from all over Natal (Fig. 4.1).

Table 4.2 Foreign migrant labour in South Africa, 1973–80.

Country of origin	1973 (June)[1]	1977 (Feb.)[3]	1979 (June)[2]	1980 (month unspecified)[4]
Angola	42	805	275	291
Botswana	46 192	43 159	32 463	23 200
Lesotho	148 856	160 634	152 032	140 746
Malawi	139 714	12 761	35 803	32 319
Mozambique	127 198	111 257	61 550	54 424
Swaziland	10 032	20 750	13 006	10 377
Zambia	684	766	809	864
Zimbabwe	3 250	32 716	21 547	19 853
total including others	485 100	391 848	326 709	285 176

Sources: [1, 2] South Africa (1981); [3] Hansard, South Africa (1977 cols 259–60); [4] House of Assembly proceedings reported in *Daily Dispatch*, East London (2 March 1981).

There have for a long time been substantial numbers of foreign migrants illegally in South Africa. As government restrictions on foreigners were tightened in the post-war period, so the incentive not to be recorded in the census, or not to indicate foreign origin, increased. The Froneman Committee estimated a total of 836 000 foreigners in 1960, of whom 650 000 were employed (270 000 of them in agriculture), against a census figure of 586 000 foreign Africans (Horrell 1964, p. 144). The committee recommended complete replacement by indigenous labour within five years, but these recommendations were not seriously implemented, *inter alia* because of the precarious financial position of the gold mining industry before prices began to rise in the early 1970s (Knight 1977, p. 52). The census figure of 490 000 foreign Africans in 1970 includes only 38 000 on white farms, which is almost certainly an underestimate.

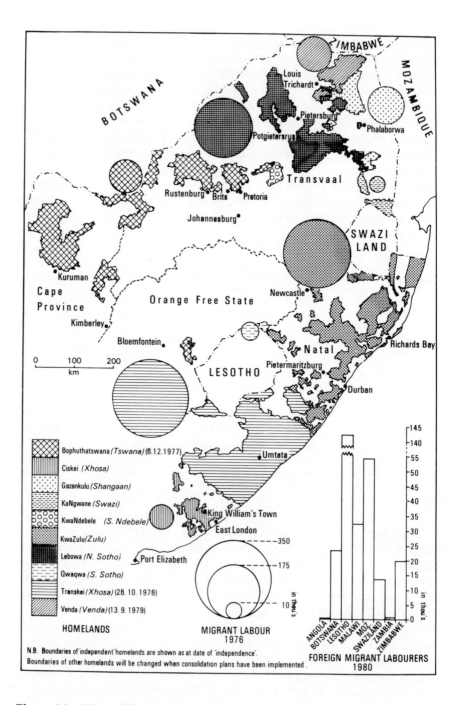

Figure 4.1 Migrant labour in South Africa, indicating homeland (1976) and foreign (1980) sources. (Sources: South Africa 1981, pp. 196 & 220.)

The major streams of clandestine migration are from Lesotho to the Orange Free State and Natal, from Mozambique to the eastern Transvaal lowveld and northern Natal, from Zimbabwe to the northern Transvaal, and from Botswana to the maize triangle. Africans from Botswana, Lesotho and Swaziland (BLS) were required to have passports after 1963, and the number of BLS citizens recorded as working in South Africa declined by 32 per cent between 1960 and 1970, despite an increase of 20 000 miners. Some 80–100 000 Zimbabweans were reportedly living illegally in South Africa in the mid-1970s (Clarke 1976, p. 65), mostly in the Johannesburg–Pretoria area. South Africa offered an amnesty in 1976 under which unregistered 'aliens' would not be liable for repatriation, but to judge from official numbers of Zimbabwean workers in South Africa since then, it appears that few workers responded.

There are also many homeland Blacks illegally working in 'white' areas, often in unpopular jobs and for extremely low wages (South Africa 1979a, pp. 152–5). Many also have their families living illegally with them, as lodgers in township houses, on the premises of white employers (in the case of domestic servants), or in squatter camps such as Crossroads near Cape Town. Their number increased in the 1970s, partly owing to some relaxation of influx control, and there are an estimated 200 000 squatters in the Cape Town area alone (see Ch. 2).

Changing perspectives of the mining companies

The 1970s have witnessed notable developments in the labour policies of the mine employers. Five aspects require consideration here, some of them clearly interrelated: a shift from foreign to domestic sources of supply, wage increases, attempts to stabilize the labour force, improvements in working conditions, and mechanization.

Ever since the 1880s, the mining companies had followed a policy of moving further afield in search of labour in the face of shortages. Independence for African territories began to reduce areas of recruitment in the 1960s, as Tanzania banned recruitment in 1962 and Zambia in 1966. The effect of Malawi's suspension of recruitment in 1974 was particularly serious, given the numbers involved and the subsequent decision by many Malawian miners to return home before the expiry of their contracts. Within South Africa, meanwhile, the mines faced growing difficulty in attracting domestic labour supplies as manufacturing employment, offering better wages as well as more congenial working conditions, expanded rapidly in the 1960s, while mining wages had not changed in real terms since 1911 (Wilson 1972a, p. 46). Thus South African Blacks employed on mines affiliated to the Chamber of Mines (including all large gold mines, the Transvaal coal mines, and a few others) fell in number from a 1962 peak of 157 000 to only 86 500 in 1971. In

1972 Mozambique and Malawi alone supplied 53 per cent of all gold mine labour. The mining companies were faced with a choice of ever increasing reliance on foreign labour or attempting to compete with manufacturing wages and working conditions.

They chose the latter option. An important enabling factor in this decision was the dramatic increase in gold prices: the average revenue received per fine ounce of gold more than quadrupled between 1970 and 1974 (Wilson 1976, p. 15). Whereas half the gold mines were state assisted in 1972, none needed assistance by 1975 (Knight 1977, p. 43). The minimum wage in June 1975 had risen to R2.20 per shift, more than five times that of 1972. These wage increases originated in the Anglo-American Corporation, whose concern about its reputation and enlightened view of company interests were themselves contributory factors in the changing situation. The changes have continued, if less dramatically, in the later 1970s, with the overall white–Black pay differential in mining declining from 18.16:1 in 1972 to 8.08:1 in 1976 and 6.72:1 in 1979, by which time the average Black miner's wage was 72.6 per cent of that in manufacturing (Table 4.3). If wages in kind are added,

Table 4.3   White–Black mine wage differentials and Black wage increases.

	White–Black pay differential		Average annual pay rate for Blacks			
			Mining and quarrying		Manufacturing industries	
	mining and quarrying	manufac- turing industries	nominal (R)	real terms (R)	nominal (R)	real terms (R)
Year						
1970	19.77	5.82	216	216	619	619
1972	18.16	5.88	266	235	729	643
1974	12.39	5.12	545	393	1053	760
1976	8.08	4.57	1059	606	1500	859
1978	7.12	4.40	1415	656	1608	746
1979[1]	6.72	4.27	1521	651	2095	897

Source: Spandau (1980, p. 215).

[1] Based on the first three months of the year, with no adjustment for expected year-end bonuses.

accepting the Chamber of Mines' evaluation of these at R40 per month (which workers would contest), the gap between mining and manufacturing wages virtually disappears.

Recruitment of Black South Africans was assisted by a relaxation in 1974 of the state requirement that workers finishing their contracts be 'repatriated' to their homelands, irrespective of where they were living when recruited. This had severely restricted urban recruitment, but now workers living near the mines may enter short-term contracts and continue to live in urban areas afterwards. Recruitment of domestic migrant labour has been aided by a

1975 agreement between the Chamber of Mines and the South African Agricultural Union (SAAU) whereby the chamber obtained selective rights of
recruitment in areas of labour supply previously reserved for and monopolized by SAAU members. The large increase in Transkeian miners is largely a
reflection of this limited relaxation in what Leys (1975, p. 201) has called a
'totalitarian system designed for the total direction of black labour'.

The combination of improved wages and easier recruitment conditions
within the republic has enabled mining companies to reduce the foreign
component of their labour force to only 35.7 per cent by mid-1979. On
mines affiliated to the Chamber of Mines the proportion of South African
labour has increased from 20.4 per cent in 1973 to 57.3 per cent in 1979
(Spiegel 1980, p. 3), thus comfortably passing the chamber's self-imposed
target of 50 per cent (Clarke 1977, p. 24). Lesotho alone has almost maintained the same volume of migrant mine labour (Table 4.4), and is now

Table 4.4   Sources of South African mine labour,[1] June 1979.

Source	No.	% of total	Source	No.	% of total
Angola	108	0.0	Transkei	163 948	22.9
Botswana	25 690	3.6	Bophuthatswana	66 155	9.2
Lesotho	128 800	18.0	rest of South Africa	229 868	32.1
Malawi	24 590	3.4			
Mozambique	53 753	7.5			
Swaziland	10 120	1.4			
Zambia	36	0.0			
Zimbabwe	10 150	1.4			
others	2 101	0.3			

Source: Gordon (1981, pp. 114–5).
[1] Figures include employment in quarries.

responsible for half the foreign supply. The skill of Basotho miners has long
been acknowledged, and the extreme dependence of Lesotho upon this form
of labour ensures its dependability as a supplier. In this respect Lesotho is
more akin to a homeland than to other foreign states which supply migrant
labour.

Numbers alone, however, do not tell the whole story. The Malawian and
Mozambiquan miners were the most experienced ones who took the longest
contracts, often up to the permitted maximum of 24 months. They were
replaced with men who had far less experience, if any, and who took contracts for 6–12 month periods which, after the repeal of the Masters and
Servants legislation in 1974, could be (and often were) broken. Turnover on
all chamber-affiliated mines increased by over two-thirds between 1974 and
1978 (Lipton 1980, p. 109) and training costs inevitably soared. Many mines

faced serious absolute shortages at times, despite the greater flexibility permitted by short-term contracts offered to urban Blacks after 1974.

This period of labour shortage and high turnover happened to coincide with a period when Blacks were permitted to do certain more skilled jobs under the Artisan Aides Agreement of 1973, which represented the first breakthrough in the face of the (white) Mine Workers Union's militant defence of job reservation. Ironically, increasing use of Blacks in skilled jobs with high training costs accentuated the problems caused by increased turnover of migrant labour.

The mid-1970s were also a period of increasing conflict on South African mines, resulting in 178 deaths in 65 incidents between September 1973 and June 1976 (Horner & Kooy 1976, p. 17). Possible causes are many. Wage grievances figured prominently, particularly questions of differentials and the Lesotho government's attempt to enforce without consultation a new system of deferred pay. Anxiety and tension are inevitable by-products of dangerous employment: there were no less than 2993 mine deaths and 110 169 serious injuries in the years 1972–5 (Horner & Kooy 1976, p. 20). Political influences, and particularly the possibility that most of the Basotho miners supported the opposition Congress Party in their own country, may have been significant. Ethnic tensions were perhaps heightened by recruitment of Zimbabweans and far larger numbers of Xhosa than hitherto, which may have made the Basotho in particular feel threatened. Above all, in the opinion of Horner and Kooy (1976, pp. 25–8), conditions of life in the compounds, including sexual frustration and total lack of privacy, together with the lack of workers' representation, explain the extent of conflict. For the mine owners, such conflicts proved costly in terms of strikes, interruptions and broken contracts, adding to problems of shortage and labour turnover.

The response of the mining companies to these problems has been twofold: increased mechanization and related research, and efforts to stabilize the workforce. Mechanization is relatively easy in the coal mines, with seams which are mostly thick, shallow and nearly horizontal, in undisturbed strata. Despite low Black wage levels, mechanized mining methods have been more competitive than 'handgot' mining since about 1958 (Spandau 1980, p. 170). Whereas 90 per cent of coal was loaded by hand in 1955, this was true of only 40 per cent by 1975 (Knight 1977, p. 55). Conventional mechanized mining is now most important, and open-cast mining small but increasing. Wage levels became a significant inducement to mechanization only in the 1970s, when the risks of relying on foreign labour and the interruption of production by riots and strikes were at least as important. Spandau (1980, p. 171) claims that in the Witbank area 'at a time in 1973 when some collieries were still prepared to delay mechanisation in an attempt to save Black workplaces, the labour riots themselves became responsible for the reduction in employment'.

On the gold mines, 'stoping' (breaking and handling of rock) is much less amenable to mechanization because of hard abrasive rock and deep, narrow, undulating seams. Machines developed elsewhere in the world require adaptation, and relatively little relevant research occurred before the 1970s. In 1974 the Chamber of Mines decided to spend R150 million over the next decade on research into mechanization. Future possibilities include the use of vehicles to handle materials underground, and of boring machinery instead of traditional blasting and drilling.

Mechanization also faces non-technical impediments. It demands a higher proportion of semi-skilled and skilled workers, which under the present conditions creates the danger that new jobs will be closed to Africans by the Mine Workers Union. However, in the newer open-cast coal mines, Blacks drive earth-moving equipment and do the simpler parts of artisan jobs (Knight 1977, p. 56). Blasting certificates continue to be monopolized by whites, but the new mechanized methods already involve less blasting in the coal mines and may do so eventually in the gold mines.

Government resistance to stabilization of miners in family housing also impedes mechanization with its demand for more skilled Black labour. Since 1952 the gold mines have been allowed to stabilize up to 3 per cent of their labour force, but only if the authorities can be fully satisfied by the circumstances in each case. Restriction to South African Blacks nullified the effects of this 'concession' since most experienced miners were foreigners, and in practice less than 1 per cent of Black miners had been stabilized by 1970. A recent new agreement allows the mines to house key Black workers in urban residential areas without this historical limitation (Spandau 1980, pp. 216-7), but only on condition that they be 'repatriated' at the end of their contracts.

The Anglo-American Corporation has pressed for changes in government policy more than other gold mining companies. Its stated objective is to create 'a proper hierarchy of jobs objectively evaluated and paid, thus providing opportunity and motivation for the individual to advance, combined with adequate training opportunities to enable him to do so' (Oppenheimer 1973, p. 69). The corporation aims to house 10 per cent of its 130 000 Black miners on a family basis, if allowed to do so (see Ch. 11).

On non-gold mines less restrictive policies are applied, especially on diamond, coal and platinum mines where several companies are building family houses. These mines are more capital intensive, more mechanized, and already have a higher proportion of skilled labour (Lipton 1980, p. 125), thus incentives to stabilize are greater. High percentages of stabilized labour are noted by Lipton at the Phalaborwa copper–phosphate mine (80 per cent), the Kimberley diamond mines (62 per cent), and at Rand Mines' new eastern Transvaal coalfields at Rietspruit, near Ogies, and Duvha, near Witbank (70–80 per cent). At Phalaborwa, government restrictions do not apply as the workers can be housed in the adjoining homeland of Gazankulu: the same applies to workers on coal mines belonging to Rand Mines in Natal, who are being helped to buy their own homes in KwaZulu. At Kimberley abundant local labour and rising mine wages enabled De Beers to make a conscious decision to replace migrant, largely Basotho, labour with local labour. In the major new mining developments in the North-West Cape, however, the Coloured labour preference policy has been rigorously applied to prevent Blacks being stabilized at these mines, which are highly mechanized and employ a high proportion of skilled workers.

The mining companies are fostering a more limited form of stabilization for the bulk of the labour force. This involves encouraging workers to enter into, and keep, longer contracts, and to induce them to return in as short a time as possible. In part this involves major programmes of upgrading hostel accommodation to reduce overcrowding and to provide more privacy and improved facilities, sometimes with special facilities for more senior men. New hostels are typically smaller buildings, with fewer men per room, and arranged in a village-type setting (Lipton 1980, p. 133). Where mines have only a short lifespan, the use of mobile homes is one solution. These developments are long overdue; Selvan's (1976) detailed description of housing conditions for migrant workers in Cape Town gives some idea of the extent to which improvement is necessary. Even the more progressive companies will clearly take many years to bring all their accommodation up to an improved standard. The situation would be eased if the government ceased to require the mining companies to house all their workers; there is a strong argument in favour of allowing workers the choice of a higher wage and responsibility for their own housing. At the Selebi–Phikwe mine in Botswana, for instance, many workers choose to live in the squatter township of Botshabelo. Such a solution would not, of course, appeal to the South African government with its characteristic concern for controlling every aspect of life for its Black population.

Re-engagement Guarantee Certificates (RGC's) and bonuses are other incentives being used to induce longer service and rapid return to the mine. Workers in certain categories are provided with RGC's if they have worked for at least 26 weeks on the mine; these expire within a certain period, often six months, after a contract is ended. Conditions which a worker must fulfil to qualify for a RGC have not yet been standardized (Spiegel 1980, p. 3). In a period of labour surplus, there may be attempts to limit recruiting to holders of valid RGC's. Men who have worked 45 weeks or longer also qualify for an early return bonus (ERB) which in October 1979 was equivalent to six and a half weeks basic pay for every 52 weeks of service (Spandau 1980, p. 176). If a worker stays at home longer than six weeks but less than six months, he loses the ERB but continues to qualify for re-engagement. RGC's and ERB's are given mainly to skilled and semi-skilled workers, but occasionally these benefits may be given to unskilled workers who perform exceptionally well. They have succeeded in lengthening the average contract. Thus the average Lesotho miner's period of service on chamber-affiliated mines increased from 10.6 months in 1976 to 14.0 months in 1979, while the mean home-stay period dropped from 5.3 months to 4.6 months; the proportion of Lesotho miners staying for the maximum two-year period rose from 7 per cent in 1976 to 22 per cent in the first half of 1980 (Spiegel 1980, p. 4). Lower turnover has meant reduced recruitment, the Lesotho figure decreasing by 24 per cent from the peak year of 1976 to 1979. This allows greater selectivity by the employers, particularly at a time when real wages have been increasing.

Farm labour

Agricultural workers have long been amongst the lowest paid Blacks. The agricultural sector was excluded from the protection afforded to Africans by the Wage Act of 1925 and the Bantu Labour (Settlement of Disputes) Act of 1953 (Lemon 1976, p. 49). The Native Laws Amendment Act 1952, discussed earlier, reinforced existing controls on the movement of farm labour. Black workers must obtain permission to leave the district from the Labour Control Board, on which local white farmers and officials sit. Once familiar with these restrictive conditions, African migrant labourers often return to the homelands, whence they can go more easily to 'white' urban areas to seek work; this tendency has been increasing in recent years (Smit 1976, p. 56).

The political leverage of white farmers is such that they managed to prevent the establishment of job reservation in agriculture and replaced white *bywoners* (squatters), driven off the land in the 1920s and 1930s, with cheaper African and Coloured workers. The latter perform many skilled and managerial jobs on white farms today, but often earn little more than labourers. White farmers' traditional complaints of labour shortages merely reflect the low wages paid. The recent improvements noted for other sectors are largely absent in agriculture. In 1976 the average annual income of Black agricultural workers was only R114.20, equal to 18.8 per cent of their counterparts in mining, 13.2 per cent of the average wage in manufacturing, and only 15.2 per cent of the average for all non-agricultural occupations. Only in those areas recently opened up to mine recruitment has there been significant pressure on agricultural wages. The Natal sugar industry is a case in point; it relies heavily on Pondo labour, as Zulu men will not accept the job, and the basic wage of a cane-cutter, excluding bonuses and payments in kind, has risen from 34 cents per day in 1969–70 to R1.75 per day in 1975–6, in order to compete with mine wages (Knight 1977, p. 50).

Since the 1950s government intervention has sought to end the labour tenancy system whereby Blacks would work part-time for a white farmer and be allowed to live on the farm with their dependants and cultivate a piece of land, or even work in the towns for part of the year. Black squatters on white farms were similarly to be eliminated; if the breadwinners were working in urban areas as migrants, their families would be moved to the homelands and the land they occupied freed for white farming. The government encountered some resistance from farmers in northern Transvaal and Natal who favoured the tenancy system, but the policy of eradicating squatters and abolishing labour tenancy went ahead in the 1960s, when 340 000 labour tenants and 656 000 squatters were removed, together with 97 000 people from 'Black spots' – areas of African settlement surrounded by white farmland – and small 'scheduled areas' set aside for Africans under the Native Land Act of 1913 (Baldwin 1975, p. 216). A further 305 000 labour tenants were removed in the years 1970–9 (Gordon 1981, p. 452). The labour tenancy system was finally abolished in August 1980, which resulted in several thousands of African families being evicted; one of the most severely affected regions was Weenen, Natal (Gordon 1981, p. 119).

As a result of these measures farmers now rely increasingly on a smaller, better trained labour force of regular workers. This should enable them to pay, house and feed their workers better than hitherto, but with a few notable exceptions there is little sign that this has happened. Whereas the need for casual labour has declined, as the Du Plessis Commission anticipated (South Africa 1970, pp. 158, 174–5), the demand for migrant farm workers has in some cases increased, as predicted by Wilson (1971); mechanization has generally increased yields rather than replaced labour.

Government intervention in the agricultural labour market may be explained in terms of apartheid ideology (Baldwin 1975) or in terms of capitalist development (Morris 1977). Undoubtedly the declining white population and increasing Black population of the *Platteland* (countryside) gave rise to concern over the *Verswarting* (blackening) of the rural areas which had long been regarded as the Afrikaner cultural heartland. The Du Plessis Commission recommended that 'white agriculture must accordingly be made less dependent on non-white labour and eventually be released from need of it as far as possible' (South Africa 1970, p. 175). This was clearly impracticable, but the policy of removing squatters and labour tenants certainly reduced the Black population in these areas. Although this stabilization of farm labour 'was consummated under the ideological umbrella of Separate Development' (Morris 1977, p. 55), state intervention has clearly restructured the relations of production and in the process permitted capitalist agricultural expansion in white rural areas. No such expansion has taken place in Black rural areas, whose essential function as labour suppliers will now be considered.

Effects of labour migration on the source areas

In assessing the disadvantages of migrant labour, it is important to make clear that the alternative with which comparison is being made is the effect of a permanent exodus of labourers and their families from the source areas, *not* simply the absence of any migration. This is the only realistic basis of comparison in South Africa, where there is no doubt that a far larger proportion of migrants would settle permanently in the urban areas with their families if allowed to do so, and where the needs of the urban economy and the paucity of opportunities in the homelands combine to make some form of exodus, permanent or temporary, as inevitable as such periphery–core migration has been even within developed countries. Thus to concede that the homelands could not support their population in the absence of migration is no argument in favour of the migrant labour system; it is merely a reflection of legally imposed constraints on long-term outmigration. In the case of foreign source countries the same argument applies, in so far as it is the refusal of South Africa to allow foreign migrants the option of permanent residence with their families, which dictates that they remain migrant labourers. In Western Europe where the use of migrant labour is comparatively recent, the receiving countries have gradually accepted responsibility for those whose labour they require as permanent parts of their population (Lemon 1980).

In favour of the system it is argued that remittances widen the spread of the cash economy. In practice homeland migrants actually spend four-fifths of their wages in 'white' areas: this money and the multiplier effect it represents in terms of job opportunities are lost to the source areas. The general practice of taxing foreign migrants in their country of origin does clearly benefit those countries, although Mozambique, Malawi, Botswana and since 1975 Lesotho have all insisted on deferred pay arrangements; perhaps the 'independent' homelands could do the same. The remittances themselves may, however, be used to clothe and feed a tighter family circle than previously (Wilson 1972a, p. 131). A further argument in favour of the system is that workers with rural links have something to fall back upon in time of unemployment. This appears to be an excuse for inadequate social security arrangements; in any case the possibility of 10 or even 20 per cent unemployment in a recession hardly justifies the insistence that more than half the total urban Black labour force (more than 90 per cent in the case of the mines) be made up of migrants.

Disadvantages for the source areas are overwhelming. First, poor rural areas are subsidizing urban economic advance. Rural and urban areas are seen, for political reasons, as separate entities, lacking mutual responsibility (Wilson 1972b, p. 175). Thus migrant labourers are paid lower wages than would be needed for family support, that is *below the cost of reproducing the labour force*. Municipalities and employers are saved the costs of housing, social security and infrastructure which the presence of families would demand, and economic growth points are able to expand 'without having to bear the cost of the human being behind the labour unit' (Wilson 1972b, p. 188). With the conferring of 'independence' on homelands, the latter suffer the same disadvantages in these respects as genuinely foreign suppliers of labour, except in so much as they receive 'foreign aid' from South Africa: thus Bophuthatswana and Venda, for instance, become responsible for housing, education and social services for a population whose productive labour primarily benefits the South African economy (see Ch. 2).

Meanwhile the rural areas become so densely populated that there is insufficient land for the rationalization and improvement of agriculture. De Wet (1980), in a study of land betterment in the Ciskeian village of Cata, shows that the population increased by 49 per cent while the land area under cultivation was reduced by more than half in an attempt to check soil erosion; 41 per cent of families were left landless and those who retained land had less than before, leaving the population as a whole even more dependent on migrant labour than before, apart from a minority benefiting from an irrigation scheme. It is abundantly clear that only a large-scale *permanent* exodus of population can establish conditions in which rural living standards can be raised. Instead of this, the South African government continues to use the homelands as dumping grounds for non-productive Blacks of all ages from both rural and urban areas of 'white' South Africa, who become primarily dependent on the migrant labour of their breadwinners for survival, and whose presence further negates rural development efforts.

Foreign suppliers are at least spared resettlement: there is no way South Africa can resettle her non-productive South Sotho or Swazi populations in Lesotho or Swaziland. Lesotho does, however, suffer from acute overpopulation, and her problems would be greatly eased by a permanent exodus of population. Unfortunately the opposite is occurring, as lowered recruitment of mine labour combined with a labour force expanding by 20 000 annually leaves an increasing number of young men with little chance of creating a rural base of security within Lesotho. The Lesotho Land Act 1979 attempts to prevent further fragmentation of holdings, but in the absence of other employment opportunities this will inevitably mean that it is the wage-earning migrant labourers who are able to 'buy' an inheritance of arable land from their parents, leaving other sons landless (Spiegel 1980, pp. 5–6).

In a further sense migrant labour may actively delay reform of a low productivity subsistence economy. If the indigenous economy were a closed system, either population would have been kept in check by mortality or there would have been an economic revolution in terms of the ideas of Boserup (1965). Instead, 'the export of male labour serves as a means of increasing the resource base of the indigenous economy without altering the present economic-social structure' (Rutman 1964, pp. 27–8). Given the nature of the land tenure system, where land is allocated by the tribal chief and cannot be sold, the migrant labourer invests capital not in land improvement but in improving his economic and social position in the village by acquiring wives and livestock. This reinforces his attachment to the village and gives him a vested interest in the survival of the indigenous economy.

Migrant labour, by making the homelands and exporting countries part of an open system, has further undermined the incentive to farm commercially. Although Africans had to be forced to sell their labour in the 1880s, they have gradually come to accept working for the white man, rather than farming, as a means of meeting cash needs. Ironically, rises in wages may actually reduce investment by migrants in their land, because earnings per unit of time are so much greater on the mines that crop production, by comparison, may seem hardly worthwhile.

It is well known that migration, whether permanent or temporary, drains the source areas of their best manpower in terms of age, enterprise and education. In the homelands the rate of migration reaches 90 per cent at the educational level of primary school plus four years (Nattrass 1976, p. 70). The South African system of limiting migrants to one-year contracts (two years in the case of mining), together with the legal and customary barriers which migrants encounter in employment, means that they receive little training and acquire few skills which they might subsequently apply in the homelands, although the governments of the latter have paid for their education.

Many of these arguments are illustrated by Williams' (1971) study of Lesotho. Decision-makers and opinion leaders needed for innovation adoption were often absent, and both morale and incentives for improvement might be lowered. Insufficient male labour contributed to low crop yields; in particular the furrows produced at ploughing time might be too shallow for maximum plant survival and growth. Young boys, uninstructed in sound techniques, were left to manage livestock, and were therefore unable to attend school. Migrant workers tended to regard spells at home as holidays. The tradition of migrant labour had produced 'an attitude of indifference to local conditions' and perhaps even 'an induced disbelief in the ability of the nation to become economically viable' (Williams 1971, p. 177).

Such attitudes are hardly surprising when, after contributing to a century of economic growth in South Africa, 'Lesotho now finds herself with no rights of access to most of the accumulated capital which her citizens helped to form' (Wilson 1975a, p. 522). Mozambique alone of the labour exporting states of Southern Africa obtained something in return from South Africa. In terms of the Mozambique Convention of 1928, 40 per cent of the tonnage in the 'competitive area' between Maputo and Durban should pass through Maputo. This has enabled Maputo to develop as a secondary core within the Southern African space economy. In addition, the payment of part of the migrants' wages to the Mozambique government in gold at the official price proved an increasing windfall as the gold price soared, but South Africa terminated this arrangement in April 1978 (Horwood 1978, p. 25). Elsewhere in the region, capital accumulation under the migrant labour system has been hopelessly one-sided. In Wilson's words (1976, p. 38): 'Surely both logic and social justice point to the imperative of extending the principle of distributing the social dividend at least as widely as the labour catchment area of any

KVCC

KALAMAZOO VALLEY
COMMUNITY COLLEGE
LIBRARY

economy.' South Africa, by giving 'independence' to the peripheral areas of her space economy, is doing precisely the opposite. This rejection of social responsibility is clearly illustrated by the study of frontier commuters which now follows.

Frontier commuters: a new apartheid concept

The notion that the homelands 'should not only become dumping grounds for the surplus rural population but should also provide accommodation for those working in adjacent urban areas' began to gain ground about 1950 (Henning 1969), when Umlazi became the first homeland town built to alleviate the Black housing shortage in a 'white' city, Durban (Smit 1979, p. 7). But it was not until the late 1960s that this new method of reducing the Black population in 'white' urban areas was enshrined in official policies (General Circular no. 27 of 1967).

In terms of the circular, white local authorities were required to obtain government approval before initiating any new Black housing schemes. The Department of Bantu Administration and Development (now the Department of Co-operation and Development) had to be satisfied that such developments, especially family housing, were essential, and that accommodation could not be provided in an adjacent homeland. From 1968 Blacks were allowed only to rent houses in townships outside the homelands; in the latter they could acquire freehold, and were encouraged to build their own homes. Extensions to Black townships in Pretoria, East London and elsewhere were subsequently suspended, and the city councils, acting as agents of the South African Bantu Trust, began large-scale construction programmes at Mabopane, Mdantsane and elsewhere in adjacent homelands (Smit & Booysen 1977, p. 20). These townships were used to accommodate not only the increased Black population but also many Blacks living in slum areas of 'white' towns such as Duncan Village (East London) and Cato Manor (Durban). In cases where distances are too great for daily commuting, Black workers may be housed on a single basis in 'white' urban areas and commute on a weekly or monthly basis between their jobs and their families who have been rehoused in the new homeland towns.

The result has been an extremely rapid growth of townships just within the homelands in areas abutting 'white' urban areas and growth points. The population of these townships can be attributed to five processes: resettlement from nearby 'white' urban areas, resettlement from 'white' rural areas, natural increase, migration from rural areas within homelands, and the existing population before incorporation into homelands. The last applies where homeland boundaries were redrawn so as to include existing Black townships, really suburbs of 'white' towns and cities, such as KwaMashu, which was transferred from Durban to KwaZulu in 1977.

These dormitory towns housed over 700 000 commuters in 1979, an increase of 147 per cent since 1970 (Table 5.5, p. 103). The pre-eminence of KwaZulu (55.7 per cent) reflects the fragmented nature of this homeland, several of whose 10 parts abut developed 'white' areas (Table 4.5). The latter include the established urban areas of Durban–Pinetown and Pietermaritz-burg, the coastal resorts of Natal, the growth point of Newcastle – site of the third ISCOR steelworks – and Richard's Bay, the major new port on Natal's north coast. Bophuthatswana, the second most fragmented homeland, accounts for 22.5 per cent of all commuters, owing to the proximity of parts of the territory to Pretoria and the 'border industries' of Rosslyn, Brits, Rustenburg and also Mafeking, which was itself incorporated into Bophu-thatswana in 1980. Lebowa and Ciskei are the only other homelands with significant numbers of commuters. Lebowa borders the rapidly growing mining town of Phalaborwa as well as Pietersburg and Potgietersrus. Most Ciskeian commuters travel from Mdantsane to East London; Mdantsane was one of the first commuter towns to be built and this, together with the economic stagnation of East London (Black 1980, pp. 65–6), explains the static number of Ciskeian commuters during the 1970s. The spatial pattern of frontier commuting in South Africa is shown in Figure 4.2.

The building of homeland townships and, in some instances, the extension of homeland borders which were not hitherto within daily commuting dis-tance of 'white' cities, have acted as a pull on rural homeland dwellers who can now move without restriction and live as families within the homelands while the breadwinners work in 'white' areas. Squatter settlements have appeared in some cases, particularly in the Winterveld, Klippan and Oskraal areas around Ga-Rankuwa, Mabopane and Temba north of Pretoria (as described in Ch. 2). The population of these squatter areas was officially estimated at 350 000 in 1976 (Smit 1979, p. 8) compared with 175 000 in all the planned towns of Bophuthatswana put together in 1975. Spatial displace-ment of these squatter settlements beyond the homeland border has conse-quences for transport provision, distance and costs of commuting which will be considered below. It also means that, as with migrant labourers' depend-ants and those resettled in new homeland townships, the responsibility is once more shifted from the South African government to its artificially created poor relations, the homeland governments.

The combination of planned townships and squatter settlements has brought considerable proportions of the homeland populations within a short distance of their borders. Nearly 50 per cent of the Bophuthatswana population already lived within a 50 km radius of Pretoria by 1970 (Smit 1979, p. 8). In Ciskei the districts of Mdantsane and Zwelitsha, serving East London and King William's Town–Berlin respectively, had 54.8 per cent of all Ciskeians according to preliminary 1980 census results.

This trend induces Smit (1979, p. 18) to believe that border urbanization has gone too far; he regrets the movement of population from the 'heart-

Table 4.5 Residence and workplace of frontier commuters, 1976.

Homeland, places of residence	Bus	Train	Other	Total	Places of work
Bophuthatswana					
Odi 1	68 400	16 900	8 000	93 300	Pretoria, Rosslyn, Brits
Bafokeng, Mankwe	11 600	—	4 600	16 200	Rustenburg
others	19 000	7 400	8 900	35 300	other urban areas
				10 100	rural areas
Ciskei					
Mdantsane	13 100	12 200	4 400	29 700	East London
others	1 700	—	5 500	7 200	King William's Town, Berlin
Gazankulu					
Nkowakowa	3 300	—	1 100	4 400	Tzaneen
others	1 100	—	900	2 000	other urban areas
				1 400	rural areas
KaNgwane					
Kanyamazane	8 300	—	1 100	9 400	Nelspruit
others	4 100	—	1 600	5 700	other urban areas
				7 900	rural areas
KwaZulu					
Umlazi, Inanda, Shongweni, Mpumalanga, Umbumbulu	56 800	70 900	31 600	159 300	Durban, Pinetown, Prospection, Hammarsdale, Kingsborough, Amanzimtoti
Edendale, Swartkop-gebied	25 600	—	4 900	30 500	Pietermaritzburg, Howick
Enseleni, Nqwelezana, Ezikhawini	11 300	—	3 600	14 900	Empangeni, Richard's Bay
Madadeni, Osizweni	17 600	—	8 800	26 400	Newcastle, Utrecht
others	37 200	—	13 500	50 700	other urban areas
				43 800	rural areas
Lebowa					
Namakgale	9 500	—	2 000	11 500	Phalaborwa
Seshego, Sebayeng, Mankweng	9 800	500	4 000	14 300	Pietersburg
Mahwelereng	3 500	—	3 400	6 900	Potgietersrus
others	4 000	—	1 400	5 400	other urban areas
				8 200	rural areas
Qwaqwa					
Witsieshoek	1 650	—	150	1 800	Harrismith
Transkei					
Ezibeleni and others	4 500	—	1 900	6 400	Queenstown and other urban areas
				700	rural areas
Venda					
Ozanani II	1 200	—	500	1 700	Louis Trichardt
others	700	—	300	1 000	Louis Trichardt
				1 000	rural areas

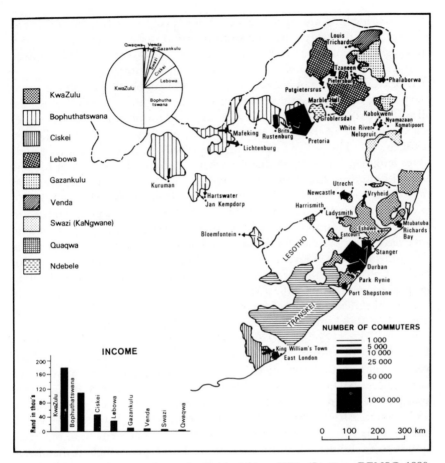

Figure 4.2 Frontier commuters in South Africa, 1976. (Sources: BENSO 1980, Table 15; South Africa 1979a, p. 2, 1981, p. 214.)

lands' of the homelands and welcomes the development of growth points deeper within the homelands. Yet there is little possibility of significant employment growth, apart from the functions of homeland government, at most such growth points. Over extensive areas of the homelands, small service centres are the highest form of urban development that can be expected (Fair 1973, p. 158; Lemon 1976, p. 190). Permanent migration of population from these areas could prove beneficial by opening up the very opportunities for agricultural development which the migrant labour system has so long denied. The problems of squatting are common to most Third World cities, and both informal housing and informal sector employment are widely viewed as logical adaptations to the Third World urban milieu; in the right circumstances, particularly a rapidly expanding urban economy (such as those of many South African urban areas), they can be a transitional stage to something more permanent. The real problem arises when the urban economy is artificially separated from the rural–urban migration, which it induces, by an international boundary, and the people concerned become the responsibility of a different state with minimal resources.

It has long been a notable characteristic of many South African cities that the poorest members of the community commute the longest distances. The displacement of Blacks from many areas zoned for other race groups under the Group Areas Act 1950 contributed substantially to this situation (Lemon 1976, p. 75). The policy of housing Blacks in homeland commuter townships lengthens the average Black worker's journey still further. At Mdantsane, 12 km from East London, the average commuter spends between two and three hours each day travelling to and from work (Matravers 1980, p. 40): this is partly attributable to public transport services poorly related to user needs, a common complaint in such townships, revolving around an inflexible linear system and the universal necessity of changing buses in the case of Mdantsane. Most commuters could not afford the economic cost of such journeys, and the fares are subsidized partly from a transport levy on employers and partly by the government. Subsidies have risen rapidly, with the establishment of more commuter townships: from R14.8 million in 1968–9 to R49.2 million in 1975–6 and R77.1 million in 1976–7 (South Africa 1979a, p. 125). The 1976–7 figure was made up as follows: employer levies for bus transport 16.0 per cent; government bus subsidies 16.7 per cent; government rail subsidies 67.3 per cent. Rail transport is important for commuters to Durban, Pretoria and East London (Table 4.5), but buses transported 63.3 per cent of all commuters working in 'white' urban areas in 1979 (South Africa 1981, p. 214). A new train service between Mabopane and Pretoria costing R85 million is currently under construction. Increased numbers of homeland commuters will clearly place high demands on expanded and co-ordinated transport systems, while far greater volumes of cars are likely to demand much improved road links as Black incomes increase. Costs of both infrastructure and subsidies could be much less were it not for the decision to house Black workers and their families within the homelands.

To the inconvenience of long-distance commuting is added the need to travel to 'white' towns for most goods and services. The displacement of Black residential areas (and squatter camps) beyond homeland borders and some distance from 'white' towns which they serve creates a highly artificial situation, in that what is essentially a single functional unit becomes divided into two centres competing to meet the same demand. The Black townships currently have very low levels of functional complexity: thus Mdantsane and Zwelitsha, the second and third largest places in the Eastern Cape, are classed by Cook (1980, p. 80) only as a minor town (6th order) and local service centre (7th order) respectively. Although the population of the Black towns may be sufficient to support a greater range of enterprises, the fact that adjacent centres of higher hierarchical order are already established means that local entrepreneurs cannot compete, unless they become members of South African national chains or retail groups. This might improve shopping opportunities, but it would provide little benefit to the homeland concerned as money would still flow out to 'white' areas rather than circulate within the homeland (Cook 1980, p. 87). These Black townships have, furthermore, few functional links within the homelands: thus to reach Mdantsane from anywhere else in the Ciskei it is necessary to cross the border and travel through South African territory. This hardly encourages internal flows within the homeland and reinforces the satellite relationship with East London which inhibits business and industrial development.

The Riekert Report (South Africa 1979a, p. 11) speaks of the need for labour agreements and 'co-operation between states and co-ordination as regards training and the maintenance of sound labour relations'. Such phrases imply relationship between equals, but they say nothing about the fundamental inequity of locating labour supplies in distinct geographical areas, at considerable inconvenience and cost to the people concerned, and then shedding responsibility for those areas by decreeing them to be part of independent states. Any pretence of bold consolidation of the latter to include major 'white' towns and growth points seems finally to have been abandoned with the April 1981 announcement that King William's Town, surrounded on three sides by Ciskeian territory, was to remain white (Koornhof 1981).

Directions of government policy

To avoid all permanent residence of Africans in 'white' towns it has been seriously suggested (Burger 1970) that high-speed transport links to major employment centres could enable Africans to travel hundreds of miles a day in a short space of time and so continue to live in those homelands remote from large cities. This futuristic extension of the frontier commuter principle is suitably dismissed by Wilson (1975b, p. 183) with the remark that 'a society that cannot afford to pay the majority of its workers a living wage is hardly in a position to turn its entire proletariat into a jet set'. Thus the migrant labour system continues, modified by employers for economic reasons in the ways which have been described. It is complemented by a rapidly growing new army of over 700 000 frontier commuters. This relatively stable labour force can undergo training and acquire the skills increasingly needed by the urban economy. The Riekert Report (South Africa 1979a, p. 165) expressed doubt as to whether such commuters could acquire Section 10 (1)(b) rights to residence in 'white' urban areas by working lawfully for one employer for an unbroken period of 10 years. It is clearly not the government's intention that they should do so and the closure of this potential loophole may be anticipated.

Meanwhile the future position of urban Blacks who do have Section 10 rights remains unclear. In 1976 the 30-year leasehold right was re-introduced and in 1978 it was extended to 99 years. In its 1979 white paper on the Riekert Report (South Africa 1979b) the government conceded that all Blacks with Section 10 rights should have the opportunity to bring their families with them, the freedóm to change jobs within the board area in which their rights were granted without recourse to Labour Bureaux, and the right to transfer their Section 10 rights to other areas. These relatively major concessions are subject to the availability of jobs and housing, as judged by officials, and they do not apply in the Coloured labour preference area of the Western Cape. There is also some uncertainty as to whether the concessions will be confined. to the present generation of Blacks with Section 10 rights, or whether they can be inherited by their children who are defined as homeland citizens by a 1978 amendment of the Bantu Homelands Citizenship Act of 1970.

In so far as the white paper represents a liberalization of the previous position, it will also widen the gap between those with and without Section 10 rights. The 'have-nots' are made worse off by a new condition for migrants seeking to remain in a 'white' area: to the offer of employment and availability of housing is added 'the non-availability of suitable local work-seekers'. Such a widening of the gap between 'insiders' and 'outsiders' (Wilson 1975b, pp. 182–3) would be consistent with the government's evident desire to create a Black middle class (see Ch. 2). Whether this will have the politically stabilizing effect intended is another matter.

Conclusion

It is debatable whether the fundamental purpose of government policy has been to create a cheap and easily controlled labour force for capitalist expansion, or to further the ideological aims of apartheid. There can be no doubt, however, of the coincidence of these aims in practice. Although some policies do create extra costs, such as transport infrastructure and subsidies for frontier commuters, not to mention the costs of administering influx control, capitalist advantage and ideological goals have undoubtedly reinforced one another to a marked degree. Conflict between ideology and economy has been most apparent in terms of the increasing demand for a stabilized, skilled Black labour force to underpin a dynamic economy. Frontier commuting and the stabilization policies of the mining companies appear to be meeting this demand within the requirements of apartheid ideology.

In the case of farm labour, wage costs themselves continue to be minimized by restrictions on labour mobility, with some exceptions. Although the stabilization of farm labour 'was consummated under the ideological umbrella of Separate Development' (Morris 1977, p. 55), state intervention has clearly restructured the relations of production in rural areas and in the process permitted capitalist agricultural expansion. Mining wages had also been minimized (by the migrant labour system) prior to the 1970s, but a combination of factors has brought about considerable improvement in wages and the beginning of upgraded living conditions. In non-agricultural employment sectors today, it is above all the social costs of labour – education of workers' children, social services, welfare benefits for the old, the widowed and the unemployed, housing of squatters – which are being effectively transferred to 'independent' states. Thus are the benefits of the South African economy being confined to an ever smaller part of its labour catchment area.

5 Urbanization in the homelands

P. SMIT, J. J. OLIVIER and
J. J. BOOYSEN

The current state and processes of urbanization in the homelands* confirm that the urban areas reflect the nature of South African society. First, the low proportion of the homeland population urbanized (16.8 per cent in 1980) is an indication of their underdevelopment. Secondly, as in the rest of Africa and other Third World countries, the rapid urbanization process in the homelands, with 14.6 per cent urban population growth per annum between 1970 and 1978, has outpaced economic and particularly industrial development (Van Eeden 1980, p. 427). In the case of the homelands a new dimension is added to the urbanization process in that it is stimulated mainly by external political–ideological forces from inside 'white' South Africa. Urbanization is considered essential for the socio-economic development and political stability of the homelands, because 'the major strategies for reversing the economic degeneration threatening many, if not most of the homeland communities revolve in one way or another around the planning of their urbanization' (Lombard & Van der Merwe 1972, p. 27). The progress of urbanization is thus crucial to the government's policy of separate development.

In this chapter, attention is focused on the most important processes underlying urbanization in the homelands. Influx control measures to restrict the flow of population from the homelands to 'white' urban areas, the resettlement of Blacks from 'white' urban areas in homeland towns, the establishment of a commuting system whereby Black workers travel daily between homeland towns and adjacent 'white' urban complexes and the leakage of Black purchasing power from homeland towns to white areas, all have a 'considerable effect upon the rates and spatial incidence of urbanization' (Fair & Schmidt 1974, p. 159). They also make it impossible to divorce the urbanization of the homelands from that of 'white' South Africa.

---

*Officially known as the National States but described as homelands in this chapter. Unless otherwise stated, this term excludes the 'independent' Black states of Transkei, Bophuthatswana and Venda. They are excluded mainly for statistical reasons, as these former homelands were not included in the 1980 population census.

Demographic features of the homelands

By 1980, 81.8 per cent of the total Black urban★ population lived in 'white' South Africa, as opposed to 18.2 per cent residing in the homelands. The 1980 population census shows that the total Black population of South Africa (excluding Transkei, Bophuthatswana and Venda) numbers almost 16 million, of which 6.5 million or 40.7 per cent reside in the homelands and 9.5 million or 59.3 per cent in 'white' South Africa (Table 5.1). Boundary

Table 5.1 The rural–urban distribution of population in 'white' South Africa and the homelands in 1980.

	Whites	Coloureds	Asians	Blacks	Total
'White' area					
total	4 444 591	2 548 041	773 576	9 468 693	17 249 754
urban	3 958 514	1 973 227	708 957	4 940 699	11 593 100
rural	486 077	574 814	64 619	4 527 974	5 654 646
Homelands					
total	8 682	5 998	6 110	6 501 326	6 522 216
urban	1 713	1 845	2 679	1 097 157	1 103 430
rural	6 969	4 153	3 431	5 404 169	5 418 786
Republic of South Africa					
total	4 453 273	2 554 039	779 686	15 970 019	23 771 970
urban	3 960 277	1 975 672	711 636	6 037 856	12 698 538
rural	493 046	578 967	68 050	9 932 163	11 073 432

Source: provisional data from 1980 population census, Department of Statistics, Pretoria.

changes, consolidation, resettlement and possible under-enumeration in the 1970 population census contribute to the abnormally high population increase shown by the homelands during the period 1970 to 1980. Compared with a growth of 29.5 per cent in the total Black population of South Africa, the homelands experienced an increase of 65.8 per cent in the period between the population censuses. Qwaqwa (512 per cent), KwaNdebele (412 per cent) and KaNgwane (201 per cent) registered an exceptionally large population increase (Table 5.2).

Figure 5.1 indicates the relative increase and decrease of the Black population (1970–80) according to data by homelands and magisterial districts. In addition to the positive changes experienced by the homelands, the South-

★ The term urban presents particular difficulties in South Africa where large numbers of Black migrant workers oscillate between their families in the homelands and their jobs in white urban areas. Many homeland towns do not have an economic base and can hardly be classified as urban in the fullest sense. Only those areas or settlements falling under the control of a local authority were regarded as urban for the 1980 population census, which excluded, for example, spontaneous settlements where the residents no longer carry on farming operations but are dependent mainly on work in the urban areas for a livelihood.

Table 5.2 Increases and decreases in homeland population (%), 1970–80.

Homeland	White	Coloured	Asian	Black	Total
Ciskei	−55.06	−21.20	−57.14	76.44	73.82
Gazankulu	60.54	402.04	−75.00	71.72	71.76
KaNgwane	−81.22	570.00	—[1]	204.12	201.56
KwaNdebele	−74.47	20.00	140.00	414.96	412.03
KwaZulu	−53.25	−14.30	−21.18	52.72	52.11
Lebowa	−38.36	110.08	−27.91	60.83	60.34
Qwaqwa	40.82	—[1]	—[1]	514.51	512.08
total	−44.69	−11.34	−21.20	66.57	65.80

Source: compiled from unpublished data from the 1980 population census.
[1] no population in 1970.

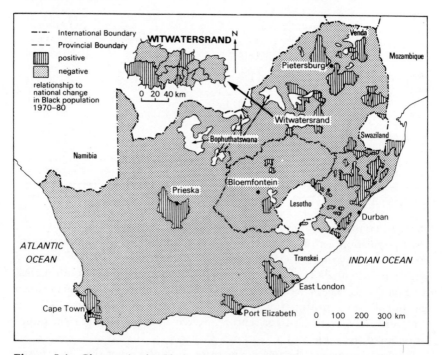

Figure 5.1 Changes in the Black population, 1970–80, expressed as positive or negative deviations from the national rate of increase in the Black population. The 'independent' homelands of Bophuthatswana, Transkei and Venda are excluded. (Source: calculated from population census data, 1970 and 1980.)

western Cape showed rapid increases in the Black population: although regarded by the government as a preferential labour area for Coloureds and whites, the population succession here whereby Blacks are increasingly taking the place of Coloureds (pointed out by Smit 1976, p. 56) is persisting unabated. Increasing numbers of Coloureds are in fact leaving the Southwestern Cape for better paid jobs on the Witwatersrand and in the Durban–Pinetown area and Blacks have to be 'imported' to replace them. Other areas that experience relatively rapid increases in the number of Blacks are Port Elizabeth (arising from industrial development) and certain areas peripheral to Johannesburg. While the inner cores of the large metropolitan areas showed decreases, relative to the national rate of change, in the numbers of Blacks, rapid increases were experienced on the immediate periphery of these areas.

Only 16.8 per cent of the homeland population is in urban areas, compared with 37.8 per cent of the total Black population of South Africa and 52.2 per cent of the Blacks living in 'white' South Africa. According to Swart and Oosthuizen (1978, p. 23), the Black urbanization process has, as a result of government control measures, not progressed rapidly compared with other Third World countries. The fact that 89 per cent of the whites, 73 per cent of the Coloureds and 91 per cent of the Asians have already been urbanized suggests that large-scale urbanization lies ahead for the Black population. Dewar (1976, p. 33) estimates that by the year 2000, 75 per cent of the Black population will have become urbanized. Attention will now be paid to the most important forces underlying the urbanization process in the homelands and 'white' South Africa and an indication will be given as to where the most important urban development is likely to occur in future.

Urbanization in 'white' South Africa compared to the homelands

The process of urbanization in South Africa could be regarded as the outcome of a conflict between ideological–political and economic forces. The interaction between economic–centripetal forces (the concentration of production factors in particular core areas or centres) and the political–centrifugal forces (the independence of the homelands periphery and the political coupling of the Black urban population in 'white' areas to the homelands) forms the framework within which the urbanization process of the Black population in South Africa is taking place (Board et al. 1970, Fair 1965).

Urbanization in 'white' South Africa   Five phases can be distinguished in the urbanization of the Black population in 'white' South Africa (Smit & Booysen 1977, pp. 5–15). In the *first phase*, which commenced after gold and diamonds had been discovered, Blacks flocked to the mining areas from all parts of the subcontinent. By 1904 there were some 353 000 urban Blacks and 233 'white' towns already had a Black component. A *second phase*, which would last until 1950, was introduced in 1923 with the passing by Parliament of the Natives (Urban Areas) Act, which provided for the clearing of Black slums. Strict influx control was introduced and the principle of impermanency, which for several decades would dominate the provision of housing and services for Blacks, was accepted. The increase in industrial development in the 1930s attracted growing numbers of Black women to the urban areas and natural population increase began supplementing the numbers of migrant labourers. During the war and in the years immediately following it, Black influx into the urban areas and the growth of slums reached a critical level. A *third phase* of intensified segregation and slum clearance was introduced in 1950 and with the passing of the Group Areas Act. More stringent influx control measures and the establishment of a network of Labour Bureaux significantly limited the growth of the Black urban population. A *fourth phase*, in which the emphasis was on homeland development, was introduced in the 1960s. Provision of housing for Blacks in 'white' areas was restricted and where possible family housing had to be provided in homeland towns. This development will be discussed in more detail below.

A *fifth phase* began in 1975. The position of the urban Blacks had become so problematic that during a discussion between the prime minister and homeland leaders on 22 January 1975, eight of the 14 items on the agenda specifically concerned urban Blacks. The prime minister stated that the government was prepared to consider sympathetically 'a form of leasehold for Black people in White areas' (House of Assembly Debates 1977, col 2767). With regard to trading rights in Black townships, the assurance was given that the relevant legislation would be reviewed. A year later, in January 1976, a home ownership scheme was introduced for Blacks in Black urban areas. The scheme would, however, not apply to large townships west of the Eiselen Line as this area was regarded as a preferential labour area for Coloureds (Fig. 2.1, p. 26). Participation in the home ownership scheme was initially subject to the possession of a certificate of homeland citizenship, while the right of occupation was limited to a period of 30 years. These restrictions were lifted in August 1976, however, and the period of 30 years would only apply to the maximum period permissible for the repayment of the housing loans.

After the riots which broke out in Black urban areas on 16 June 1976, a number of reforms relevant to urbanization were introduced. The language question (i.e. insistence on Afrikaans in Black schools) was initially regarded as the major cause of the riots but it soon became apparent that lack of housing and services had also played a role (South Africa 1979d, pp. 603–6). The most important reforms were the following:

(a) The Urban Foundation was established in December 1976 to promote and co-ordinate the private sector's involvement in improving the quality of life of urban communities in South Africa (Steyn 1979, p. 109). Contrary to the view generally held by the private sector that provision of housing and services was the responsibility of the government alone (the private sector was responsible for only about 11 per cent of the 45 877 houses built for Blacks in 'white' urban areas between 1972 and 1976: Theron 1979, p. 64), Mr H. F. Oppenheimer as Chairman of the Urban Foundation stated that 'directors of public companies are more coming to accept a measure of responsibility for the environment in which they operate' (Steyn 1979, p. 109).

(b) In 1977 the Community Councils Act was passed by Parliament. In terms of this Act, Blacks obtained control of local affairs pertaining to their own residential areas. It was agreed that the powers of the community councils would eventually extend beyond those of local authorities (municipalities and city councils). The establishment of community councils without doubt confirmed the permanency of Blacks in the urban areas. By March 1981, 227 community councils had been established. Although a low polling percentage was recorded for the first community councils (5.6 per cent in the two contested wards in Soweto), an average polling percentage of 41.27 was achieved in the election of the first 112 community councils (Department of Co-operation & Development 1979, p. 27).

(c) A 99-year leasehold system was introduced in 1978. Although Blacks may own only the houses and not the land, leasehold is generally regarded as permanent ownership. By March 1981, 795 houses had been sold under the 99-year leasehold. In most of the Black townships more than 75 per cent of the number of houses sold were under the 30-year home ownership scheme.

(d) In the interim report of the Commission of Inquiry into the Constitution (South Africa 1980a) provision was made for Coloureds, Asians and Chinese representation on the president's council but Blacks were excluded. Because Coloureds and Asians were not prepared to serve on the council if Blacks were excluded, provision was made for a Black council in an advisory capacity in the fifth Constitution Amendment Bill (House of Assembly Debates 1980, col 7954–5). After opposition from and negotiations with Black leaders, the government officially announced the abandonment of plans to establish such a Black council. It remains the view of the government that urban Blacks should exercise their political rights via the homelands and that those who cannot be accommodated in this way should 'in some or other co-ordinated form' be given representation in a constellation of states (House of Assembly Debates 1980, col. 245).

Homeland urbanization: a new dimension   There are two basic reasons for the fact that there were only three homeland 'towns' by 1960 and that the urban Black population numbered only 33 486. In the first place, the Black population of South Africa, as in the rest of the subcontinent, had never established an urban tradition. Secondly, economic development and urbanization in the core areas inhibited urbanization in the homelands (Henning 1969, p. 169). The more Blacks left the periphery to go and work in the core areas (particularly large 'white' cities), the more economic conditions deteriorated and the more unfavourable became the climate for urbanization in the homelands.

After 1948 the idea began to gain ground that towns in the homelands should not merely become repositories for the surplus rural population but should also provide accommodation for Blacks working in adjacent 'white' areas. Umlazi, established in 1949–50, was the first town to be established in a homeland to relieve the Black housing shortage in a major 'white' city (in this case Durban). This represented the beginning of the frontier commuting, described in full in the previous chapter.

Up until the end of the 1950s the question of independence for the homelands had not been raised. The rate at which countries in the rest of Africa were gaining independence influenced government policy, however, and in 1959 the Promotion of Black Self-government Act was passed by Parliament. This changing view of the political future of the homelands brought about greater awareness of the fact that an urban structure was absolutely essential if these areas were to be guided towards independence. High priority was given to the establishment of homeland towns and 66 per cent of the budget for the physical development of the homelands was voted for this purpose under the first five-year plan (1961–6). More than 80 000 houses were to be built in the homelands within five years. In political circles the idea was beginning to gain ground that the different Black peoples should be settled in the homelands in their own political, social and ethnic context. Apart from these objectives it was also realized that the establishment of towns in the homelands or on the periphery would counteract the influx of Blacks to the 'white' urban core areas.

By the end of 1965, 38 500 houses had been completed in 37 homeland towns. Under the second five-year plan (1966–71) R121.5 million was allocated (74.7 per cent of the total physical development programme) for the building of 93 480 houses. From 1961/2 to 1977/8 more than R520 million was spent by the Development Trust, homeland governments* and development corporations on the establishment of towns in the homelands. The annual expenditure by these bodies increased from R21.8 million in 1970/1 to R75.5 million in 1977/8. Up to now 88 towns (including towns in Transkei, Bophuthatswana and Venda) have been proclaimed (Fig. 5.2). The urban Black population in the homelands increased from 33 486 in 1960 to 594 420 in 1970 and was estimated at 1.5 million in 1978. In 1980 the urban Blacks in the seven non-independent homelands numbered 1 097 157. Urban development and population settlement constituted a considerable percen-

*During the 1960s all the Black towns were financed and administered by the SA Development Trust. Since 1972 the legislative assemblies of the homelands have been granted the authority, subject to the approval of the South African government, to pass certain laws in respect of homeland towns. For the first time in the history of the homelands, decision-making was transferred from the core areas to the periphery.

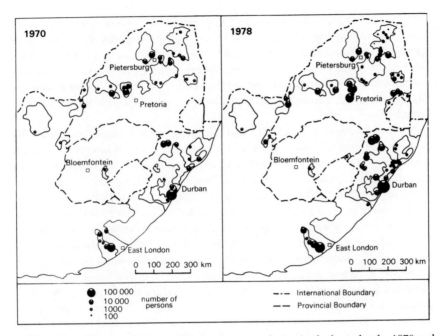

Figure 5.2 The distribution of Black urban population in the homelands, 1970 and 1978. (Source: Smit & Booysen 1981.)

Table 5.3 Total Black homeland population, 1980.

Homeland	Urban no.	% of total	Rural no.	% of total	Total
Ciskei	228 559	36.3	401 796	63.7	630 355
Gazankulu	14 330	3.0	462 364	97.0	476 694
KaNgwane	4 620	2.8	155 262	97.2	159 882
KwaNdebele	23 109	13.8	143 368	86.2	166 477
KwaZulu	695 155	21.8	2 482 414	78.2	3 177 569
Lebowa	118 073	7.3	1 540 052	92.7	1 658 125
Qwaqwa	13 311	5.7	218 915	94.3	232 226
total	1 097 157	16.8	5 404 171	83.2	6 501 328

Source: compiled from unpublished data from the 1980 population census.

tage (e.g. KwaZulu 20.9 per cent, KwaNdebele 36.5 per cent) of the total expenditure of homeland governments during the period 1974/5 to 1978/9.

Three main reasons can be advanced for this rapid urbanization in the homelands. In the first place, large numbers of Blacks from the 'white' areas were resettled in the homelands and the homeland towns in particular. From 1960 to 1970, for example, 68 144 Blacks were moved to the homelands from 'Black spots' in 'white' rural areas and homeland areas which in the consolidation process had to be merged into 'white' areas. According to Venter

(1976, p. 35) some 275 000 Blacks from within and outside the homelands were resettled during the period 1970–5. Of greater significance to urbanization in the homelands, however, was that virtually all those Blacks who were moved from 'white' urban areas were resettled in the various homelands. Since 1967 it has become official policy to resettle non-productive Blacks (the aged, handicapped, widows, etc.) from the 'white' areas to the homelands.

A second reason for the rapid urbanization in the homelands was the decision to freeze all family housing for urban Blacks in 'white' areas as from 1 January 1968. Family housing was as far as possible to be provided in neighbouring towns in the homelands. Slum areas were cleared and the residents resettled in the homelands (e.g. Blacks from East London's Duncan Village were moved to the neighbouring homeland town, Mdantsane). In this way certain urbanization problems from the core areas were transferred to the periphery (Smit & Booysen 1981, p. 28). The effect of this is indicated in Table 5.4, clearly showing how the provision of housing for Blacks has decreased in 'white' areas since 1968. Although the provision of housing has increased in the homelands, it cannot compensate for the decrease in building programmes in 'white' areas where a tremendous housing backlog has developed. By the end of 1977 the shortage was estimated at 141 000 family housing units and 126 000 hostel beds in the 'white' areas (South Africa 1979b, p. 111). In the homelands the housing shortage was put at 170 000 units (Van der Merwe & Stadler 1977, p. 1). It is estimated that during the 1980s 110 000 houses will have to be built annually in the homeland towns (Gordon 1980, p. 403).

Table 5.4 Number of houses built and expenditure on housing for Blacks in 'white' areas and in the homelands from 1967/8 to 1976/7

Year	'White' areas		Homelands	
	number of houses	expenditure (R1000)	number of houses	expenditure (R1000)
1967/68	14 369	7 770	4 233	5 656
1968/69	14 950	8 571	15 753	9 515
1969/70	12 127	6 880	567	18 515
1970/71	8 566	6 289	11 364	24 030
1971/72	6 710	6 278	8 664	35 662
1972/73	5 149	5 670	13 141	25 790
1973/74	7 573	6 026	7 963	30 504
1974/75	8 111	6 611	7 561	45 985
1975/76	7 835	9 811	5 405	67 215
1976/77	6 109	5 619	29 241[1]	—

Source: South Africa (1979a, pp. 110 & 116).
[1] Transferred to homelands from certain Black residential areas, namely KwaMashu 15 415 houses, Edendale 4984 houses and Clermont 2840 houses.

After the riots of 1976 housing programmes in the 'white' areas were stepped up and the provision of family housing was tackled on a large scale. The restrictions on the provision of family housing in 'white' urban areas, which had been in force since 1968, were lifted. In the 1979/80 financial year, R100 481 200 was spent by the government on the provision of housing in 'white' urban areas. Although houses can be rented or purchased in the homeland towns at lower prices than in the 'white' urban areas, building society loans are more readily available in white urban areas. The provision of utilities such as sewerage and water services is far more satisfactory in Black residential areas in the major cities than in homeland towns and townships in rural areas (e.g. see Fig. 5.3). In Soweto, for example, an electricity

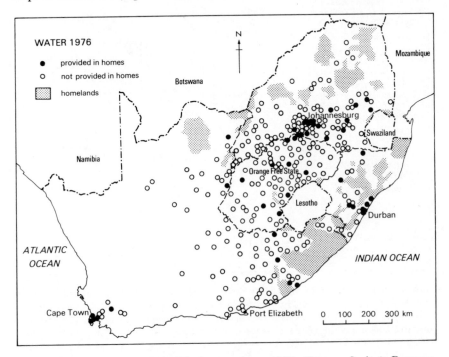

Figure 5.3 Water services in Black townships, 1976. (Source: Smit & Booysen 1981.)

supply scheme is currently being developed at a cost of R150 million. In this respect South Africa is following a typical African pattern, in that funds allocated to the major urban areas and particularly the main conflict areas (e.g. Soweto) constitute a large proportion of the total expenditure on housing and urban development. It can therefore be expected that in future urbanization will occur less rapidly in the homelands than in the 'white' areas because the pull exerted by the 'white' urban areas will be much stronger than in the past.

In an analysis of the increase in the urban Black population from 1936 to 1970 (Fig. 5.4), it is clear that the major metropolitan areas have absorbed the largest part of the Black population (Smith & Booysen 1981, p. 62). In 1970 more than 60 per cent of the urban Black population was in the major metropolitan areas (the P–W–V area, Durban–Pinetown, Southwestern Cape, Port Elizabeth–Uitenhage and East London) and the future growth will un-

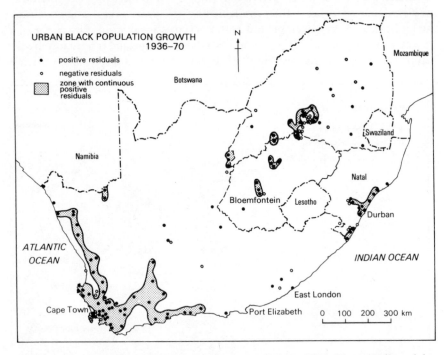

Figure 5.4 Growth of the Black urban population, 1936–70, as indicated by residuals from regression. The variables used in the regression analysis were the total urban Black population of each town or city against the percentage growth rate of the urban Black population for each town or city between successive intercensus periods: 1936–46, 1946–51, 1951–60, 1960–70. (Source: Smit & Booysen 1981.)

doubtedly also occur in these areas (Du Pisanie 1980, p. 15). Economic forces are increasingly gaining the upper hand over political–ideological forces. Homeland governments are becoming increasingly opposed to resettlement of Blacks from the 'white' areas and the establishment of homeland towns without economic bases. The KwaZulu government has made it clear that there will increasingly have to be shared decision-making regarding the location of urban areas (KwaZulu Government Service 1979, p. 4).

Thirdly, the decentralization of industries (see Ch. 3) has also contributed towards homeland urbanization. Since 1968 and especially since 1973, restrictions have been placed on the number of Blacks that may be employed in industries, particularly in the Pretoria–Witwatersrand–Vereeniging area. A total of 360 industries have been established up to April 1981 in the homelands (including Transkei, Bophuthatswana and Venda) with a capacity to provide job opportunities for 31 000 Blacks. In addition 250 small Black industrial enterprises (each employing between two and seven people) were established in the homelands while the commercial and service sectors supply jobs for 35 000 homeland Blacks. Decentralization has occurred on the periphery of Johannesburg in the Babelegi, Rosslyn, Brits and Rustenburg areas, however, so that while there has been a decrease in the number of Blacks in the core area of the Pretoria–Witwatersrand–Vereeniging industrial complex, the Black population on the periphery has increased rapidly (Fig. 5.4).

During the period 1972–5 approximately 100 000 Blacks annually entered the labour market in the homelands, including Transkei, Bophuthatswana and Venda (Van Eeden 1980, pp. 418–19; Du Plessis 1980, pp. 436–67). Only about 28 per cent of these Blacks could find employment in the homelands. Some could find jobs in adjacent 'white' areas and commute daily between their homes and their work. However, more than one-third (roughly 34 000) per annum should be regarded as migrant labourers or unemployed (Van Eeden 1980, p. 419). The government is currently intent on decreasing the number of industrial growth points and has intensified its efforts to concentrate industrial development in a few growth points in and near the homelands. Also rapidly gaining ground is the idea of 'co-operative areas', for example East London, Berlin, King William's Town, etc., which will be jointly developed and perhaps in future, jointly governed by the Black government concerned and the South African government.

Consequences of homeland urbanization

The most important consequences of urbanization as it has occurred in the homelands can be summarized as follows.

The freezing of extensions to Black residential suburbs in 'white' urban areas and the resettlement of Blacks in neighbouring homeland towns helped to bring about a decrease in the urban Black population of 197 'white' cities and towns during the period 1960–70. Towns such as Pietersburg, Potgietersrus and Rustenburg, which are situated close to homelands, divested themselves of their Black residential areas while the old Cato Manor in Durban has disappeared altogether. These factors contributed towards the finding by the South African Labour and Development Unit of the University of Cape Town that there is an increase in the flow of Blacks back to the homelands and that administrative measures 'have had the desired effect as far as the Government was concerned' (Die Beeld 18 Mar. 1981).

As a result of the artificial stimulation of homeland urbanization, the majority of homeland towns are situated on the borders of the homelands (Fig. 5.2). Most of these towns lack an economic base and none of the homeland towns can be regarded as an urban area in the full sense of the word. They are little more than appendices to or domitory towns for 'white' urban areas. It is evident from Table 5.3 that Ciskei and KwaZulu have achieved the highest percentage of urbanization of all the homelands. The main reasons are that both these homelands border on major metropolitan areas (East London and Durban respectively). Ten of the largest homeland towns are situated within 4 to 35 km of the nearest large 'white' urban area. As is the case with primate cities elsewhere in Africa, the largest homeland towns such as Umlazi and Mdantsane are also those with the most rapid population growth and the most serious squatter problems (Smit 1979, pp. 13–14). In 1975 more than 60 per cent of the total urban population of the homelands was living in only 10 towns, and by 1979 this had increased to 65 per cent. The largest towns grow the fastest and also receive the lion's share of the capital expenditure. In 1979, 64 per cent of the Ciskei's urban population and 70 per cent of the houses were concentrated in Mdantsane. In 1978 roughly 42 per cent of the total urban population of KwaZulu lived in Umlazi and KwaMashu (Smit & Booysen 1981, p. 85).

As a result of the artificial character of the homeland towns and the fact that they lack an economic base, there are substantial leakages of purchasing power from the homelands to adjacent 'white' cities and towns, resulting in relatively insignificant multiplier effects in homeland towns. In certain homeland towns it was found that the inhabitants spent only about 20 per cent of their money outlay on clothing in the town itself while the balance was spent in adjacent 'white' towns. Chief Buthelezi, Chief Minister of KwaZulu, has warned that in the future this could lead to a boycott of white businesses (*Star* 20 Nov. 1980). Large concerns, however, are allowed to establish businesses on an agency basis in Black urban residential areas such as Soweto as well as in homeland towns, endangering the future of the small Black businessman. Free trading areas where trade can be carried on by all race groups are planned in some 'white' urban areas, as proposed by the Riekert Commission: a black business group has recently been given permission to occupy premises in the heart of Johannesburg's central business district (*Star*, 22 Oct. 1981).

A commuting system has developed, giving a new dimension to migrant labour. In 1979 an estimated 719 000 Blacks commuted daily between their homes in homeland towns and their jobs in 'white' areas; the frontier commuting phenomenon is described fully in Chapter 4. Table 5.5 shows that the vast majority of commuters come from urban areas. KwaZulu and Bophuthatswana were responsible for roughly 75 per cent of all commuter traffic. The 718 900 commuters earned about R1 280 million in 1979 (more than 25 per cent of the Gross National Product of the homelands). Com-

Table 5.5 Estimated number of commuters from homelands, 1979.

Homelands	1970	1976	1979 urban	rural	total	% of grand total
'Independent'						
Bophuthatswana	84 000	154 900	148 500	13 400	161 900	22.5
Transkei	3 400	7 100	8 200	700	8 900	1.2
Venda	3 000	3 700	4 000	1 600	5 600	0.8
total	90 400	165 700	160 700	15 700	176 400	24.5
Other						
Ciskei	40 000	36 900	37 100	—	37 100	5.2
Gazankulu	3 400	7 800	5 100	2 700	7 800	1.1
KaNgwane	3 000	23 000	20 300	12 800	33 100	4.6
KwaNdebele	—	—	2 400	1 100	3 500	0.5
KwaZulu	127 000	325 000	332 000	68 600	400 600	55.7
Lebowa	26 000	46 300	44 300	13 600	57 900	8.1
Qwaqwa	1 000	1 800	2 500	—	2 500	0.3
total	200 400	441 400	443 700	98 800	542 500	75.5
grand total	290 800	607 100	604 400	114 500	718 900	100.0

Sources: BENSO (1980), South Africa (1979a, 1981); data for 1970 and 1976 courtesy of Dr A. Lemon.

muting patterns are having a decisive effect on the entire transportation system and network in South Africa. The subsidies for the transportation of Black workers by rail and bus currently amount to more than R100 million per annum. As a result of rising costs, subsidized transportation of Black workers on a daily basis can no longer be regarded as the solution to the problem of Black urbanization.

Housing shortages in the homelands and Black residential areas in 'white' towns and cities have inevitably led to squatter conditions on a large scale. If the term 'squatting' is interpreted in the broadest sense of the word, South Africa has between 1 and 1.5 million squatters (of all race groups). It is an open question, however, whether an area such as Winterveld north of Pretoria in Bophuthatswana (see Ch. 2) should be regarded as a squatter area or as a spontaneous settlement. President Mangope of Bophuthatswana, regards the Winterveld, where between 200 000 and 300 000 'squatters' are living, 'as the biggest and most pressing problem confronting my administration' (Mangope 1980, p. 20). It is estimated that there are roughly 250 000 squatters in the area surrounding Edendale and Zwartkop in KwaZulu. Squatter camps are emerging around virtually all homeland towns but Black leaders have neither the will nor the administrative machinery to take positive action. In recent years a large number of Blacks (mainly from Transkei and Ciskei) have settled on the Cape Flats at places such as Crossroads,

Modderdam and Unibell (see Ch. 2). Many of the squatter towns have been cleared, but so great was the public outcry as well as resistance from the Transkei and Ciskei governments that the South African government is currently engaged in resettling the approximately 20 000 squatters from Crossroads in a new urban area on the Cape Flats. Squatting also occurs to a considerable extent around 'white' urban areas such as Germiston and Krugersdorp. It is obvious that the provision of housing for Blacks can no longer be the responsibility of the government alone. The private sector is playing a larger role in the provision of housing but the Blacks will have to be assisted to an increasing extent to build their own houses.

Conclusion

Economic forces are to an increasing extent gaining the upper hand over the political–ideological forces which have dominated the urbanization of the Black population for several decades. The relaxation of influx control measures, linking the stay of Blacks in 'white' urban areas with the availability of work and suitable housing, will step up the process of urbanization in the 'white' areas. The stipulation that Blacks may not stay in a 'white' urban area for longer than 72 hours without prior permission will be removed (1981 legislation) and the period extended to 30 days. The proposed new Black Community Development Act published on 31 October 1980 recommended that new administrative machinery for influx control should be introduced and that a considerable number of current laws be struck from the statute book. The above draft Bill was published along with two others with a view to receiving comments on the proposed legislation prior to its submission to Parliament. There was wide reaction to the draft Bills and the Minister of Co-operation and Development referred the matter to a committee to consolidate all the comment and to propose new legislation before 15 April 1981. Of particular significance is the fact that Blacks were appointed to the above committee.

Community councils responsible for carrying out influx control functions will experience tremendous pressure from persons seeking to enter 'white' urban areas, and from those already employed in these areas and with permanent obligations in respect of housing, hire purchase agreements, etc. who may regard 'outsiders' as a threat to their positions. The establishment of community councils has given urban Blacks some right of say in the running of their own local affairs. How long this will satisfy them remains to be seen. Homeland governments appear to be reluctant to grant greater local autonomy to Blacks in homeland towns. Most homeland governments hold more traditional views while the urban Blacks in the homelands have a more modern outlook. In Africa, the conflict between 'modern' and 'traditional' has led to more than one *coup d'état*.

Up until now there have been virtually no links between homeland towns and their hinterlands. Homeland towns are not only dependent on 'white' South Africa for the provision of food and job opportunities but also remain islands in a sea of underdevelopment. If the borders of independent homelands should ever be closed to commuter traffic, these towns would inevitably die. In this respect the homeland towns resemble primate cities in Africa where there is often more interaction between the urban areas and the Western world than between them and their immediate hinterlands (Friedmann & Alonso 1977, pp. 266–304). The advantages of modernization and economic development do not filter through to the heartlands with sufficient strength to have a stimulating effect, particularly on the stagnating agricultural economy.

The most stringent test of whether the policy of separate development can succeed or not centres to a great extent on the urban areas of South Africa, where not only the white and Black population groups but also the various Black ethnic groups have the closest contact with one another, and where their common interests are to a very large extent entwined. The urbanization of Blacks in South Africa is therefore entering a new era of change and challenges, the course of which should be highly interesting to monitor.

6 The informal sector of the apartheid city: the pavement people of Johannesburg

K. S. O. BEAVON and
C. M. ROGERSON

In common with many Third World countries, there exist in both urban and rural areas of South Africa a significant proportion of the workforce engaged in economic activities that are insecure, do not provide full employment and which, almost invariably, generate low incomes. Amongst the activities which may be described by the rubric of 'the informal sector' are the home brewing of traditional African beer, the operation of shebeens (illicit drinking places), baby-minding, street barbering, the running of 'informal' schools, garbage scavenging, newspaper-vending and street hawking in food, clothing and flowers (Rogerson & Beavon 1980). The numbers of persons involved in such activities in South Africa is not accurately recorded. Nevertheless, from the limited studies so far undertaken (Maasdorp & Pillay 1978, Maree & Cornell 1978, Biesheuvel 1979, Webster 1979a, Wilsworth 1979, 1980, Morris 1980, Dewar & Watson 1981) it appears that participation in the urban informal sector in South Africa is relatively small compared to many Third World cities (cf. McGee & Yeung 1977, Bromley & Gerry 1979, Sethuraman 1981). Moreover it appears likely that the population 'employed' in the informal sector of South Africa is still only a fraction of that formally employed in industry and service activity. But despite recent increases in the numbers of those classified as formally unemployed, informal sector occupations exhibit a rapid upward advance. As Dewar and Ellis (1979, p. 25) observe, in future years 'the informal sector of the economy will have to play an increasingly important role in providing the job opportunities that will be severely in demand'. Alarmed by the potential threat posed to the apartheid system by the burgeoning levels of unemployment, policy makers in South Africa are reassessing their attitudes towards the informal sector. In the context of the state's attempts to foster a politically stabilizing Black *petite bourgeoisie* in the townships that fringe the cities of 'white' South Africa, the current national development plan speaks cautiously of encouraging the informal sector (South Africa 1979e).

This chapter examines aspects of life in one component of the informal sector of the apartheid city. It must be acknowledged, however, that the informal sector as an analytical concept has serious shortcomings (Bromley 1978a, McGee 1978, Moser 1978, Bromley & Gerry 1979, Gerry 1979). Most important for the present discussion is the marked heterogeneity of the activities comprising the informal sector. Nevertheless the growing rejection of the terminology of an informal sector does not detract from empirical studies into the organization and operations of those activities in which the working poor scrape out a daily existence (Williamson 1977). Indeed, the urgency for further contributions towards an 'asphalt pavements' geography has been emphasized on several occasions (McGee 1974a, 1979a; Bromley 1981).

The focus of attention here is on the conditions of existence of a group of the 'pavement people' of Johannesburg, to reveal something of the organization, characteristics and spatial distribution of the city's street traders. In investigating the street traders of Johannesburg as a micro-study of life in the urban informal sector of South Africa, it is imperative 'to show the manner in which processes at the individual level fit within the national level of which they are a part' (Moser 1977, p. 471). Accordingly the initial concern is with the root causes of structural unemployment in the South African economy: the existence of an increasing body of surplus workers gives rise to the continuing expansion of informal economic occupations. The discussion follows in the vein of those pioneering geographical works on informal economic activities in Third World cities contributed notably by Bromley (1978b, 1978c, 1981), McGee (1971, 1974a, 1974b, 1976, 1979a; McGee & Yeung 1977), Santos (1976, 1979) and Forbes (1979, 1981). The literature of urban geography on South Africa largely has eschewed investigations of the informal sector (Rogerson & Beavon 1980, Beavon & Rogerson 1981, Beavon 1981) notwithstanding that it is apparent that such informal activities have historically constituted persistent features of the urban milieu (Beavon & Rogerson 1980, Rogerson 1980, Van Onselen forthcoming).

Informal activity as a response to structural unemployment

The growth of a community of pavement peoples in South Africa, working in a variety of informal income niches, must be situated against a backdrop of the generally low wage levels paid to Blacks in formal employment, the meagre unemployment security benefits open to Blacks and most importantly, to the creation of a mass of 'structurally' unemployed workers (Webster 1979a). As distinguished from cyclical unemployment, the term structural unemployment connotes the existence of a large and permanent body of workseekers 'surplus' to the requirements of capitalist production (Maree 1978, Simkins 1978, de Klerk 1979). The extent of this surplus labour pool is revealed in detailed studies of unemployment by Simkins (1978):

between 1960 and 1977 the volume of unemployed persons almost doubled (from 1.2 to 2.3 million) in a period which included a sustained 'boom' of the national economy. These figures (that include underemployment) suggest a rate of structural unemployment in South Africa of approximately 19 per cent of the labour force. The structures of apartheid serve to ensure that the burden of this unemployment falls almost exclusively upon the country's Black population (Legassick 1974b).

The roots of the present dilemma of structural unemployment are as follows. First, the participants in the street occupations of South Africa represent 'the highly visible casualties' (Cohen et al. 1979, p. 20) of the out-workings of twin processes of peasantization and proletarianization. A second source is the limited extent of employment creation in conditions of peripheral capitalism. This retarded rate of employment expansion has been worsened by the third and fourth causes, namely the restrictive effects of the industrial colour-bar or job reservation legislation and the destruction of employment opportunities occasioned by the Environment Planning Act. Finally, a source of specifically urban unemployment is that resulting from the spatial immobilization of Black labour consequent upon South Africa's notorious pass laws. Each of these origins of structural unemployment are briefly elaborated.

Peasantization and proletarianization   The beginnings of South Africa's sur-plus population of potential workers are located in the processes of peasant-ization and proletarianization. The era of mercantile capitalism in South Africa (pre-1870) was associated with the growth of peasant commodity production in pre-capitalist African societies (Bundy 1978). By the end of the 19th century there emerged a class of peasant producers both anxious and able to respond to early market opportunities being generated by the expand-ing capitalist economy. Colonial capitalism, however, began inexorably to weaken and eventually destroy the peasant class it had earlier created and nurtured (Palmer & Parsons 1977). Of critical importance was the ascent of mining over mercantile capital: whereas the latter was interested primarily in securing commodities produced within the pre-capitalist economy, the former was centrally concerned to extract labour from the regions in which pre-capitalist elements had been perpetuated (Bundy 1978). From this period henceforward processes of peasantization were superseded swiftly by those of de-peasantization and proletarianization (Webster 1979b).

Increasing pressures began to be applied to the erosion of peasant classes as the forces favouring their creation and maintenance weakened relative 'to those who had come to define the desirable future in terms of the creation of a mass labour force' (Bundy 1978, p. 240). The basic elements and institutions of what Legassick (1977) styles as South Africa's 'labour-coercive economy' were now shaped and later modernized to meet the exigencies of capitalist development. As the expanding capitalist economy required ever-increasing amounts of cheap labour, Blacks were confined to smaller and increasingly overcrowded vestiges of territory, the 'reserves', which were set on a course of rural pauperization and decay (Magubane 1975, Legassick 1977, Bundy 1978). The progressive dissolution of the pre-capitalist economies of these areas and the advance of processes of underdevelopment assured that the reserves would furnish a vast reservoir of migratory labour for the mines, the farms and later the manufacturing industries of South Africa. Over the years, however, the rural economies of these areas have collapsed such that the supply of labour from them has turned into an embarrassing surplus contributing, particularly since 1948 (Simkins 1981a), a continuing stream of persons into the ranks of South Africa's structurally unemployed. The proletarianization of Blacks means that the reproduction of an increasing proportion of the workforce now had to be provided within the urban milieu.

Employment creation in conditions of peripheral capitalism   The South African economy manifests several of the distinguishing traits of peripheral capitalism. Most important for the present discussion is a recognition of the economy's failure to absorb the growing numbers of workseekers in consequence of the application of increasingly capital-intensive technologies of industrial (and agricultural) production (Maree 1978). Such technologies are designed in the context of advanced capitalist economies where capital is relatively plentiful and cheap with labour relatively scarce and expensive. In the context of South Africa's domestic resource endowments, in particular its vast reservoir of cheap labour, the import of such foreign technologies is inappropriate (Maree 1978, de Klerk 1979). The continuing introduction of such technologies in South Africa is inseparable both from the country's dependent position in the world economy and from the weakness of local research and development in producing alternative and more appropriate technologies. The important position of multinational corporations in the South African economy (Seidman & Makgetla 1978) further reinforces the trend towards the importation of foreign technologies. Finally, both Maree (1978) and de Klerk (1979) emphasize that the adoption of capital-intensive techniques of production is promoted by a suite of tax measures which have caused factor-price distortions which artificially reduce the cost of capital in South Africa. Accentuation of the dilemma of structural unemployment has been the by-product of the pursuit of such policies.

The industrial colour-bar   The term 'industrial colour-bar' refers broadly to the array of legal, institutional, social, political and economic practices that retard or block the occupational advancement of Blacks in the South African economy (Maree 1978). The industrial colour-bar legislation firmly placed white workers on the favourable side of South Africa's unfolding dynamic of development and underdevelopment (Legassick 1977). But, for Blacks, this body of legislation served to augment the numbers of unemployed. Maree (1978, p. 33) elaborates:

> By virtue of the Industrial Colour Bar Whites have been able to retain a near monopoly on skilled jobs, particularly those for artisans, over the past fifty years or more. Consequently, one of the ceilings put on the growth rate of the economy has been the growth of skilled White labour. Because of relatively fixed ratios between the number of skilled and unskilled workers in any industry, the growth of demand for unskilled and semi-skilled African workers has been limited by the growth rate of the predominantly White skilled labour force.

Shortages of skilled white labour accompanied by the higher rate of increase in the supply of Black relative to white workers therefore supplemented the growing pool of unemployed Blacks in South Africa.

The Environment Planning Act It is ironic that the chief legislative instrument designed to promote employment growth in the peripheral areas of South Africa should have the consequence, albeit unintended, of reducing total employment opportunities in manufacturing. The Environment Planning Act was introduced in 1968 and provides, *inter alia*, for the control over the establishment or extension of factories in certain areas of South Africa. Under Section 3 of the Act written ministerial permission is required before industrialists in the proscribed areas may undertake a 'factory extension', defined exclusively as any increase in the number of a firm's Black employees. In later amendments to this legislation industry was to maintain a strict ratio of Black to white employees (Rogerson 1975, Gottschalk 1977).

The net impact of this legislation has been to destroy employment opportunities in manufacturing as firms either failed to expand or sought to introduce labour saving technologies. Between 1968 and 1978 government vetoed the additional employment of over 100 000 Black workers in the metropolitan areas (most importantly in the Pretoria–Witwatersrand–Vereeniging region) in terms of this legislation. To this net employment loss must be added the further job reductions that flowed from firms forced to close plants as a consequence of the Act and also the losses stemming from government's refusal to permit the zoning of new industrial land, in particular in the Pretoria–Witwatersrand–Vereeniging area. As compared to the slight progress of employment creation in the decentralized areas of South Africa the Environment Planning Act has severely reduced the total number of manufacturing job opportunities in the country (see Gottschalk 1977, Rogerson in Ch. 3 of this vol.).

The spatial immobilization of Black labour The measures introduced by the state to counter the process of Black urbanization have been so forcefully applied that it has been suggested by Horrell (1973, p. 162) that there is no more coveted right, including the vote, anywhere in the world, than the qualification of a Black South African to a degree of permanency in the country's 'white' cities in terms of what is called Section 10 rights (see Ch. 7). The recent government commission into manpower in South Africa, the Riekert Commission, recorded with alarm that those Blacks with Section 10 residence qualifications dared not move even when they were unemployed for fear of losing their residence rights (South Africa 1979a, b). The report draws attention to the growing volume of unemployment in the metro-politan areas of South Africa as a direct consequence of the spatial immobil-ization of Blacks with Section 10 rights (South Africa 1979a, b).

In summary, the growing crisis of structural unemployment compels many Black South Africans to seek an existence in one of a variety of pave-ment occupations. In examining such occupations it is necessary to under-stand that the entrepreneurship of these people is contingent upon their social conditions of existence under apartheid. The strategy of working on the streets of South Africa is one which is essentially a replacement for an un-available or perhaps inadequate wage income. With these comments in mind, the discussion now shifts to the street traders of Johannesburg as a micro-level case study of life in the urban informal sector of one South African city.

The urban informal sector under apartheid: a case study of street trading in Johannesburg

Street trading in many Third World cities is often portrayed as a 'marginal' occupation, an example of how the poor 'make out', or as one dimension of the coping responses of the urban poor to the shortages of alternative employment (Bromley 1981). These interpretations also could be applied to street traders in the South African city. But it is important to stress that street trading plays a vital role in the commodity and service distribution of the Black sub-system of the apartheid city (Beavon 1981). Accordingly, far from being simply a marginal occupation, street trading is potentially functional to the socio-economic system as a whole (Bromley 1981). It may contribute to a lowering of the cost of living in the city by keeping down the prices of foodstuffs and commodities for the urban poor and, in so doing, hold down pressures for rising wage labour costs in capitalist enterprises (Gerry 1979, Forbes 1981). Moreover, street traders fulfil a further role in encouraging consumption, both by selling at relatively low prices and by making items available at a wider range of locations and for longer time periods (Bromley 1981). The functionality of street traders for capitalism is simply 'that even when the poorest consumer has a need which capitalism can satisfy, someone is there to ensure the realisation of even a minute quantity of surplus-value'

(Gerry 1979, p. 70). In this fashion, the street traders of the Third World are viewed as contributing to 'the reproduction and dominance of the higher-order groups within the city' (Forbes 1981, p. 853).

In view of such interpretations, it is necessary to account for the seeming paradox of the small-scale development of street trading in the apartheid city and of the associated tradition of suppressing rather than supporting this activity by Johannesburg municipal authorities. The urban managers of Johannesburg overwhelmingly view street hawkers as a nuisance, making the city look untidy by their presence or through their litter, the cause of traffic congestion and even, on occasion, of the spread of disease. The anti-informal policies pursued by local authorities in Indonesia (Forbes 1981) and Colombia (Bromley 1978b) were explained as policies of containment rather than of elimination, their goal being merely to restrict the expansion of these activities to some imaginary optimum size and, in so doing, to pre-serve the *status quo*. In South Africa, however, municipal authorities have constantly pursued policies directed towards the total removal of street trading (see Rogerson 1980). Imbued by the powerful ideology of modern-ization, city administrators in Johannesburg have perceived the street traders as a community standing 'in the way' (cf. Cohen 1974) of their modernizing goals. In addition, since implementation of the racist apartheid ideology, the largely Black community of street traders constitutes a further obstacle towards attaining the objective of creating a pure white city (Proctor 1979). Unlike the situation in many Third World cities where street traders vote in local elections and occasionally evince the interest of populist politicians (cf. Bromley 1978b), the Black street traders of Johannesburg neither have a vote in the white municipal elections nor does their plight attract a sympathetic vote amongst the mass of the white electorate. In these circumstances it is not surprising to record the existence of a battery of controls, at both national and municipal levels, upon the conduct of the pavement peoples of Johannes-burg. A brief examination of these controls is essential to understanding the organization, geography and characteristics of the street traders operating in the city.

Legislative controls on street trading   Access to land and markets in South Africa is primarily exercised through the Group Areas Act No. 36 of 1966. This legislation prevents Blacks from either buying land, owning businesses, or trading within a so-called white Group Area. As the business districts of South African towns and cities are almost invariably part of a white Group Area this legislation prevents Blacks from being trader-owners within such areas, thereby precluding the possible evolution of enterprising hawker businesses into retail outlets with fixed premises.

Whereas the Group Areas Act has an indirect effect on Black street traders, the Black (Urban Areas) Consolidation Act No. 25 of 1945 (as amended) affects them more directly. In the case of Black hawkers in Johannesburg the

Act requires that they obtain the permission of the West Rand Administration Board (WRAB) in order to trade in the downtown area of the city. The WRAB in turn is required to be empowered by the Minister of Co-operation and Development to grant or refuse such permission. Only once permission has been accorded can an application be made to the local authority (in this case the Johannesburg municipality) for a street trading licence.

An application to the Johannesburg City Council for a street trading or hawker's licence must be accompanied by a fee of between R1 and R10, depending on the nature of the goods to be traded and their method of sale. But before a licence can be granted the application is scrutinized by various municipal departments including Health, Traffic and Planning. An objection from any one of these departments can result (and frequently does), in the rejection of the application. In addition, at the discretion of the licensing board the prospective Black street trader may be required to advertise his intentions to trade through the medium of at least two newspapers in both official languages, English and Afrikaans. The advertisement will solicit objections to the intentions of the hawker. The total cost of this complex procedure (including the cost of the licence if it is granted) varies between R100 and R130. Even equipped with a licence to trade as a hawker, the individual seller is constrained further by the regulations that govern street trading in the central area of Johannesburg.

As is the case in many Third World cities, the municipal authorities of Johannesburg possess a variety of additional legal instruments and controls designed to keep hawkers out of prestigious areas of the city (cf. McGee & Yeung 1977). In this respect the central business area of Johannesburg is 'the defended space' of the city (Bromley 1978b, 1978c). This space, as defined by the licensing and business control laws promulgated under the provincial authority of the Transvaal, is officially termed 'the restricted area' of Johannesburg (Fig. 6.1) because even with a licence the operations of hawkers are severely curtailed. Within the defended space both national and local authority agencies are empowered to enforce the controls on street trading. For example, the trader who successfully negotiates the maze of procedures and duly obtains a licence finds that hawking in the restricted area is only permitted before 7 a.m. and after 6 p.m. Furthermore within this defended space there exist several defined 'restricted streets' (Fig. 6.1) where trading is prohibited between 7 a.m. and 9 p.m. on any Saturday. In addition, on Christmas Eve and New Year's Eve, and on the Saturday preceding such days if they should fall on a Sunday, the prohibited hours of trading throughout the restricted area run from 7 a.m. to midnight. It is hardly surprising that even licensed hawkers operate 'illegally' in the restricted area notwithstanding that they expose themselves to arrest, confiscation of their goods and fines of R100.

Control over street trading in the defended space of the city is further complicated by a distinction between hawkers operating from 'fixed stands' and

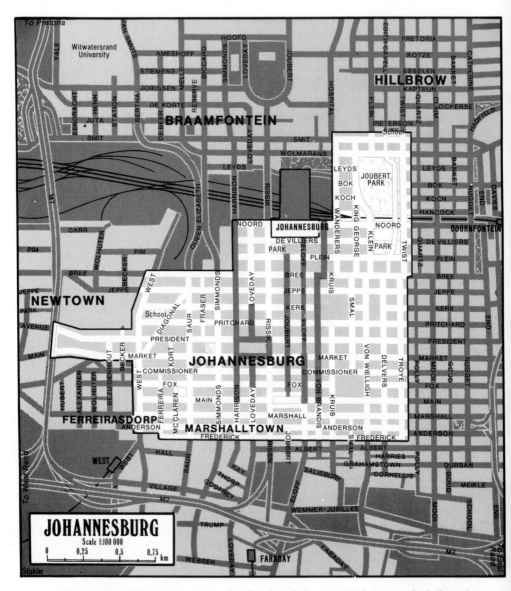

Figure 6.1 The restricted area (outlined) and the restricted streets (shaded) within the central business district of Johannesburg. (Source: Johannesburg Municipal By-laws.)

the remainder who are considered to be mobile hawkers. The latter group find themselves subject to the municipal 'move-on' regulations that require them to move their goods and barrow or stall to a new site at least 25 m distant every 20 minutes. Furthermore the hawker may not sell at any site so vacated within the next 24 hours. These legislative controls are prime influences upon the organization and geography of street trading in Johannesburg.

The organization and spatial distribution of street trading in Johannesburg The focus here is upon the organization and spatial attributes of street trading conducted in the 'white' city of Johannesburg. Within the limits of this chapter no consideration is accorded to those thousands of hawkers who operate in the Black townships of Soweto, 20 km to the west of the city, or Alexandra immediately north-east of Johannesburg. Also excluded from this study are the traders of the indigenous craft market known as Mai-Mai Bazaar, in the heart of the 'white' city, which falls under a different set of controls to those governing street traders.

The street trading community of Johannesburg comprises mainly the vendors of foodstuffs (cooked and uncooked), clothing, flowers, soft goods, newspapers and African curios or handicrafts. Less numerous are the hawkers of beverages, furniture, firewood, paper carrier bags, watches and car hubcaps (Biesheuvel 1979). Within this varied group of superficially independent entrepreneurs it is possible to recognize, following Bromley and Gerry (1979), a complex mix of work relationships. These range from 'disguised wage work' to situations of 'true self-employment'. For example, the newspaper sellers of the central city are effectively disguised wage-workers of the newspaper companies, without the normal benefits available to employed labour (Biesheuvel 1979). The earnings of this group are based upon a commission on each newspaper sold (*Rand Daily Mail* 21 Mar. 1973). Within the sector of flower selling there exist relationships, best termed 'dependent working', where poorer traders borrow monies and become dependent upon better-off traders or where certain flower sellers acquire a variety of obligations which substantially reduce their freedom of action (see Tomaselli 1981). It appears that dependent work relationships exist also within the sector of soft goods sales as many hawkers enter into such dependent roles with their suppliers, small wholesale businesses located in the central city (Biesheuvel 1979). Only within those street trading operations requiring the least capital, such as the sale of foodstuffs and second-hand clothing, is there a work relationship approaching that of 'true self-employment' where the trader enjoys relative freedom in terms of both the choice of supplier and outlets for his goods (Bromley & Gerry 1979). Even within these activities there exists a possibility for the formation of dependent work relationships as hawkers obtain merchandise on credit from other sellers or wholesalers (cf. Bromley 1981).

The growth of street trading within 'white' Johannesburg has been such that since the 1960s it has been described by municipal officials as 'one of the city's biggest problems' (*Star* 17 Jan. 1964). Yet, in total there are no more than perhaps 1000 street traders regularly working in the whole city. Hawking activities are widespread throughout the city, including also its suburban zones. Nevertheless, as Forbes (1979, p. 19) observes of the pedlars in Ujung Pandang, 'there is an important spatial variation in the distribution of the informal sector'.

Within Johannesburg, the geographical pattern of traders is broadly a function of the spatial distribution of income opportunities (potential consumers), of complementary and competing trades and of the regulatory behaviour of the municipal authority (cf. Bromley 1978c). Hawkers operate at a range of locations including railway stations, taxi ranks, bus stops; at major shopping concentrations; outside hospitals; alongside the Black hostels in the industrial areas; at road intersections and outside places of entertainment and sports stadiums (Biesheuvel 1979, p. 64).

The map of hawking activities in Johannesburg is marked by clustering along the line of railway stations, stretching from Industria in the west to Denver in the east (Fig. 6.2). But, by far the greatest concentration of street

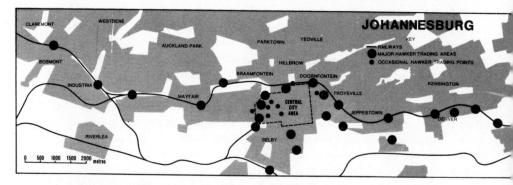

Figure 6.2 The geography of hawking in Johannesburg. (Source: modified from Biesheuvel 1979.)

trading occurs within the central business district of Johannesburg. In this zone are the mass of the city's newspaper vendors, flower sellers, African curio hawkers and sellers of cooked and uncooked foodstuffs. The latter activities are found particularly around the central transport termini for Black commuters, and around the mini-bus and taxi ranks that fringe downtown Johannesburg. For these activities, the peak business periods are associated with the early morning and late evening rush hour for Black commuters into and out of the city. With the exception of the lucrative business of flower selling, which is dominated by the Indian community (Tomaselli 1981), the overwhelming majority of street traders are Blacks. Until recently there was one further and very notable exception to this pattern. In the vicinity of Diagonal Street, in the northwestern part of the restricted area long occupied by the Indian community, there existed a group of Indian hawkers trading from barrows parked in the gutters of the streets outside the shops. The barrow traders were engaged primarily in the sale of fruits, food-stuffs and small items of clothing, giving to the area the character of an Indian bazaar. However, with the relocation of the Johannesburg Stock Exchange from the heart of the CBD to Diagonal Street in the late 1970s, the city's 'move-on' regulations were ruthlessly enforced to excise this group of hawkers from the environs of the new Stock Exchange (*Rand Daily Mail* 24 Apr. 1979, *Sunday Express* 21 Oct. 1979).

The final element in the spatial mosaic of street trading in Johannesburg is the pattern of pavement traders operating from 'fixed stands' in the city. These are sites that may be hired from the city council for the specific desig-nations given to that site, and offer the trader immunity from the 'move-on' regulations. In the case of only a small number of these stands does the city council rent out an actual structure as well as the site; rather, a shelter is usually erected by the stand tenant. Separate stands are designated respec-tively for 'white' and 'non-white'★ traders in respect of a variety of com-modities and services. Nevertheless, in practice, it is only the sellers of flowers, fruit and vegetables that occur in any numbers (Tomaselli 1981). The current spatial pattern of the stands is portrayed in Figure 6.3. The recent history of these stands is summarized on Table 6.1, which shows the numbers and uses of stands by race categories. Of greatest significance is the redistribution of stands between whites and non-whites over this period and, in particular, the drastic reduction in the number of flower stands available to non-whites. The formal apartheid period witnessed an effective increase in the numbers of stands available for occupation by whites, notwithstanding that white street photographers are a phenomenon of past years and that white shoe-blacks no longer operate. By contrast, in a period of great demand for access to selling points in the restricted area by Black and Indian traders there has been a net reduction in the number of available sites (Beavon 1981). The consequence of this reduction is an intensified competition for the remaining stalls. Competition has been particularly severe amongst the city's Indian flower sellers with tenders in 1980 of up to R6000 for the annual lease of one stand in Market Street in the city centre (*Sunday Express* 30 Mar. 1980).

The Black and Indian street traders operating in Johannesburg have sought through various means to resist both their progressive removal from the city central zone and their constant harassment by the municipal authority. The traders have formed a number of organizations, most importantly of flower sellers and hawkers, to defend their common interests in the face of attempts to destroy their livelihood. But as has been the experience of similar organ-

★The authors regret that it is necessary to use these racial tags here and in Table 6.1 and Figure 6.3. However, the controls discussed in this chapter are couched in such terms. Non-whites in this context refer to both Black Africans and Indian and Coloured persons.

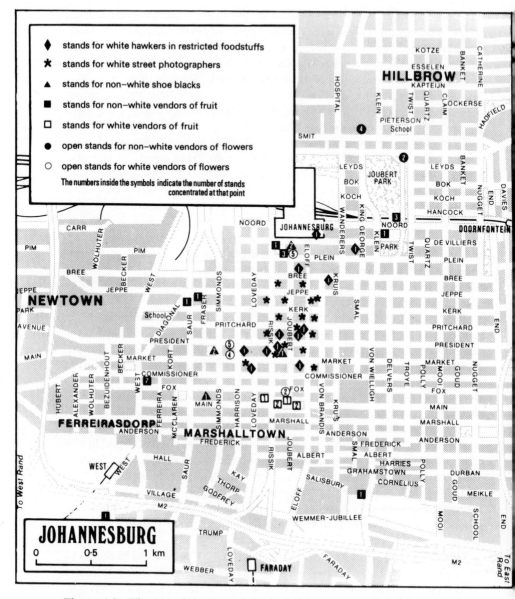

Figure 6.3 The sites of 'fixed stands' in the Johannesburg CBD. (Source: Johannesburg Municipal By-laws.)

izations (cf. Bromley 1978b, Peattie 1979), these associations tend to represent primarily the interests of better-off traders aspiring to 'middle class' status. There has been no solidarity of the Johannesburg street traders with other groups of the working poor in the apartheid city. For the majority

Table 6.1 Numbers of fixed stands in the restricted area of Johannesburg.

	1953–57	1957–66	1966–80
Non-white operated stands			
shoe blacks	6	6	6
fruit stands	9	9	9
flower stands	33	33	16
total	48	48	31
White operated stands			
foodstuffs	0	0	12
street photographers	0	0	16
flower stands	0	0	0
fruit stands	5	5	6
total	5	5	34

Source: Johannesburg municipality.

of traders, resistance to municipal harassment is reflected in the day-to-day attempts to flee from officialdom whenever possible, to offer fictitious names and addresses when apprehended, to leave small children in charge of hawker stalls when raids occur (in the knowledge that these children will not be arrested), and to seek to confuse officials with receipts of applications for hawker licences rather than the difficult-to-obtain hawker licence itself. These efforts at resisting the repression of municipal authority in Johannesburg have done little, however, to improve the plight of the ordinary street trader.

The characteristics of street traders in central Johannesburg A picture of the street hawking community operating in Johannesburg is obtained from the results of a questionnaire survey undertaken during 1979–80 in the restricted central area of the city. At the time of the study between 200 and 250 hawkers were working daily in this part of the city. One hundred hawkers were approached; 72 provided data suitable for inclusion in the study. The survey provides the basis for discussion of the varied backgrounds, incomes, educational levels, nature of goods traded and earning capacities of street traders (see Table 6.2).

The hawkers of the central Johannesburg are engaged in the sale of a variety of commodities, the majority (some 57 per cent) in aspects of food distribution, either of cooked or uncooked foods. The market is the commuter Black workforce daily disgorged at the central railway station and bus termini. Many workers entering the city in the early morning buy food from the hawkers in lieu of a prepared breakfast. Excepting food, the most important trade items are cosmetics, clothing, small jewellery and leather goods. Again, for these goods, it is the Black workers of Johannesburg's factories and offices who are the major buyers. Hawking is conducted primarily from stalls made out of cardboard boxes or planking which are

Table 6.2   Characteristics of hawking in central Johannesburg.

Types of business (%)

fruit	28.8	clothing	11.4
vegetables	15.9	leather goods	5.3
cooked meat	0.8	jewellery	6.1
corn on the cob uncooked	3.8	cosmetics	14.4
corn on the cob toasted	6.1	household items	1.5
porridge	0.8	other goods	4.5
other cooked food	0.8		

Earnings from hawking
(a) per day
minimum R2.20, maximum R82.28, average R17.45

	%		%
less than R5.00	11.1	R15.01–R20.00	16.7
R5.01–R10.00	25.0	R20.01–R30.00	19.4
R10.01–R15.00	16.7	R30.01 or more	11.1

(b) per week
minimum R12.85, average R109.67

Size of hawker's household (%)

single	8.3	7–9	20.9
2–3	18.1	10–12	7.0
4–6	45.9		

Number of years in hawking (%)

up to 1 year	8.3	11–15 years	9.8
2–5 years	33.3	16–20 years	12.6
6–10 years	25.0	21 years or longer	11.2

Previous occupations (%)

unemployed or housewife	37.5	scullery hand	2.8
factory worker	19.4	ticket collector	2.8
domestic servant	15.3	market labourer	1.4
shop assistant	8.3	plumber's assistant	1.4
waiter	5.6	cleaner	1.4
driver	2.8	hotel assistant	1.4

Age of hawkers (%)

16 and under	2.8	41–50	16.7
17–20	2.8	51–60	19.4
21–30	26.4	61–70	2.8
31–40	27.8	71–80	1.4

Level of education (%)

none	20.8	std 7–std 9	7.0
sub A–std 3	32.0	matriculation	1.4
std 4–std 6	38.9	post-matriculation	0.0

Source: survey by authors, 1979–80. Figures based on response of 72 out of 200–250 hawkers (not including those with fixed stands); subject to rounding errors.

regularly set up in one place on a daily basis. Virtually all businesses in the sample were owned and operated by the hawkers themselves; instances of hawkers in the central city operating stalls owned by other traders, and thereby functioning as the category of dependent workers, were rare.

The survey revealed that over half the street trading community were women (see also Biesheuvel 1979). Further, paralleling the findings of studies in urban areas of the Third World, there emerges a marked sexual division of labour in the most important types of street trading (Nelson 1979, Heyzer 1981). Women predominate in the hawking of food, more especially of cooked foods, whereas men are dominant in the sale of soft goods (Biesheuvel 1979). The former activities require very little capital outlay and are simply extensions of women's domestic roles. By contrast the soft goods business requires a far greater financial outlay and more expertise (Biesheuvel 1979). Although hard evidence relating to the profitability of different forms of trading is slim, studies of Third World cities (Heyzer 1981, Moser 1981) suggest a tendency for the women street traders of Johannesburg to be found in activities which provide lower returns.

The spectrum of gross weekly and daily earnings of Johannesburg street hawkers is recorded in Table 6.2. In interpreting these data the caveat must be added that traders, on the whole, were reluctant to speak of this facet of their existence. Answers were tabulated for the question 'What do you make per day?' and from these responses the gross daily and weekly earnings were computed. In seeking to reduce this to an index of net income earned, it is necessary to consider also both the average costs of purchases of R66 per week and the mean costs of transport from Soweto to central Johannesburg, an average of R24 per week. Relative to the estimated minimum budget for a Black household of six persons at the time of the survey, calculated at R180 per month (Potgieter 1980), it is evident that street trading is overwhelmingly a low-income activity in Johannesburg. Indeed, for several households the income of women hawkers is only a supplement to the male worker's wage. However, for those households dependent solely upon street trading or for those with large numbers of dependants, the majority exist below the minimum recommended budget levels. The data on earnings of hawking in central Johannesburg reveals also a striking spread of incomes, with a minority of earnings higher even than is paid to lower echelon wage-employees in the formal sector (Biesheuvel 1979). This finding lends credence to the complexity and differentiation that exists among what might appear superficially as a homogenous group of traders all operating in marginal profit situations (cf. Moser 1977, Bromley 1978b, McGee & Yeung 1977, McGee 1979a).

The stereotype view of street trading as a temporary 'refuge' occupation for newly arrived migrants to the city is not borne out by the Johannesburg study. Almost 60 per cent of traders have been so engaged for more than five years; nearly a quarter of the sample had been hawkers for 16 years or more (Table 6.2). Moreover, the mass of the hawkers are long-term continuous residents of the Johannesburg area. No cases were recorded of newly arrived migrants from the Bantustans entering street trading as a stopgap prior to entry into formal employment. For many of the traders, street hawking was entered into only after having alternative jobs in the city. Most commonly, male hawkers had experience of factory life and women hawkers of the exigencies of life as a domestic servant. Nevertheless it is apparent also that hawking is a survival niche commonly taken up at times of household crisis, such as unemployment, illness or death of the household breadwinner. It is striking that whereas the hawker community derives from a range of job backgrounds, the largest single group, including nearly all women hawkers, were formerly either unemployed or housewives. The data relating to the ages of hawkers and the number of years they have been hawkers lends support to the notion that once a person decides, or is forced through circumstance, to become a hawker, he or she is likely to remain one of the pavement community of Johannesburg. Undoubtedly, many of the street traders would have great difficulty in obtaining wage–employment in light of their meagre educational achievements. The discriminatory nature of education in South Africa is mirrored in the poor educational levels attained by the Black populace. In the case of the street hawkers, over half possess less than a Standard 4 qualification and are therefore functionally illiterate (Table 6.2).

Finally, it is worth noting the long hours of work that characterize the daily life of this group of the pavement people of Johannesburg. The bulk of hawker stalls operate between 9 to 14 hours per day, five or six days per week. The hours of business differ as between the different trade items: the vendors of cooked and uncooked foodstuffs are the earliest to take up their positions on the streets, many beginning as early as 5 a.m. (Biesheuvel 1979), to catch morning commuters on arrival in the city. Moreover it is important also to recall the prohibitions in the by-laws that hawking within the restricted area is not allowed after 7 a.m. The majority of the trader community disregard this time constraint and therefore hawk in constant fear of police harassment. Long hours of toil and a permanent feeling of insecurity are thus features of life working on the streets of the 'city of gold'.

Conclusion

This chapter has focused upon the modes of existence, organization and characteristics of a group of the pavement peoples of Johannesburg. In the shadows cast by the glittering skyscrapers of the city the story played out on the pavements is one of a struggle for bare survival. The actors in this drama daily run the gauntlet of apartheid legislation and petty municipal regulations in order to eke out a living in the city.

The street traders of Johannesburg offer a glimpse of the complexity and differentiation that exists among one typical informal sector activity. That said, any micro-study of life-conditions of informal sector participants necessarily must be linked to an understanding of forces operating at the wider national (and even international) level. What may be interpreted as the entrepreneurship of participants in the informal sector is quintessentially a response of the Black community to the social conditions of their existence under apartheid. With increasing levels of structural unemployment in South Africa growth in the numbers of persons engaged in street trading and similar informal occupations appears inevitable. Accordingly, further investigations into the mechanisms of survival in the apartheid city are urgently needed. Human geography in South Africa is only beginning to penetrate behind the apartheid city's mask of glass and steel to reveal the hard times of life on her city pavements.

Acknowledgements

The authors are grateful to Mr P. Stickler of the Geography Department at the University of the Witwatersrand for the preparation of the diagrams. The co-operation of the Town Planning Department of Johannesburg in providing some of the raw data is acknowledged. Financial assistance has been provided by the Human Research Council, Pretoria.

7 Urbanization, unemployment and petty commodity production and trading: comparative cases in Cape Town

D. DEWAR and V. WATSON

Introduction

Historically, a major characteristic of both advanced and peripheral capitalist economies has been the steady movement of people from the rural to urban areas. However, the form of this movement in South Africa has been unique. While development of mining and industry was initially based on the removal of labour from the rural areas to the Witwatersrand and the major port cities, urbanization of the Black (African) population in the 20th century has become increasingly constrained by influx control laws enacted initially under a British policy of segregation and thereafter under Nationalist apartheid policy. The most important instruments used to constrain this urbanization relate to employment and housing.

The major legislation regulating Black employment in 'white' urban areas, and the movement of Blacks between areas, is the Black Labour Act 1964, and the Natives (Abolition of Passes and Co-ordination of Documents) Act 1952. In terms of this legislation, no Black person may remain in a 'white' urban area for more than 72 hours, unless he has obtained a contract of employment (valid for one year, but renewable) through a government Labour Bureau. The award of contracts is related to the number of 'jobs for Blacks' available in the urban areas. In effect, these controls create a cycle of permanent migration. The position of the Black population in the 'white' urban areas of South Africa is therefore characterized by a high degree of insecurity and severe economic disadvantage.

In the Western Cape region these conditions are exacerbated. First, the Black population is affected by the Coloured labour preference policy in terms of which a Black person may be employed only in a job for which there is no suitable Coloured applicant. Secondly, both the Black and Coloured populations are affected by the relative economic disadvantage of the Western Cape region, where wages are lower and jobs scarcer than in the other metropolitan areas of the country.

The Black (Urban Areas) Consolidation Act 1945 regulates Black residence *within* 'white' urban areas. Under this legislation the only Black people
who are entitled to remain permanently in the 'white' urban areas are those
who qualify under section 10 (1) of the Act: those who have resided continuously in a 'white' urban area since birth (10 (1) (*a*)), or who have worked
continuously in such an area for one employer for a period of not less than 10
years, or have resided continuously in the areas for not less than 15 years, and
who have not, during this period, been subject to a fine of more than R500 or
imprisonment for a period exceeding 6 months (10 (1) (*b*)). Officials, implementing influx control legislation, have interpreted the term 'continuously'
as excluding people who technically have to return to the homelands each
year to reapply for a job. Thus even though a man has worked with one
employer, and therefore lived in the area, for more than 15 years and has only
taken annual leave to the homelands (in the process reapplying for a permit)
he is regarded as a temporary sojourner.

The number of people who qualify to remain permanently in 'white'
urban areas is a very small percentage of the total Black population. It is only
these persons who are legally allowed to have their wives and unmarried
children residing with them (section 10 (1) (*c*)) and who therefore qualify for
state subsidized housing in the urban areas. In addition to people who are
allowed permanent residence, section 10 (1) (*d*) allows for migrant workers
to remain in 'white' urban areas for the duration of their contract, due regard
being given to the availability of accommodation in a Black residential area.
In this case accommodation is generally provided by employers in the form
of barracks, single quarters or compounds.

However, even for those who legally qualify to remain in 'white' urban
areas under one of the above sections, there is a critical housing shortage.
Soweto for example, has a current official housing backlog of 35 000 units
(*Rand Daily Mail* 21 July 1981) and it can be assumed that the actual backlog is
much greater. For those who are legally resident in these areas and who do
have housing, there is still no permanent security of tenure. Until recently all
Black housing stock in 'white' urban areas was owned by the state and rented
out on a short-lease basis. In 1978 this was improved somewhat by the introduction of the 99-year leasehold Act. This system had, however, been
viewed with suspicion by Blacks and to date there have been few takers. In
the Western Cape, the Coloured labour preference policy excludes even the
99-year lease system on the grounds that Blacks are to be gradually phased
out of the area.

Over time, controls relating to housing and employment have become
increasingly interlinked. This tendency has recently been reinforced
by the Riekert Commission's recommendation that 'influx control should
be linked only with availability of work and approved housing' (South
Africa 1979a). It is now necessary for a Black person to be in possession
of proof that he is suitably housed, before he can take up employment;

similarly, he requires proof of a job before he can obtain access to housing.

These policies have had some success in containing urbanization. A recent study by Simkins (1981b) has revealed that there has been *a net outflow* of the Black population from the major cities and towns in South Africa, as well as from the 'white' rural areas, into the homelands. Between 1960 and 1980 this outflow from the white urban areas amounted to 0.75 million people and from the 'white' rural areas into the homelands to 1.25 million. Total control of urbanization has, of course, been impossible. The option facing many Blacks is either to return to the rural areas and face starvation, or 'make do' as best as they can in the 'white' cities. There is, therefore, a great deal of illegal urbanization: for example, a recent government estimate reported in *The Cape Times* (in Aug. 1981) has stated that 42.8 per cent of the Black population in Cape Town (or 85 436 people) are 'illegals'. This primarily takes the form of migrants from the rural areas and homelands seeking jobs, or families joining the breadwinner who has migrated to the urban area. For people such as these, barred from legal access to both jobs and housing, two of the most important survival strategies are squatting and petty commodity production. The majority of people in the 'informal' settlements burgeoning around the major cities, as well as most people engaged in petty commodity production, are so-called illegal immigrants. However, neither the informal settlements nor the petty commodity sector are exclusively populated by illegals. On the one hand, the housing backlog and the fact that many people cannot afford the costs associated with even the cheapest forms of state pro-vided housing, swell the squatter settlements. On the other, petty com-modity production and trading becomes an outlet for all sections of the working class during periods of unemployment, ill health or severe financial strain and is used by many as a means – sometimes on a permanent basis, sometimes intermittently – of supplementing household income.

Historically the reaction of the state to survival strategies such as these has been one of repression. Squatting has, for many years, been illegal: a 1977 amendment to the Illegal Squatting Act empowers local authorities to demolish shacks without a court order and without the onus being upon the authority to provide alternative accommodation. Similarly, petty producers and traders have been severely constrained by a gamut of legislation includ-ing health measures, building regulations, planning legislation and licencing laws (see Ch. 6). The combined effect of these regulations has been to control the numbers and locations of petty commodity producers and traders as well as the nature of their operations.

However, more recently there has been a notable change in the attitudes of policy makers towards informal settlement and economic activity. This must be seen against a general climate of international pressure for observ-able reform and increasing internal dissent and dissatisfaction. Specifically, the attitudinal changes have been fuelled on the one hand by the increasing realization that the state simply does not have the resources necessary to remove the housing backlog through conventional systems of delivery or to create sufficient employment through the mechanisms of the formal economy; and, on the other hand, by the increasingly politicized nature of both the housing and unemployment issues.

A bitter division of opinion on appropriate forms of housing policy presently exists within government circles and has resulted in the appointment of a committee of inquiry to investigate alternative methods of housing procurement. However, there appears to be widespread agreement (at least at the level of rhetoric) that the stimulation of small business should play a leading role in the state's self-proclaimed assault on unemployment and that the informal sector should be promoted. This agreement has taken overt policy form through the creation of a Small Business Development Bank to finance and promote small businesses.

Given that the stimulation of small businesses is now official policy, two important questions are raised. First, what will be the developmental consequences of the stimulation of small businesses and secondly, if this stimulation, is desirable, what form should it take. To answer these questions, it is necessary to understand more of the form and nature of the so-called informal sector in South Africa and the possible impact which a policy of stimulation is likely to have.

An empirical study

To this end a study was launched into the operation of petty commodity producers and traders within metropolitan Cape Town (Dewar & Watson 1981). The kind of activity under consideration here, and subsumed under the heading 'petty commodity production and trading', is that most generally known as the informal sector. Theories of economic development concerned with this kind of activity differ on the question of whether the unit of analysis should more correctly be the *business or activity*, or the *household*. If the primary concern is with 'welfare' (and from a developmental point of view this must be the case: there is no point in increasing the provision of jobs unless this also implies a decrease in poverty) then the household, as the primary income sharing unit, is most important. However, if the concern is with policy and the impact on these activities of outside stimulatory agents, then the emphasis is better placed on the business as a unit: by stimulating the *activity*, the household is better placed to improve its own position. Moreover, a major factor which affects small business activities is their competitive position in relation to larger businesses; for this reason, businesses are best conceived in terms of an interlinked size continuum.

This study is concerned with businesses falling at the lower end of the size continuum, whether measured by turnover, profits, capital investment, labour, or some combination of these. Defining a cut-off point raises severe difficulties: indeed it can be argued that any attempt to do this precisely (for instance, statistically) is invalid, by virtue of the continuum-like nature of business activity and the complexity of business operations. In practice, however, the problem of definition is much easier, for the factors characterizing the businesses which are the focus of this study (small size, often marginal, often impermanent, often located in informal settlements and so on) tend to coincide.

Stratification of the study In order to obtain a representative coverage of activities, an initial distinction was made between place-related producers and traders and those who are mobile (i.e. hawkers). The mobile vendors tend to locate as near as possible to points of most intensive business and pedestrian activity in the city. Consequently, major areas of hawker concentration, both in the city centre and smaller outlying business areas, were identified and included in the study (Fig. 7.1). To investigate factors affecting place-related activities, a comparative approach involving four sample areas was utilized. The selection of areas was made on the basis of the distribution of conditions which initial investigations revealed may affect the form and distribution of petty commodity activity: these included socio-economic conditions, layout, density and the degree of local authority control imposed upon them. Each area is of roughly the same size (0.38 km^2). However, densities and consequently the number of people in each area vary considerably (Table 7.1). The areas are shown in Figure 7.1 and will now be considered in turn.

Table 7.1 Comparison of sample areas.

	Crossroads	Vrygrond	Mitchells Plain	Heideveld
area (km^2)	0.32	0.42	0.44	0.34
approx. no. of people	25 000	4472	6250	4532
no. interviewed	91	20	34	28
average income (weekly)	R26	R25	R87 (household)	R31 (household)
housing type	squatter	squatter	local authority	local authority
tenure	legal but temporary	legal but temporary	ownership	rental
zoning	none	none	residential	residential

Source: Dewar and Watson (1981).

Crossroads is a Black squatter camp situated some 15 km from the centre of Cape Town. The camp was established early in 1975 after the Cape Town Divisional Council (a local government body), in an attempt to control the growing number of squatters scattered throughout their area of jurisdiction, encouraged people to move their shacks to a pre-designated point where a check could be kept on numbers and, in particular, on health conditions.

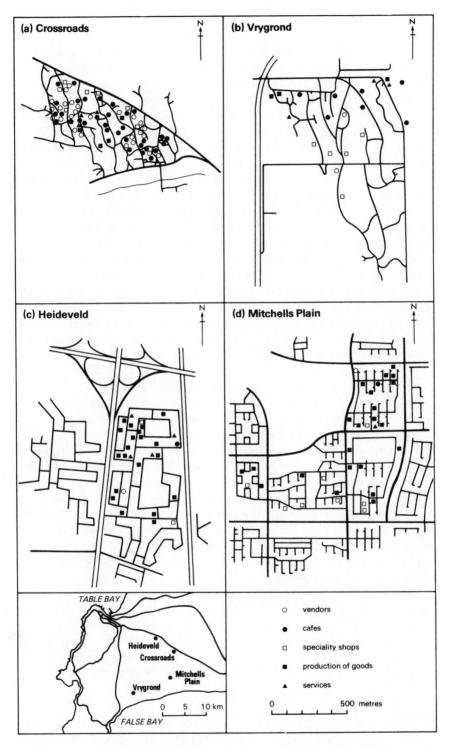

(a) Crossroads

(b) Vrygrond

(c) Heideveld

(d) Mitchells Plain

TABLE BAY

Heideveld
Crossroads

Mitchells
Plain

Vrygrond

0   5   10 km

FALSE BAY

○	vendors
●	cafes
□	speciality shops
■	production of goods
▲	services

0   500 metres

Figure 7.1 Sample areas of petty commodity production and trading in greater Cape Town. (Source: Dewar & Watson 1981, pp. 52–5.)

Although it was made clear that the camp could not be regarded as permanent, basic services were installed and within weeks some 20 000 people had established themselves in Crossroads. Over the following few months a complex social and economic infrastructure developed, consisting of schools, churches, crèches, cafes, repair shops and other forms of economic activity.

Initially, the 'problem' of squatting at Crossroads was seen purely as an housing issue. Inevitably, however, it became intertwined with the issue of influx control. The government, alarmed by the exploding size of the camp and the fact that many of the inhabitants were 'illegals', in the sense that they did not have permits to be in the Western Cape, ordered that the camp should be demolished and the 'illegals' removed to the homelands. The Crossroads inhabitants, however, refused to demolish their shacks and indicated that they would meet any forcible attempts to do so in the courts and, if necessary, with violence. Skirmishes with police and officials of the Bantu Administration Board occurred and the government decided to use troops to accomplish their aim. By this time, a powerful community organization and solidarity had developed and the plight of Crossroads had become both a national and an international issue. When a large-scale, violent confrontation seemed inevitable, the Minister of Co-operation and Development personally intervened and, through the offices of intermediaries from the universities, churches and private sector, negotiating channels between the government and the Crossroads Committee were opened.

The outcome was that Crossroads was to be treated as a 'special case' on 'humanitarian grounds'. The minister agreed to allow all people who were gainfully employed (and the fact that people in the so-called informal sector were included in the classification of employed was a significant departure from policy) should be allowed to remain in the Western Cape with their families. He further undertook to mobilize state housing finance to provide houses for these people and agreed to let them stay in the camp until the houses were completed. Some 180 houses have been built and occupied and the government is carrying out its stated intention of destroying shacks as people move in, although there are some indications that the actual population may have increased, with previous non-residents attempting to gain access to security and housing.

To a large extent therefore, the case of Crossroads is unique in South Africa. It is not regarded as permanent, but an official blind eye has been turned to it. Of significance for any study of petty commodity production and trading is the fact that Crossroads is not subject to the wide range of legal controls which affect formal townships and official (Coloured) squatting areas such as Vrygrond: business licences, land use controls, traffic regulations, building regulations, policing and so on.

Vrygrond is a 'legitimate' squatter camp. There are significant differences between it and Crossroads, which, it was considered, might have an impact on the operation of petty commodity production and trading. First,

Vrygrond is a Coloured area. The implication of this is that both men and women in the camp stand a better chance of securing a job in the so-called formal sector of the economy and family incomes are higher. Secondly, the origin and development of the camp has been different: Vrygrond came into being some 10–15 years ago to house 'temporary' persons on the waiting list for Cape Town City Council housing, and consequently there has been a steady (if slow) turnover of persons living in this area. This, together with the fact that the present residents of the camp have never been threatened as a community with mass eviction and demolition, has meant that a far less social cohesion exists. Consequently police action against petty operators has taken place to a greater degree, without the threat of organized community resistance. Further, crime is more prevalent and acts as a deterrent to small operators, whereas in Crossroads crime has been held in check by locally developed system of justice and 'vigilante' groups.

Heideveld is a Coloured low-income council housing estate. The area consists of a mix of 'economic' and 'subeconomic' dwellings, almost entirely rented; overall the socio-economic status of residents is slightly higher than those of Vrygrond or Crossroads. As part of the formal city structure, Heideveld is subject to the full range of regulations which generally affect petty producers and traders, as well as to specific regulations written into the leases of council tenants which prevent trading from houses.

Mitchells Plain (see Ch. 2) is a more expensively built, newer housing estate. It comprises a mixture of tenants and home owners and is located some 27 km from the city centre. While incomes in the area are significantly higher than those in the other areas chosen, the high cost of living in this suburb (resulting from large monthly repayments or rents, high transport costs and expensive goods and services) has resulted in severe financial strain for many families. Further, the area has become a government showpiece and consequently regulations controlling land uses are rigorously enforced.

Method of investigation   Within each of the place-related sample areas, a door-to-door investigation was carried out over a three month period by a senior researcher accompanied by an interpreter. All forms of economic activity acknowledged by the resident were recorded. In cases where visible evidence of economic activity existed, but its presence was not acknowledged, the activity was noted. In every case where economic activity was recorded, an attempt was made to interview the person in charge. In the case of hawkers, an attempt was made to interview each hawker present at the point of hawker concentration at the time of the visit. Obviously it was not possible to conduct an interview in all cases. In cases where an interview was held, a standard questionnaire was used to structure the discussion and to ensure the completion of comparable information, but of necessity the breadth of the interview was not confined by the questionnaire: discussions were as free ranging as possible.

Of necessity, studies of this kind are carried out within constraints of time and resources and are subject to severe limitations. Primary limitations of the study are as follows. Houses were visited during the day-time only, and were not revisited if the occupants were out; this means that businesses carried on in the evenings or at weekends only were unrecorded. Operators of illegal businesses were obviously reluctant to give information and it can therefore be assumed that significant numbers were also unrecorded. Accurate information on profits, turnover, or expenditure is extremely difficult to obtain, especially as few businesses have any kind of accounting system and many are very irregular. Generally, this information had to be pieced together from queries as to how much had been spent, earned or whatever in the week (or day) immediately preceding the interview, and to what extent this varied during the month, or year. These results in particular, therefore, should be treated as being broadly indicative, rather than final and absolute. In a statistical sense, therefore, the results must be regarded more as indicators than precise measurements.

Results   The percentage of people employed in petty production and trading appears to be lower in the low-income urban areas of South Africa than in other Third World countries. Since levels of employment in South Africa are not significantly lower than in other developing countries, there must be blockages in existence in South Africa which hinder the ability of these businesses to accumulate. Typically, 30–40 per cent of employment in Third World countries is in petty production and trading (Table 7.2). Localized

Table 7.2   Petty production and trading: some international comparisons.

Location		Employment in petty production and trading
South Africa		
Clermont, Durban[1]	20%	economically active
Crossroads, squatter area, Cape Town[2]	9.5%	of households
Vrygrond, squatter area, Cape Town[3]	5%	of households
Mitchells Plain, township, Cape Town[4]	4%	of households
Heideveld, township, Cape Town[5]	5%	of households
Other countries		
Kenya[6]	28–33%	urban African employment
Abidjan, Ivory Coast[7]	43%	all employment
Khartoum, Sudan[8]	23–5%	all employment
Accra, Ghana[9]	53%	all employment
Jakarta, Indonesia[10]	45%	all employment
Belo Horizonte and Sao Paulo, Brazil[11]	35–40%	all employment
Lagos, Nigeria[12]	33%	all employment

Sources: [1] Maasdorp and Pillay (1978); [2–5] Dewar and Watson (1981); [6] ILO (1972); [7] ILO (1976a); [8] ILO (1976b); [9] Steel (1977); [10–12] United Nations (1976).

Note: in the Cape Town cases the inclusion of 'illegal' activities (shebeens, drug pushing, etc.) could double these figures.

pilot studies in South Africa, conducted almost entirely within informal settlements, indicate that between 10–20 per cent of households are involved in this type of activity. These figures roughly accord with the findings in Crossroads (9.5 per cent of households) but in the other sample areas the equivalent figure is considerably lower. Clearly, therefore, the forces negatively affecting small business operation occur at both national and local levels. The national forces depress the overall level of small business activity and are primarily though not exclusively, legislative in form. The most significant Acts in this regard are those which directly outlaw informal activity, those which promote high levels of insecurity (particularly the Group Areas Act), and those Acts and practices which reduce access to credit by small business operators. The local forces result in significant variations in intensity of activity *between* areas. The primary factors here are population density, location in relation to the major exchange and production centres in the city, the physical structure of environments and the form and degree of enforcement of local authority regulations.

Contrary to widely held belief, petty producers and traders are not primarily concerned with the manufacture of articles (and traditional craft products in particular). Highest profits are to be made in the retailing sector and, where evasion of the many rules and regulations permits, it is here that operators primarily concentrate. In the Cape Town sample 59 per cent of operators interviewed were in retailing, 31 per cent in production and 10 per cent in services. Table 7.3 indicates a breakdown of kinds of activities. Table 7.4 shows the distribution of income, expenditure, profit and capital investment by sector. It is apparent, however, that there is a direct correlation between type of economic activity and level of harassment.

The highest intensity of retailing concentration was found in Crossroads, which provides a useful indication of operations in this sector. Retailing activities in Crossroads may be classified into three types: cafes (or general dealer outlets), vendors, and speciality shops. Cafes generally operate from a front room of a dwelling. They build up a regular clientele drawn from shacks in the immediate vicinity and thus tend to be of a similar size, offer a range of goods at similar prices, and are more or less evenly distributed throughout the settlement. Vendors and speciality shops are small and usually highly specialized, often selling one type of good. They therefore require exposure to a larger number of potential customers and locate along the main movement routes through the settlement and on the western edge of Crossroads where some 90 vendors have formed themselves into a street-market which operates daily. A similar classification and pattern of activities is to be found in Vrygrond squatter camp. In the two township areas (Mitchells Plain and Heideveld) selling is highly susceptible to official action and less visible manufacturing of articles (in particular the knitting and sewing of articles by housewives) is preferred. There is, as a result, a far higher proportion of petty producers and traders engaged in manufacturing

Table 7.3 Distribution of petty production and trading according to activity, in Cape Town sample areas.

	Crossroads	Vrygrond	Mitchells Plain	Heideveld	
Selling					
foods	26 (45)	4	3	1	
general cafe	41	5 (7)	1 (4)	2 (5)	total
clothes	5 (35)	–	1	–	
household goods	– (1)	–	4	1	219
liquor	– (6)	3 (10)	–	–	58.8%
wood	–	2	–	–	
herbalists	3 (4)	–	–	–	
	75 (91)	14 (17)	9 (4)	4 (5)	
Production					
knitting	1 (4)	–	9 (13)	9 (12)	
sewing	3 (2)	1	8 (10)	5 (7)	
crochet	–	–	3	4 (6)	
household	–	–	–	–	
hardware	–	–	1	3	total
foods	– (3)	–	1	1	
sjamboks	2	–	–	–	114
metal boxes	1 (1)	–	–	–	30.6%
paper flowers	–	–	–	1	
macrame	–	1	–	–	
wreaths	–	1	–	–	
toys	–	–	1	1	
	7 (10)	3	23 (23)	23 (25)	
Services					
stove repair	1	–	–	–	
watch repair	1	–	–	–	
shoe repair	2	1	–	1	
mechanic	– (3)	–	1	1	
painter	–	–	–	1	total
washing	–	–	–	1	
landlord	– (10)	2 (5)	–	–	39
disco	–	1	–	–	10.5%
child minding	– (2)	–	1	–	
radio mending	1	–	–	–	
photography	2	–	–	–	
framing	1	–	–	–	
	9 (15)	4 (5)	2	4	
total	91 (116)	21 (22)	34 (27)	31 (30)	372

Source: Dewar and Watson (1981).
( ) indicate businesses noted but not interviewed.

Table 7.4 Petty production and trading in Cape Town: weekly turnovers, expenditures, profits and capital investments.

Rand per week		Crossroads			Vrygrond			Mitchells Plain			Heideveld			Hawkers	Total		
		ret.	prod.	serv.	ret.	prod.	serv.	ret.	prod.	serv.	ret.	prod.	serv.	ret.	ret.	prod.	serv.
income (turnover)	av.	380	106	62	302	23	26	95	31	—	181	35	58	369	265	45	48
	med.	170	80	65	100	15	8	36	20	—	171	17	27	190			
expenditure	av.	275	57	21	298	18	3	37	7	—	144	8	29	348	202	22	18
	med.	132	23	18	45	10	4	4	4	—	114	5	—	169			
profit	av.	96	49	41	69	13	13	57	25	—	36	27	30	50	61	29	28
	med.	49	46	51	18	15	6	36	10	—	16	10	27	37			
capital invested	av.	1099	1251	27	689	183	255	358	235	—	883	210	540	333	672	469	274
	med.	1200	920	115	200	200	250	21	200	—	40	50	50	60			

Source: Dewar and Watson (1981).

av. = average, med. = median, ret. = retail, prod. = production, serv. = services.

in the township areas; in the squatter camp the opposite holds true.

Most businesses operating in the so-called informal sector are smaller and more fragile than is generally believed to be the case. Of the petty producers and traders interviewed in the Cape Town study, 55 per cent had weekly turnovers of under R99, and 48 per cent generated a weekly profit of under R24. The differences in average profit levels between sample areas indicate that relative security and freedom from harassment strongly affects the ability to accumulate (Table 7.5). However, even within the more favour-

Table 7.5   Percentage of petty producers and traders generating under R50 profit weekly.

Cape Town 1979[1]		
squatter areas	{ 49%	Crossroads
	{ 75%	Vrygrond
townships	{ 77%	Heideveld
	{ 77%	Mitchells Plain
	64%	hawkers
Comparisons		
Clermont, Durban[2]	80% earned under R50 per week	
hawkers, Johannesburg[3]	45% earned under R50 per week	
Hartley, Zimbabwe[4]	average weekly income $9	
Soweto, Johannesburg[5]	53% earned under R50 per week	

Sources: [1] Dewar and Watson (1981); [2] Maasdorp and Pillay (1978); [3] Beavon (1979); [4] Davies (1978); [5] Urban Foundation (1980b).

able conditions existing in Crossroads, only half of the operators interviewed were able to generate an income greater than the Household Effective Level of Living estimate of R206 a month, and 26 per cent of operators were not able to generate more than R100 a month. Average profits in the Vrygrond squatter camp, where police harassment is more frequent, were somewhat lower. Lowest profits were recorded amongst producers in the township areas.

A significant percentage of these operations are intermittent. They may be carried out on a regular part-time basis (either by the housewife or by the head and other members of the family in evenings or at weekends), or erratically during those periods when family finances are strained (that is, during periods of unemployment or when unforeseen expenditures have to be made) and they are then discontinued when family finances improve. Cycles of intermittency therefore occur – daily (particularly evenings), weekly (corresponding to main shopping days), monthly (corresponding to the employment and financial position of family members) and annually (corresponding to seasons of traditionally high turnover particularly close to Christmas). The interviews showed that intermittency was more prevalent in the Coloured squatter camp of Vrygrond and in the township areas, where people are more easily able to move into the formal labour market. In the case of Crossroads a large number of people (men and women) are not in possession of passes allowing them to work, and there is consequently a greater tendency for businesses to operate on a more permanent basis.

The supposed employment potential of petty production and trading has, on the whole, been greatly overestimated. Of those businesses investigated in the Cape Town area, the majority (66 per cent) are one person concerns and only 4 per cent employ more than three people. Crossroads has a higher percentage of people in employment in petty production and trading than the other areas, undoubtedly a function of better profits in this area, as well as of the large number of 'illegals' (Table 7.6). Nevertheless, Crossroads has an average of only 1.24 persons per business, compared to an average of 1.1 persons in other areas.

Table 7.6 Average number employed per business.

Cape Town 1979[1]			
Crossroads	1.24		
Vrygrond	1.40	retail	1.67
Heideveld	1.14	production	1.31
Mitchells Plain	1.05	services	1.09
hawkers	1.66		
Comparisons			
Clermont, Durban[2]	62% of businesses employed one person only		
Nairobi, Kenya[3]	57% employed one person only		
Howrah, Calcutta[4]	80% of businesses employed less than 10 people		
Jakarta, Indonesia[5]	40% of street trading businesses employed one person		

Sources: [1] Dewar and Watson (1981); [2] Maasdorp and Pillay (1978); [3] Chana and Morrison (1975); [4,5] United Nations (1976).

The majority of small businesses are only able to survive on the basis of extreme exploitation of labour and the use of non-remunerated family labour. The belief that the informal sector is a 'cradle of entrepreneurship' for people who 'want to make it on their own' simply does not hold true. Most operators, when questioned, related their reasons for involvement in these operations to factors such as unemployment, the need to supplement household income, lack of child care facilities, old age or poor health. In Crossroads especially, the low wages paid to formal sector employees, and the difficulties involved in obtaining permission to work, have resulted in a significant number of people being forced into petty production and trading. Clearly the existence of these producers and traders is primarily a symptom of the inadequacy of the present form of the political economy.

However, the analysis reveals a significant distinction between two broad types of small businesses. On the one hand there are subsistence-type activities, which tend to be small and which do not, either in terms of profit motivation or in terms of relationships to the means of production, qualify as capitalist operations. On the other hand there are profit-motivated operations, which are often larger, employ labour and have greater capital assets. In the case of the Cape Town study over half (58 per cent) of operators interviewed were of the subsistence-type, although this varied with sample area. Crossroads and, to a lesser extent, Vrygrond had a far higher proportion of profit-motivated operations; township areas consisted predominantly of subsistence-type activities. This distinction has important implications for any attempt to stimulate petty production and trading. While it is not impossible for subsistence-type operations to develop into fully fledged capitalist enterprises, they are far less likely to respond to market-related incentives such as training programmes, repayable loans and so on.

Initial capital requirements of most small operations are extremely small; 48 per cent of operators interviewed in Cape Town started with an initial capital outlay of less than R25 and almost without exception, the source of capital was family savings. This pattern prevails in Crossroads as well as the other areas. There is an observable link, however, between profit and size of available capital. Two capital thresholds are particularly important. First, those operators who possess transport are in a position to buy in bulk from the (often distant) cheaper wholesalers, and can therefore undercut their less mobile competitors. Secondly, those who possess refrigerators are able to store bulk buys and sell foods in fresher condition, thereby capturing a larger share of the market and increasing profits. This distinction is especially clear in Crossroads where comparatively few households own either cars or refrigerators. Invariably it is the largest of the retailers (cafe-owners in particular) who have reached these capital thresholds and who are generating significant profits. While a similar pattern is evident in Vrygrond, car and refrigerator ownership is not so significant in the township areas since trading is less common.

The policy response

It is apparent that stimulation of small businesses, even if carried out effectively, will not solve problems of poverty and unemployment in South Africa. The employment potential of these concerns is usually limited to the operators, profits and wages are exceptionally low, hours are long, working conditions are poor and there is little security. Only a small percentage of these concerns ever become stable and lucrative (see Dewar & Watson 1981 for further discussion). It may further be argued that the continuing existence of petty production and trading in this form is in many ways functional to processes of capital accumulation: it extends the distributive network of large-scale producers into areas where big capital would not find it efficient to operate, and it supplements low wages and poor social security in a manner which does not directly compete with the interests of big capital.

Clearly the only solution to problems such as these lies in a total restructuring of the South African political economy. This can only be viewed in the long term, however, and the most significant issue becomes the definition of an appropriate short-term position on the stimulation of small businesses. The *status quo* is resulting in a progressive weakening and fragmentation of the working class. It can be argued therefore, that the definition of an appropriate action is whether or not it improves the position of that class. Further, there is no chance of co-option if that action is directed towards the weakest and most vulnerable members of the class. Specifically, in the field of job creation, this means that action must be directed towards enabling people at the *lowest income levels* to supplement their incomes through petty production and trading. This in turn implies directing action at those businesses at the bottom end of the size continuum. Measures which simply succeed in stimulating those somewhat larger businesses which are established and profit generating, will in fact worsen the competitive position of the smallest producers and traders. This is because the smallest businesses are more directly challenged by 'middle' capital than by monopoly capital, and the result of their erosion will be an exacerbation of poverty and unemployment.

A dual approach is therefore required. On the one hand, pressure must be brought to bear on the state and on capital, to improve wages and social security and to expand job opportunities in wage labour. At the same time, concessions must be obtained to allow the very smallest producers and traders to operate. This implies, in particular, that subsistence-type activities must be given every opportunity to function.

It is in the light of considerations such as these that the new state policy of 'small business stimulation' in South Africa must be considered. The primary mechanism upon which this policy rests is the Small Business Development Corporation (SBDC), established recently as a joint undertaking between the private sector and the state. Originally it was proposed that the initial working capital of the corporation should be R100 million with the private sector and the state contributing on a 50–50 basis. Immediate response from the private sector, however, yielded R65 million, and it now appears as if the initial working capital will be in the order of R150 million.

The terms of reference of the corporation have not yet been formally announced. It seems, however, that its primary objectives will be: to finance small business by providing share and loan capital on a short-, medium- and long-term basis; the provision of infrastructure such as factory units, industrial parks and business centres; the underwriting and guaranteeing of loans granted by the private banking sector; and the provision of 'end-use' or quality control supervision and managerial guidance on projects financed or guaranteed by the corporation. It seems that the major thrust will be in guaranteeing commercial bank loans and in providing risk capital on a temporary or minority shareholder basis. Further, it is intended that the corporation will pay dividends (and initial yields as high as 8 per cent per annum have been mentioned) to private sector investors.

The critical question of what constitutes a 'small business' is presently under review by the directors of the corporation. The best indication of the probable outcome is the definition used by the Small Business Development Corporation launched by the Rupert Group in 1979 and since incorporated into the national corporation, since the idea of the national corporation is the acknowledged brain-child of Anton Rupert, who is also chairman of the board of the national body. The initial corporation's definition of 'small business' is one which is privately owned and managed and of which the turn-over does not exceed R500 000 and which does not have more than five branches. It is quite clear that this upper limit does not focus on the majority of small businesses: those which lie at the bottom end of the size continuum, and which are subsumed under labels such as the informal sector, the working poor, the urban poor, the casual poor, the self-employed or petty commodity producers. In fact the measures proposed by the SBDC will be totally inappropriate for these kinds of activities.

The inadequacy of this policy response can be explained as follows. First, as revealed in the analysis above, the procurement of initial capital is not a particularly severe barrier to entry into petty production and trading. Secondly, the implication of guaranteed dividends for shareholders is that safe and high-yielding investments will be preferred, yet a significant feature of most small businesses is that they are high risk operations. Further, they require loans of very small size (probably averaging between R50–100): the cost of administering loans of this size is high and will prove a major deterrent to a development corporation bent on making profits. Thirdly, the plan to provide infrastructure such as factory units, industrial parks and business centres is totally out of keeping with the *modus operandi* of the majority of petty producers and traders. Most of these operators can survive only because their overheads are almost nil: the home doubles as the shop or workshop, the family car doubles as business transport, family labour is used, and the business is often carried on in spare time. Perhaps 10 per cent of the operators interviewed in the Cape Town study would be able to bear the cost of renting even highly subsidized factory or shop accommodation, let alone the other expenses which such a move would entail. Fourthly, managerial guidance, training and end-use supervision may be useful for a full-time, profit-motivated operator employing several people. It will not, however, help the housewife producing three or four garments a week in order to pay her electricity bill, whose knowledge of accounting methods is, to say the least, rudimentary.

The impact of the policies of the SBDC will be to stimulate *middle-sized* capital, that is, those businesses which are already established to some degree and which stand a good chance of being able to pay back loans with interest.

While a strategy such as this may certainly create additional jobs (although it is unlikely that sufficient will be created to make a significant difference to the size of the reserve army of labour), its impact on wages and overall levels of poverty is highly questionable. It can be argued that the SBDC will not only be ineffective in improving the conditions of the working class, but will actually be negative. First, it will create the impression that social and economic reforms are taking place, when in fact they are not. Secondly, the proposed measures will result in further co-option into the growing South African middle class (as have selective state policies in relation to home ownership, Black urban rights and so on – see Ch. 2), thereby retarding fundamental processes of change. Thirdly, the competitive position of petty producers and traders will be undermined and, as a result, poverty and unemployment will be made worse.

The study carried out in Cape Town indicates that there are three primary areas in which action is necessary to allow the most vulnerable forms of petty commodity production and trading to operate.

(a) The repeal of certain legislation and local authority regulations, particularly: those which prevent trading or production from the home, for this is the only way in which overheads can be cut sufficiently to make many of those operations viable; those which restrict the production and trading of foodstuffs (especially cheap meat), for it is in the trading of these products that the highest profits are to be made; and those which restrict entry of hawkers and small traders into the busiest parts of the city, especially the city centre, where the concentration of potential customers is greatest.

(b) Manipulation of sources of finance and wholesale supplies. The aims of the SBDC may indeed be suspect, and every effort must be made to expose its likely effects on problems of unemployment and poverty. However, it represents substantial resources which could be used to great effect if properly directed. Pressure must be brought to bear on the SBDC for the provision of very small loans (i.e. R20 up), without surety. A further field of investigation must be that of the establishment of co-operatives, particularly in relation to transport and the establishment of wholesale outlets.

(c) Manipulation of the physical structure and population densities within urban areas. In capitalist societies, the spatial structure and the density of population to a large degree controls both the pattern and intensity of economic activity (particularly small-scale activity) for it is these factors which determine the pattern and intensity of population flows (thresholds) through a city and through local areas. Three aspects of spatial structure are important here. The first and most important involves the provision of service infrastructure for small traders (i.e. water, shelter, clean surfaces, electricity, and rubbish removal) at points of concentrated pedestrian flow, and culminating, at points of greatest economic opportunity in the city, in full-scale market infrastructure. Particularly this means manipulating the spatial and rental structure to allow small-scale operators, including intermittent operators, to produce and trade in the city centre, and other major trading areas, without substantially increasing their overheads. The second relates to the increase of population densities in local areas in order to make viable not only additional economic activity but also community facilities, transport and other supportive services. The third is the integration and channelling of flows of people through the city (as opposed to the present pattern of dispersed flows) in order to concentrate thresholds, which in turn create opportunities for petty producers and traders.

The most significant aspect of the approach presented here is that the aim is not to stimulate a comparatively few informal sector activities to become fully fledged businesses. Instead, the emphasis is on the creation of opportunities at the lowest level so as to allow those most in need to supplement incomes. The approach does not solve any fundamental problems: it does, however, strengthen the position of the working class while at the same time improving the living conditions of the very poor. The process of attempting to initiate and stimulate these changes (through a variety of channels) has begun. Clarity on the precise nature of the difficulties, reaction and appropriate responses will only emerge as the process gathers pace.

Acknowledgement

This chapter is based largely on the findings of a research project undertaken by the Urban Problems Research Unit, University of Cape Town, reported fully in Dewar and Watson (1981).

8 Informal housing and informal employment: case studies in the Durban Metropolitan Region

GAVIN MAASDORP

The First and Third Worlds meet in South African metropolitan regions, with regard both to housing and employment. The dichotomy is due partly to different demographic profiles and technological backgrounds, and partly to differential access to political power. Housing and labour market conditions have been shaped by race laws, particularly since the adoption of apartheid as official policy in 1948.

Legislative impediments and official policies

The enforcement of racial–residential segregation has led to the large-scale relocation of African, Coloured and Asian families, usually towards the outskirts of cities. There is no overall housing market but instead a set of racially segmented markets characterized by different systems of financing and tenure. The government's view that Africans are merely 'temporary sojourners' in 'white' cities recently has given way to an acceptance of their permanence and the institution of a 99-year leasehold scheme in townships, except those in the homelands where freehold title is available. However, these schemes are still in their infancy and the absence of a housing market among Africans, together with the restricted area of land made available to them for housing and legal problems in the way of obtaining institutional finance, has inhibited the private construction of housing. All three black population groups rely largely on state housing, but the shortage of such housing means that informal settlements play an important role in providing shelter. In the case of Africans, most privately supplied housing is in fact in these settlements.

Many of these settlements are not officially classified as 'urban', and this gives a grossly underestimated urban population. The inhabitants are part of the metropolitan economy although many are illegally present in the area in the sense that influx control prevents them from obtaining work permits. Nevertheless, many are employed illegally in the formal (wage) sector while others are absorbed in the informal sector.

Since South Africa is not a developed country, the urbanization process displays certain Third World characteristics. However, government policy towards informal settlements has lagged behind that of Third World governments and international aid agencies, which recognized in the early 1970s that conventional housing programmes for low-income families could not keep pace with urban population increase (itself boosted to historically unprecedented rates by rural–urban migration). Moreover, what housing was provided was too costly for the target group. Instead, low-income households tended to congregate in squatter settlements in which they provided their own shelter. Although such shelter did not meet official standards, it was often substantial, it suited the pockets of the poor and it could be improved as and when required by changes in family size and financial circumstances. Clearly, new approaches were called for, and upgrading and site-and-service schemes became enshrined in housing policies (see Grimes 1975, Maasdorp 1977). Indeed the term 'squatter' has itself been replaced by less pejorative terms such as 'spontaneous', 'informal' and 'unauthorized'. In South Africa there has been much entrenched resistance on the part of government (at all tiers) to any housing scheme other than that of conventional 'townships'. All the old stereotypes of 'squatters' and 'squatter settlements' have been steadfastly adhered to.

The applicability of a revised approach in the South African context may be illustrated by examining the results of a number of sample surveys of households in informal settlements. This paper is concerned with three such areas – two Indian and one African – in the Durban Metropolitan Region (DMR). Haarhoff has developed a typology of urban settlement in terms of types of land occupation and status of building improvements (see Maasdorp & Haarhoff 1981, p. 46): the two Indian areas would be regarded as 'spontaneous informal' and the African area as 'unauthorized informal', but for the sake of brevity we use the term 'informal'.

The Durban Metropolitan Region

The DMR is depicted in Figure 8.1. It straddles the developed and developing world, both administratively and in the range of problems it faces. It is centred on the city of Durban from which it stretches along the coast to Amanzimtoti in the south and Umhlanga Rocks in the north, and inland as far as Hillcrest. It includes many different local governments within the province of Natal, and spills over into the African homeland of KwaZulu to the south and north. A narrow corridor of Natal – through Pinetown and Kloof – separates the southern and northern urban blocks of KwaZulu. The city and its white suburbs are part of the rich world, KwaZulu part of the Third World. The DMR suffers from the typical problems facing the industrial cities of the rich countries – pollution, traffic congestion, urban sprawl –

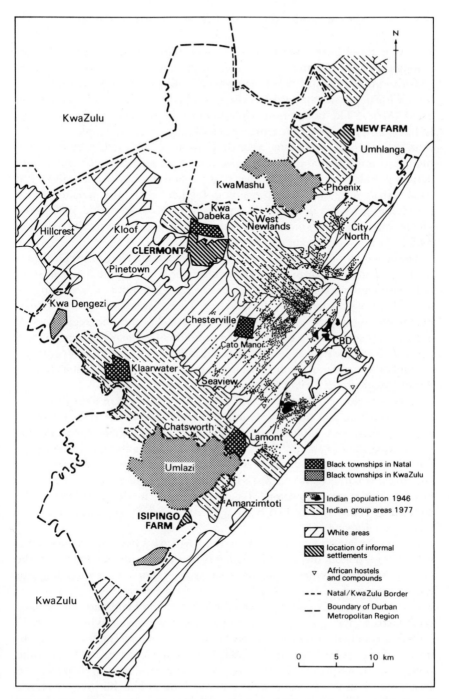

Figure 8.1 The Durban Metropolitan Region, indicating location of informal settlements referred to in the text. The location of Group Areas and of African compounds and hotels in the 'white' city (see Ch. 9) is also shown. (Source: based in part on a map prepared by Errol Haarhoff, School of Architecture, University of Natal 1981).

as well as those facing Third World cities – high population growth rates among the lower-income groups, and a lagging supply of physical services.

With a population in 1980 of between 1.67 and 1.86 million, depending on how it is calculated, the DMR is the second largest metropolitan region in South Africa. The population is predominantly African (52–57 per cent); Indians comprise 22–25 per cent, whites 18–20 per cent and Coloureds 3 per cent. Africans are increasing as a proportion of the total; they have the highest average annual growth rate (7.2 per cent) reflecting not only a high natural population increase, 2.8 per cent per annum, but also a high rate of rural–urban migration (the remaining 4.4 per cent). The overall annual population growth rate of 4.5–5.0 per cent between 1970 and 1980 in the DMR is not high by Third World standards, large cities typically growing by 5 to 11 per cent per annum (Grimes 1975, pp. 112–13).

The economy of the DMR is reasonably diversified. The port of Durban is the largest on the African continent in terms of cargo handled, and serves a rich hinterland which includes the Pretoria–Witwatersrand–Vereeniging industrial region (the largest in the country). There has been a rapid growth of manufacturing industry in the DMR since 1925, and the region today accounts for some 14 per cent of total employment in the manufacturing and construction industries in South Africa. In addition a wide range of commercial and other service activities is found in the area, and Durban itself is South Africa's major tourist and vacation centre.

Since the white population enjoys a very high standard of living by international comparison, and the Coloured population is not only relatively small but also receives higher average incomes than elsewhere in the country, it is among the Indian and African population groups that the low-income housing problem poses the greatest challenge and is manifested in the existence of informal settlements. Such settlements are nothing new in the DMR; however, after the provision of new townships in the early 1960s, the authorities believed they had been eliminated and we are concerned with their re-emergence.

During the last 25 years, Indians in the DMR have been subjected to considerable residential displacement, mainly due to the implementation of the Group Areas Act which imposed strict racial–residential segregation, but also as a result of urban freeway schemes, railway development and land-use zoning. Because they have involved the destruction of large housing stocks, these factors have aggravated the demand for new housing which is already high as a result of social changes within the community (such as the breakdown of the extended family system) and population growth. Housing policy for low-income Indians is considered in detail in Chapter 10. Displaced households have been relocated in public housing schemes, e.g. Chatsworth, as well as in privately developed residential areas, e.g. Reservoir Hills. The former provide a variety of housing ranging from sub-economic to private purchase, while the latter accommodate the higher-income groups. But the supply of housing, whether public or private, has lagged behind demand. With some 24 000 families on the waiting list and considerable overcrowding in formal residential areas, it was not surprising that a number of informal settlements arose in the metropolitan periphery.

The African population grew rapidly during and after World War II when Durban experienced industrial expansion. By 1950 some 50 per cent were illegally housed in shacks rented from Indian landlords in Cato Manor. In 1952 an 'emergency camp' was established in the area. This was essentially an attempt at providing the type of informal housing associated with current World Bank site-and-service schemes in Third World countries. Basic services were provided by the municipality and terraced sites were laid out on which families could erect shacks under supervision. In its heyday the population of the camp was probably about 90 000; population estimates for Cato Manor itself varied, but at its peak the area probably contained some 120 000 inhabitants. But the Cato Manor area was cleared by 1964 and the population relocated in two large new townships (KwaMashu and Umlazi – see Fig. 8.1).

On the surface it appeared that the situation had been contained – shacks had been replaced by townships. Yet evidence was accumulating that this was not the case. One indication was that, according to township managers, dwellings invariably contained more than the number for which they had been planned. There was a large undisclosed population consisting of lodgers who frequently lacked the necessary work permits to make their presence legal. The second indication was that, although shacks might have been eliminated within the Durban municipal area, they had started mushrooming elsewhere in the region, particularly from about 1965 onwards. The new shack areas were located on the periphery of the built-up areas, often in valleys where they could not be seen easily. They were centred mainly to the south of Pinetown and from Clermont stretching along the Umgeni River to the New Farm–Phoenix areas of the Inanda district north of KwaMashu.

Surveys in informal settlements

In 1975–6 sample surveys were conducted in three informal settlements, viz. the Indian areas of New Farm (near Mount Edgecombe to the north of Durban) and Isipingo Farm (just to the south of Umlazi township) and the African area of Clermont (near Pinetown) – see Figure 8.1. The results appeared in a series of interim reports between 1977 and 1978; for the final report see Maasdorp and Haarhoff (1981). More recent studies of informal settlements in the Durban Metropolitan Region are Stopforth (1978), Moller (1978), Moller and Stopforth (1980) and J. Maasdorp (1981).

The New Farm and Isipingo Farm areas were both previously given over to Indian smallholder agriculture (sugarcane and market gardening). However, farming units became increasingly fragmented and uneconomic over the years and the land-use pattern changed, particularly from the late 1960s onwards, the area being converted to residential use.

Clermont was declared a private township for Africans in 1937; it is therefore one of a handful of townships outside the homelands which provide Africans with freehold title. It is controlled by the Chief Commissioner for Co-operation and Development, Natal, who administers it on behalf of the South African Development Trust, and is situated on the border of KwaZulu within which homeland it ultimately might be incorporated.

All these areas contained modern dwellings as well as informal structures. New Farm contained 550 and Isipingo Farm 400 shacks; their shack populations were 3800 and 3900 respectively and the occupancy rates 6.9 and 7.4 persons per dwelling respectively. The estimated population of Clermont in 1976 was approximately 57 000 of whom some 22 000 were residing in unauthorized dwellings, i.e. they were there with the permission of the owners but the dwellings had not been sanctioned by the authorities.

Displacement, migration and overspill Why did these informal settlements exist? Why were the people not housed in official townships? In the Indian areas, the Group Areas Act was responsible for between 25 and 40 per cent of the households having to vacate their previous dwellings; others moved because of overcrowding or for various family reasons. The reasons for choosing the particular informal settlements rather than townships related mainly to low rentals and the shortage of official housing. The households generally would have preferred to remain in their previous areas and it may therefore be said that many had already suffered a net welfare loss (in terms of type and location of dwelling, costs of housing and transport, accessibility to employment and availability of community facilities) in the move.

If the Indian settlements owed their origin mainly to displacement, African informal housing at Clermont was due to the twin forces of rural–urban migration and urban overspill. Two distinct types of inhabitants were distinguished, namely, rural–urban migrants and native-born persons, i.e. born in the DMR. Migrants comprised 57 per cent of the sample population. One-third of the population consisted of ethnic groups from outside Natal and KwaZulu, two-thirds were single and there was a marked preponderance of males. The shack area of Clermont was therefore a reception area for people from many parts of Southern Africa, for single persons and for males. The demographic features were not those of a settled community. In this respect it differed markedly from other African informal settlements (cf. the other studies referred to above). Although the results of all the studies conducted to date in the DMR tend to confirm the general features of similar studies in Third World countries, each settlement has its unique characteristics.

An understanding of the factors determining the decision to migrate is necessary for planning prescriptions at both the urban and rural ends.

Empirical evidence in the Third World has shown that economic motives are the most important factors determining the decision to migrate (see Yap 1977, p. 244). This decision is determined mainly by the individual's expectation of earning a higher income in the urban area.

In addition to economic influences, the social determinants of migration also have to be taken into account. The most important of these appears to be the presence of relatives and friends in the city. Other destination contacts – migrants from the same rural locality or from the same language or ethnic group – also have a positive effect on migration to a particular urban centre. Such contacts, by providing emotional comforts, deflect the psychic costs of migrating. But even here there is an economic factor, namely, relatives and friends might provide temporary support, in the form of food and accommodation, to new arrivals in the city. Thus it is not always easy to separate the economic and non-economic determinants.

Nevertheless, the large number of reasons advanced by the Clermont respondents for migrating from their areas of origin have been divided into those which appeared to be mainly economic and those which seemed primarily non-economic in nature. The economic reasons cover answers relating to rural poverty and unemployment, and the desire to undertake specific types of work. The non-economic category includes answers relating to family or community problems, preferences regarding lifestyles, the intention to marry or other reasons relating to family, and political reasons such as unrest and war. The reasons for migrating are depicted in Table 8.1. The Table shows that economic reasons were far more important than non-economic. These results confirm those of studies in other countries, namely, that the major reasons for rural–urban migration are economic in nature.

The reasons for migrating could also be divided into 'push' and 'pull'

Table 8.1 Percentage distribution of migrants by reason for migrating, Clermont.

Reason	Total
economic	
rural poverty	22.8
rural unemployment	20.2
earn money	27.3
specific work	4.9
sub-total	75.2
non-economic	
family, community problems	6.0
lifestyle	4.5
marriage, family	12.3
political	1.9
sub-total	24.7
total ($n = 100\%$)	618

Source: Maasdorp and Haarhoff (1981).

factors as is commonly done in the literature (see Oberai 1977, pp. 214–15). 'Push' factors are those which relate to conditions in the migrant's home locality, e.g. population pressure on the land, climatic conditions, shortage of paid employment, technological change in agriculture, etc. 'Pull' factors relate to conditions (real or perceived) in the receiving area which attract migrants, e.g. higher incomes, availability of jobs and educational opportunities, presence of relatives and friends, etc.

According to Table 8.1 the 'push' factor, in the form of rural poverty and unemployment, rural family and community problems (family and faction feuds, and quarrels with neighbours), and the political climate (guerilla warfare) had induced 51 per cent of the sub-sample to head for the city. But this may, in fact, understate the impact of 'push' factors; it is not easy to distinguish the 'push' from the 'pull' in respect of those who migrated in order to change their lifestyles or who moved with their parents or spouses. Such decisions could have been prompted by either force, or by a combination of the two.

The majority of migrants came straight to Durban from their rural areas. They moved mainly on their own and the movement took place principally from the late 1960s onwards. Some two-thirds moved straight to Clermont but about one-quarter had lived in authorized townships before moving to Clermont. This is not unusual; studies in Latin America indicate that many migrants 'invade' spontaneous settlements only after several years residence in the urban area. The major reasons for the respondents not living in township housing were because they were ineligible in terms of Section 10 of the Black (Urban Areas) Consolidation Act, or because they felt they could not afford the rental, or because the newer townships were too far from their work places.

The growth of African informal settlements also received an impetus from urban overspill. Almost four-fifths of the Durban natives in the sample had been born in formal townships in the DMR but had left there because of a shortage of housing.

Urban commitment   It is clearly an important aspect of housing policy to ascertain to what extent migrants plan to remain permanent urban dwellers as opposed to returning to their rural homes after a spell – short-term or prolonged – of urban employment (see Nelson 1976 for further discussion). Migration may be permanent or temporary, and migrants in the latter category may be short-, medium- or long-term sojourners in the city. These different groups have different behaviour patterns which are influenced by expectations. It is therefore important for policy makers, both in rural and urban areas, to know the distribution of intentions within a migrant population. In the urban areas different degrees of urban commitment affect the integration of migrants into the labour force, their demand for services and housing, and their willingness to invest in urban housing and improve their neighbourhoods.

The Clermont study showed that a slight majority (52 per cent) of migrants were committed to permanent urban residence. Those who regarded themselves as 'temporary' urban residents were asked when they planned to return to their rural homes. With few exceptions, the respondents did not advance a specific year but rather mentioned factors which would determine the date of their departure from the DMR. The responses are shown in Table 8.2. The responses indicate that urban and rural factors were

Table 8.2 Percentage distribution of temporary urban dwellers by sex and factors influencing date of return migration, Clermont.

Date related to	Male	Female	Total
termination of employment	37.3	17.1	32.1
financial target	24.9	4.3	19.6
period, age target	7.0	12.9	8.5
rural, homeland conditions	10.9	20.0	13.3
social factors	3.5	20.0	7.7
children	4.0	5.7	4.4
housing, legal factors	3.5	11.4	5.5
uncertain	5.0	2.9	4.4
unspecified	4.0	5.7	4.4
total (n = 100%)	201	70	271

Source: Maasdorp and Haarhoff (1981).

both important influences. The major factors related to termination of employment, the attainment of a financial target and conditions obtaining in their rural area or homeland. The attainment of retiring or pensionable age was clearly an important issue, particularly among males. The Table shows, too, that the attainment of a financial target remains important among rural––urban migrants. Among the specific targets mentioned here were the accumulation of sufficient savings for an unspecified purpose or in order to further their studies, purchase oxen or other livestock, or to pay *lobola* (bride price). Financial targets were more important among males than among females; for the latter, rural–homeland conditions, social factors such as marriage and shack demolition were more important.

Employment and incomes A popular stereotype of informal settlements is that they are refugees for the unemployed. But this has not been true of most settlements in the DMR. There was virtually no unemployment in the Clermont sample while the unemployment rate in the Indian areas was only 3–4 per cent. In the former area, the activity rate of almost 75 per cent was much higher than in a 'normal' population.

The Indian settlements were inhabited by low-income families, the mean household income of R180 per month being considerably less than the mean for Durban Indian households of R320 per month. In contrast, the Clermont population comprised mainly single persons, and the mean individual monthly income approximated the mean monthly wage for Africans in Durban of R117. Shack-dwellers in Clermont, therefore, were not in the lowest-income strata within the African community. Although artisan, factory-type work was the major occupational category, a number of professional persons lived in the three areas. The proportion was small but it consisted of teachers, lawyers and nurses. The presence of professional persons in squatter areas has also been remarked upon in studies undertaken in other countries.

Tenure and rentals   Arrangements with regard to tenure were similar in the three study areas. Three distinct groups were found, namely, owners of land and dwellings, tenants-at-will and tenants.

In Clermont, shack-dwellers who were the owners of the land and the dwelling received approximately one-eighth of their total income from rental and were thus not primarily dependent on rent as a source of income. This group comprised between 4 and 12 per cent of sample households.

Tenancy-at-will, i.e. an arrangement whereby a household rents the land but constructs and owns the dwelling, predominated in the two Indian areas where it accounted for 60–70 per cent of the samples. In Clermont, in contrast, only 2 per cent of the sample were tenants-at-will. Site rental was R30–R50 per annum in the Indian areas and R10 per month in Clermont. But tenants-at-will in Clermont were receiving just over R60 per month in rental from sub-tenants; this was therefore a profitable activity for them.

Whereas in Clermont 90 per cent of the households were tenants, i.e. they rented both the land and dwelling, the figure dropped to 10–40 per cent in the Indian areas. Rentals were higher in Clermont, the median being R9.82 per month. This was very close to the monthly rental of R9.76 being charged in a new adjoining township but was higher than the average of R6.71 per month in the older Durban townships. It appeared that, because of the shortage of official housing, tenants were paying a small premium for accommodation in unauthorized dwellings in Clermont.

The overall median monthly cost of accommodation in New Farm was R2.40 and at Isipingo Farm R4.09. At New Farm, tenants-at-will spent only 1.4 per cent of their median incomes on housing. This may be contrasted with the 25 per cent level adopted in South Africa and the 10 per cent level set in World Bank-financed projects.

Tenure arrangements may be different in a homeland. For example, in Malukazi, an informal settlement in the KwaZulu section of the Durban Metropolitan Region, the majority of households obtained their sites by paying to the local chief a once-and-for-all lump sum (usually between R20 and R80 plus a bottle of brandy!).

Costs of construction and quality of housing   In the Indian settlements three types of construction were common, namely, (a) by the family with some community assistance, (b) by the family with hired labour or (c) by a building contractor. At 1975 prices the median cost of construction at Isipingo Farm was R714. It was lowest (R588) when the dwelling was constructed by the family itself with some community help, and highest (R975) when a building contractor was employed. The median cost of construction when a family hired paid labour to assist it was R782. These figures may be compared with the 1975 cost of R3000–R3500 of constructing a township dwelling.

Costs of construction were lower in Clermont where they varied from a median of R101 (owner-built) to R75 (in the case of tenants-at-will). The most common building materials were wood and iron but stone, cartons and mud were also used.

At New Farm and Isipingo Farm a reasonable investment had been made in housing and, although costs of construction were considerably below that of public housing, the dwellings could not be considered hovels. According to a physical study, housing conditions in the Indian settlements were reasonable; spatial standards were in fact at least as good as those of the 'Housing Code'. (No physical study was conducted at Clermont, but at Malukazi spatial standards were found to be at least equivalent to those of township housing.) Lightweight building materials were used, and thermal performance could have been improved if some guidance in construction techniques had been available. Moreover investment in housing would undoubtedly have been greater had the future of these areas not been uncertain. This uncertainty militated against the use of more durable building materials.

The New Farm and Isipingo Farm dwellings illustrate the extent to which private funds, even among relatively low-income groups, may be mobilized for housing investment. This is clearly an important consideration in countries experiencing rapid urban population growth.

Perceived needs The Indian areas contained only few standpipes and no electricity, while in Clermont the majority of households had access to communal water and toilet facilities. The perceived needs of the households are compared in Table 8.3. A roughly similar order of needs was expressed in the other recent studies in Durban referred to above.

Although the order differs, the importance of security of tenure, water, electricity, sanitation and streets shows up strongly in all three areas. Housing rated low in the list of priorities; it was mentioned by one-third of the households in Clermont and by fewer in the Indian areas. But this is not surprising, and the results are in line with those in other recent studies which indicate that squatters place far more emphasis on security of tenure and the quality of services rather than on housing *per se*.

Table 8.3 Comparison of major perceived needs – African and Indian squatters.

	% of respondents		
Item	Clermont	New Farm	Isipingo Farm
security of tenure	99.3	86.0	76.1
water	98.6	100.0	79.8
electricity		84.9	94.5
streets	98.4	41.9	61.5
sanitation, individual toilets, bathrooms	73.2	52.7	61.5

Source: Maasdorp and Haarhoff (1981).

Housing preferences   In all three areas, households were asked to choose their future housing preference from among five alternatives, all of which were carefully explained to them. These alternatives, and the responses, are listed in Table 8.4.

Table 8.4 Comparison of housing aspirations – African and Indian squatters.

	% of respondents		
Alternative	Clermont	New Farm	Isipingo Farm
status quo	2.2	7.0	—
upgrading	17.8	73.0	68.2
site-and-service	41.9	7.0	17.1
township house	21.8	11.0	4.6
core house	10.0	—	9.1

Source: Maasdorp and Haarhoff (1981).

This Table shows that Indian squatters placed far more emphasis on squatter upgrading, and less on the other approaches, than did African shack-dwellers in Clermont. An important point in all three studies, however, is that only a small minority opted for the conventional township approach. The studies illustrate that aspirations vary from one area to another, and that any low-income housing policy should contain a number of different alternatives. By doing so it would widen the range of choices available and therefore increase public welfare.

The informal sector

Informal settlements are often thought to be conterminous with informal sector employment. Although this is an erroneous view, studies of African informal settlements in the DMR suggest that some 20 per cent of income-earners are engaged in this sector; the proportion appears to be lower in Indian areas.

Definition   In the Clermont study the informal sector was defined as comprising unlicensed and unrecorded activities. This definition accords with that of Hart (1971), who coined the term informal sector. However, the International Labour Organization (ILO 1972) broadened Hart's concept to include 'small-scale' firms, and this has given rise to considerable definitional confusion. Added to this is conceptual confusion as well as the ideological divide between reformists and neo-Marxists (see Bromley 1978a). The result is that much of the literature represents a mere caricature of the informal sector.

Following the ILO, the terms 'small' (in an African context, less than 20 workers) and 'informal' have often been used synonomously. Yet this seems to be incorrect. If it is not, i.e. if informal is small and *vice versa*, the entire economy of certain platteland towns in South Africa must be considered informal. To regard such enterprises as informal is patently ridiculous. They might be part of the small-scale, self-employed sector, but they *are* licensed, they *do* submit tax returns and they *are* enumerated in censuses.

Enterprises which are licensed and recorded in various official returns surely cannot in any sense be regarded as informal. In our view the distinguishing characteristic of the informal sector is precisely that it is unrecorded. By this we mean that (a) activities are not recorded in any official returns, and (b) incomes earned are not disclosed. In many respects the informal sector is best described as the unrecognized, harassed sector – the 'furtive' sector in that it is operated by stealth because it contravenes regulations of one sort or another or goes against conventional standards or behaviour patterns (Maasdorp 1980a). Thus builders of shacks contravene building codes, roadside vendors contravene health by-laws, pirate taxi operators contravene transport regulations, shebeen keepers contravene liquor laws and prostitutes offend middle class morality.

Although the idea of the informal sector is associated with Third World countries, it has its counterpart in the developed countries, viz. the 'underground economy'. This may be defined as that sector of the economy forced by government interference to make its own rules, i.e. to cheat to survive. The underground economy flourishes the world over – in the United States and Britain where there is a growing tendency to barter services in order to avoid taxation, in Italy and behind the Iron Curtain. It is therefore independent of the type of economic system in operation in a country. The underground economy or informal sector operates among all races in South Africa, and probably represents a considerable proportion (possibly 20–50 per cent) of the Gross Domestic Product in most countries (Louw 1981, pp. 3–4), although it does not figure in national accounts.

Informal economic activities in informal settlements cover an extraordinarily wide range. Louw (1981, pp. 7–8) has categorized them into three, namely:

(a) 'ordinary' businesses of a manufacturing or commercial nature, e.g. building, painting, tailoring, repairing, shoemaking;
(b) prohibited businesses, e.g. drug peddling, prostitution;
(c) common crime, e.g. theft, fraud, mugging.

The illegality of the 'ordinary businesses' stems simply from the fact that they are unlicensed; the operators voluntarily or involuntarily have circumvented bureaucratic red tape in order to make a living or to exercise their entrepreneurial skills.

A number of additional points should be made in order to clarify some of the confusion surrounding the concept. The informal sector (a) contains a wide range of incomes – it is not confined to the very poor; (b) provides a considerable amount of permanent, full-time employment although it may also contain many jobs of a temporary or casual nature; (c) is not synonomous with sub-contracting, much (probably most) of which occurs within the formal sector.

The usefulness of our definition of the informal sector as the unrecorded, unenumerated sector may be queried. For example, is there a clear line dividing what is informal from what is formal? Louw (1981, p. 2) thinks not, simply because nobody complies 100 per cent with all laws relating to the submission of returns or records all information accurately. But we think that the dividing line is clear; an *individual* may operate in both sectors, e.g. in two different jobs, but the *activity* should be capable of classification on the basis of whether it is licensed or registered and incomes are declared. Thus, for example, a registered domestic servant would be in the formal sector, an unregistered one in the informal sector; a teacher in the formal sector, his undisclosed income from giving extra lessons in the informal sector.

Informal activities in Clermont   In the Clermont sample 79 per cent of income-earners were engaged entirely or predominantly in the formal sector, with the balance in the informal sector. The division cannot be a hard and fast one as some individuals were engaged in both sectors. Overall, however, the proportion engaged in both sectors was only 3.5 per cent.

The informal operators were engaged in numerous activities which are summarized in Table 8.5. This Table illustrates that approximately one-third of the operators were engaged in selling, foodstuffs being the major traded line. These activities were conducted mainly from fixed premises, either indoors or along the roadside, with a minority of itinerant sellers hawking or peddling their goods from street to street. The brewing and selling of liquor absorbed another one-third; the great majority of these operators were

Table 8.5 Percentage distribution of operators in the informal sector in Clermont by category, sex and origin.

	Migrant			Native			Total		
Category	M	F	T	M	F	T	M	F	T
seller:									
foodstuffs	22.7	15.9	19.0	28.8	18.0	22.7	25.5	17.0	20.8
clothing and related									
goods	12.0	6.8	9.2	9.1	7.2	8.1	10.6	7.0	8.7
household, medicinal									
goods	2.7	2.2	2.5	4.5	1.2	2.7	3.5	1.8	2.6
manual:									
building, machinery	17.3	—	8.0	4.5	—	2.0	11.3	—	5.1
clothing, footwear	13.3	10.2	11.7	18.2	16.9	17.5	15.6	13.5	14.5
traditional crafts	1.3	2.3	1.8	—	—	—	0.7	1.2	1.0
traditional medicine	13.3	3.4	8.0	6.1	—	2.7	9.9	1.8	5.4
transport	—	—	—	6.1	—	2.7	2.8	—	1.3
service	9.3	—	4.3	9.1	—	4.0	9.2	—	4.2
brewers, sellers of liquor	6.7	52.3	31.3	13.6	50.6	34.2	9.9	51.5	32.7
entertainer, gambler	1.3	6.8	4.3	—	6.0	3.4	0.7	6.4	3.8
total (*n* = 100%)	75	88	163	66	83	149	141	171	312

Source: Maasdorp and Haarhoff (1981).

M = male, F = female, T = total.

females, and the size of this category helps to account for the overall majority of females in the sample.

Migrants were more likely than natives to be engaged in manual work related to building and machinery and in traditional crafts and medicines, while natives were more likely to be found in the more sophisticated lines such as transport and manual work relating to the production of clothing and footwear. It was in the field of liquor that the contrast was greatest – migrants were the brewers while natives were the shebeen keepers. Here again natives were found in the more sophisticated (and more profitable) line.

One activity which does not appear in Table 8.5 is that of 'landlordism'. Landowners and tenants-at-will received incomes from letting or sub-letting, but this was not investigated separately in the informal sector survey. There is no doubt, too, that many other activities also did not fall into the sample.

Because of the great variety of activities, it has been suggested that the informal sector should be divided into two distinct categories (Sethuraman 1976, p. 73). These are: (a) an irregular sector consisting of low-status but nevertheless legitimate fringe activities (such as car washing, casual gardening and begging) and illegal activities; and (b) the informal sector proper which would then refer to small-scale economic activities as well as to non-wage and family concerns. If we relate this division to the activities listed in

Table 8.5, we find that the irregular sector would consist largely of illegal rather than of low–status activities. Patently illegal and frowned–upon activities (brewing and selling of liquor, prostitution, gambling) accounted for 37 per cent of the operators; other illegal (unlicensed) activities, to which official response is often more passive, e.g. selling of foodstuffs and clothing, for 33 per cent; and other fringe activities, e.g. traditional medicine, for 5 per cent. At most, 25 per cent (mainly the manual workers) could be regarded as producers of 'socially acceptable' goods in the eyes of the authorities.

Employment   One of the most important issues in framing a policy towards the informal sector is the extent to which the sector is capable of providing employment and incomes, not just for the operators themselves but for other individuals as well. Of the 312 operators less than one-third (31 per cent) were providing employment for others, the overall mean number being 1.3 per operator. The most labour-intensive activities were those of builder, mechanic and seller of foodstuffs. But, all in all, the employment-generating capacity of the operators was low.

Approximately three-quarters of the operators were engaged on a full-time basis in their operations. Not only are activities in the informal sector sometimes regarded as unproductive, but it is often thought that the sector does not provide full-time work opportunities and that it is therefore characterized by disguised unemployment or underemployment. We ascertained the number of hours worked per day and the number of days worked per week, and found that over 60 per cent of the operators worked between 7 and 12 hours per day. A small minority in fact worked for more than 12 hours daily. The majority worked on all seven days of the week and approximately 85 per cent worked on either six or seven days. However, some of the 'work' might have involved 'waiting' for customers and the figures do not enable us to infer anything about the intensity of work. One survey (Wegelin 1978, p. 162) had classified all persons working less than 25 hours per week as 'underemployed' and if we adopt a similar classification, we see that at most some 16 per cent would be 'underemployed' (working less than 5 hours per day for 5 or 6 days per week). There was clearly an employment problem among the *operators* but its precise extent was not measurable. In contrast, there might well have been a sizeable amount of 'underemployment' among the *employees* in these operations; the majority (72 per cent) of employees were stated to be in 'full-time' employment but almost two-thirds of male and just over one-half of female 'full-time' workers were occupied for 5 hours or less per day.

Incomes   A very interesting result obtained in the Clermont *household* sample was that median earnings were higher in the informal than in the formal sector. Many writers consider that the informal sector offers employment of a 'marginal' nature, but amongst the Clermont shack dwellers it offered an important and financially rewarding form of economic activity. The survey amongst *operators* revealed a mean monthly income from informal activities only of R133; this was net of purchases, rent and wages, and exceeded the mean monthly African wage in Durban of R117. The survey showed that operators could be divided into three categories, namely, those with a single informal sector operation only, those operating in both the informal and formal sector, and those with another (subsidiary) informal sector activity. Almost 75 per cent of the operators were in the first group, almost 20 per cent in the second and 5 per cent in the third. The mean monthly incomes in the three groups were R143, R209 and R150 respectively. However, in the case of those operating in both sectors, mean monthly incomes were higher in the formal than in the informal sector – R120 compared with R89 – and it appeared that the majority in this group 'moonlighted' in informal activities, i.e. the informal sector was a subsidiary source of income.

In contrast to the operators themselves, employees in the informal sectors earned incomes far below the average wage for Africans in Durban. The low wages could perhaps be explained partly by the short hours worked and partly by the fact that many were relatives who received lower remuneration than non-relatives. The overall mean wage was R30 per month.

Other aspects   Apart from the 20 per cent of operators who were active in both sectors, a further 50 per cent had previously been employed in the formal sector. Some had been dismissed or retrenched but the majority appeared to have left their jobs voluntarily, the major reasons being the desire for self-employment and the prospect of higher incomes.

The majority (72 per cent) of the operators stated that they had experienced ease of entry into the informal sector, thereby confirming the results of other studies (ILO 1972). However, competition appeared to be more limited than might have been expected, 52 per cent stating that they had no competition. Harassment by the authorities, which is often mentioned in the literature as militating against the more effective growth of the informal sector, was experienced by 39 per cent. This harassment took the form of arrests, fines and destruction of premises and/or goods.

When we sought to ascertain whether the operators planned to stay in the informal sector, they answered that they were largely committed to the informal sector. Thus 85 per cent planned to remain in their existing activities and the majority had plans to improve their businesses. A further 27 per cent planned to obtain new business premises.

One of the major advantages of informal sector operations identified in the literature (ILO 1972) relates to the small amounts of capital required to establish businesses. This is borne out by the results. Only 20 (6 per cent) of the operators did not require any capital to start their businesses, while the median amount of R28 meant that the operators were able to start with very small amounts of money. Those sellers who had no capital requirements were itinerant traders with no fixed premises and who purchased on credit. Capital requirements were highest for manual work of an artisan or manufacturing nature – operators in the building field, mechanics, dressmakers and shoemakers – presumably because of the nature of the equipment required.

Respondents were asked to state the type of equipment or goods they required for conducting their activities. The answers illustrated (a) the simple nature of much of the equipment used, e.g. by sellers of clothing, (b) the ingenuity of some of the operators, e.g. the use of old car tyres for shoe-making, and (c) the extent to which some operators went towards creating a convivial atmosphere for their customers, e.g. the shebeen keepers. Some 83 per cent purchased their equipment or goods. The great majority (93 per cent) obtained their materials, equipment or goods from wholesalers or retailers. They purchased from Indian-owned shops in Durban's Grey Street area, the Durban produce market, bottle stores and factories. There were thus linkages between the formal and informal sectors. Less than 1 per cent in each case obtained their supplies from private households, hawkers or from within the shack area. A few sellers of second-hand clothing bought their goods from white families while some supplies, e.g. *dagga* (marijuana), grass for mat-making and *muti* for traditional medicine were obtained from rural areas, often being collected by the operator. The operators drew their supplies almost entirely from the DMR. In only a minority of cases (35 per cent) were goods delivered to the operator's location.

Customers were drawn from both the shack area as well as the authorized housing area of Clermont. Thus 72 per cent of the operators drew their customers from both areas, 26 per cent from shack dwellers exclusively. Moreover some sellers of liquor and *dagga* appeared to draw customers from the white and Indian areas as well.

Several studies have found that an important feature of informal sector operations is that prices are subject to negotiation. However, this was apparently not the case in Clermont; 78 per cent of the operators stated that they had fixed prices. An important advantage of the informal sector identified in the literature is that the operators are usually willing to sell their commodities in broken lots in order to satisfy the ability of the lowest-income households to pay; 61 per cent of the sample sold in broken lots.

Conclusion

A number of conclusions result from the case studies which by and large support the informal housing and employment policies recommended by major aid agencies today.

First, there is no option but to incorporate upgrading and site-and-service schemes in housing policy. Informal settlements have continued to grow in the DMR since the studies were undertaken. The major concentrations are in the Inanda area and to the south of Umlazi. It has recently been estimated that, in 1980, informal settlements contained 36 per cent of the urban African population of Natal–KwaZulu and 300 000–333 000 (or 31–35 per cent) of the total African population of the DMR. Between 195 000 and 214 000 were accommodated in the Inanda–Richmond Farm–Clermont area on the northern periphery, and between 105 000 and 119 000 on the southern periphery.

The growth of informal settlements, fuelled by rural–urban migration, has been an uninterrupted process in the DMR since at least the 1930s. Attempts to clear the region of shacks in the 1950s and 1960s might have looked like succeeding, but housing provision by the state could not keep pace with demand. Recent public housing schemes for Africans are equally unlikely to make any significant impact on the overall balance of formal–informal housing. At a conservative estimate, if the African population of Natal–KwaZulu is 65 per cent urbanized in the year 2000, it could then be 2 615 000–2 816 000 in the DMR, i.e. it would increase over the next 20 years at an average annual rate of 5 per cent per annum. Yet, based on present plans for township housing projects, some 1 730 000–1 770 000 Africans could be living in informal settlements in the DMR in the year 2000. This would represent 63–66 per cent of the African population of the region. In 1970 only 11–12 per cent, and in 1980 some 31–35 per cent, of the African population of the DMR resided in informal housing. Thus the proportion of the African population in informal settlements could double over the next 20 years.

Fortunately there are now more encouraging signs on the policy front. First, the Department of Co-operation and Development has given its blessing to site-and-service schemes and the Department of Community Development in 1980 appointed a committee of inquiry into 'unconventional' housing.

Secondly, although cost–benefit analysis of the Little–Mirrlees type did not appear applicable because of the difficulty of quantifying benefits, a financial analysis showed that a revised housing policy would achieve considerable economies. Cost economies could be achieved by design optimization in housing layouts as well as by the use of alternative (lower) standards and self-help. The present method of charging for housing in homeland townships contains a large subsidy element which is, however, misallocated – more than two-thirds went to households not requiring a subsidy whereas 20–25 per cent of households received inadequate subsidies. The size of the subsidies required is closely related to the capital cost of housing. The average subsidy per household and the number of households requiring a subsidy decline as the capital cost of housing falls. It is therefore possible to provide housing more cheaply and more suited to affordability. Capital costs and subsidies could both be cut significantly by reducing the standards of housing and infrastructure. Thus the government could obtain more for each R1 invested in low-income housing. This is very important in view of recent statements in Parliament regarding the number of dwellings actually built in 1980 compared with the housing backlog. For example, in 1980–81, the government constructed only 3.6 per cent of its own estimated shortage of houses for Africans in urban areas (*Natal Mercury* 24 Sept. 1981).

Thirdly, if the size of the informal sector hangs largely on the dividing line between being licensed or unlicensed, the concept may not be useful, particularly from the angle of employment creation. If the sector is freed of restrictions – if licences are freely granted – it could be reduced substantially at the stroke of a bureaucratic pen (it would not be *eliminated* – there would always be some incentive for underground economic activities, e.g. drug peddling and prostitution would continue). It is not clear that the legalizing of operations would of itself stimulate employment. But the real point is that the law makes it difficult for people in the informal sector to earn incomes. If it is made easier, some employment might be stimulated and the income-earning potential of Africans enhanced. Money would circulate more rapidly in the townships and informal settlements, the economy of these areas would be stimulated and the income distribution impact would probably be favourable.

The informal sector appeared to have positive as well as negative aspects. Operators were receiving higher incomes than wage-employees in the formal sector, and we found no clear evidence of the 'subordination and exploitation' of informal sector operators that is sometimes claimed in the literature. It may well be that, in the peculiar economic, social and political climate of South Africa, with its many imperfections in the labour market, the informal sector offers more favourable *relative* income-earning opportunities to Africans (particularly females) than it does elsewhere in Africa. On the negative side, the following features stood out:

(a) The great majority of the activities were commercial (selling) rather than manufacturing (artisanal). In this particular sample, therefore, there did not seem to be much scope for the introduction of a programme of technical training.

(b) The operations were very small in terms of employment generated. There appeared to be some underemployment particularly among 'employees' and, given the nature of the activities, the scope for employment growth appeared limited.

Finally, the informal housing and employment sectors must be seen in perspective. They are a mixed bag and some writers have tended to glamourize them while others have been entirely negative in their approach. Governments have an important role in providing for the housing and welfare of the lowest-income groups, and for many families informal arrangements are probably not optimal in terms of shelter, employment and income. But informal housing often has greater potential for improvement and expansion than has state housing, and some informal activities are productive and provide a good livelihood to the operator. In a mixed as opposed to a centrally planned economy, the enterprise and initiative displayed, together with the investments made, in informal housing and employment, are factors which could be encouraged by sympathetic government policies. In South Africa the legislative rigidities inherent in the policy of apartheid are a major obstacle to the adoption of such policies.

Acknowledgements

The author wishes to acknowledge constructive comments from Jane Maasdorp, and the collaborated work of Nesen Pillay, Errol Haarhoff and Julian Hofmeyer in the case studies. This chapter is based largely on the author's contribution to Maasdorp and Humphreys (1975), Maasdorp and Pillay (1977), Maasdorp and Haarhoff (1981), and Maasdorp (1981). Grateful acknowledgement is made to the Human Sciences Research Council, Pretoria, for sponsoring the project.

9 Segregation and interpersonal relationships: a case study of domestic service in Durban

ELEANOR PRESTON-WHYTE

One of the cornerstones of the policy of separate development and, indeed, one of the few areas in which apartheid has been pursued to its logical conclusion, is in the provision of separate living areas for members of each race group in South Africa. Through various acts of Parliament the country has been transformed into a chequer board of black and white states and homelands, while in towns and urban centres where black and white mingle in the work situation the members of each race group must be housed in residential areas set aside for their use alone. When not at work blacks and whites have, theoretically at least, nothing in common and no right to be in the residential areas of groups other than their own. The ideal and practice of race segregation has thus created within every South African town and city a series of geographically and racially isolated suburbs, which over time have become increasingly differentiated from each other socially and even culturally.

There are exceptions to every rule. Blacks not only work, but also live, in many of the white suburbs of South African cities. They constitute a largely ignored category of 'non-people' whose presence is tolerated because of the services they offer to whites but whose existence is socially ignored both in planning and in the day-to-day community life of these 'white' areas. Blacks who work and live within 'white' cities have, however, created a distinct subculture which serves and expresses those particular needs which stem from the geography of residential separation. It is the object of this chapter to describe black social and cultural adaptations to working and living in an area set aside for whites in South Africa. This is done by focusing attention on the lives and social relations of black women employed as domestic servants in the homes of whites in the city of Durban.

The majority of domestic servants in the Republic are African. Indians and Coloureds do enter this field, but, in Durban at least, not in great numbers and the few who do seek domestic employment work largely on a part-time basis and are seldom offered or accept accommodation on the premises of their employers. It is the employment only of African women which is considered in this chapter. The material used was gathered as part of a wider investigation into the working life, social ties and inter-personal relations of African (i.e. Black) women working as domestic servants in Durban.

The racial ecology of Durban

Durban is unusual amongst South African cities in that, because the boundaries of KwaZulu abut the white and Indian residential areas of the city (Fig. 8.1, p. 145), the greater part of the African population and particularly of the labour force of the metropolitan area live in a Black state, crossing its borders each day to work. These KwaZulu citizens are either housed in one of two massive townships of Umlazi and KwaMashu, or else have found their own accommodation largely in the mushrooming shack or informal settlement areas which are now a feature of the city's periphery. The majority of Africans who live in the white controlled areas of Durban are theoretically accommodated in one of the relatively small municipal townships of Lamontville, Chesterville or Clermont, or in their associated men's hostels. These areas are situated, if not at great physical, then at least at some social distance from the centres of white activity and, indeed, can only be entered by whites with the permission of the township manager. There are, however, other pockets of African residence in the heart of the 'white' city and these make the inter-racial interaction at the *personal* level far more complex than would appear from the accepted apartheid model.

Dotted largely around the Bay and in outlying areas of the city there are various compounds (Fig. 8.1), ranging in size from 50 to 1000 inmates, which are run by municipal, provincial and governmental bodies as well as by a few private organizations. Together these house approximately 27 000 Africans, mostly men. There is one black woman's hostel in the centre of Durban which offers 677 permanent beds and limited temporary accommodation. Of greatest interest to this chapter are the thousands of domestic servants, both men and women, who live scattered over the white and Indian residential areas of the city on the premises of their employers. In 1970 their numbers were estimated to be between 30 000 and 55 000 (Maasdorp & Humphreys 1975, p. 71) and given the fact that the municipal authorities estimate that in 1980 there were some 66 577 Africans living in the white areas of central Durban, Pinetown, Hillcrest and Queensborough, this figure is probably about the same today. It must be remembered, however, that despite possible prosecution, by no means all servants are registered by their employers and also at any time there are numbers of visitors and other illegal occupants in many servants' quarters.

For all these Blacks the official *locus* of social and recreational life is in the African townships. At one time there were numerous churches, halls and an active social centre serving Africans in the heart of Durban. With the inexorable implementation of apartheid all but a few of these facilities have been closed or moved to the townships, and all new recreational ventures must be established in these areas. The halls and amphitheatres open to Blacks are in one or other of the large townships and there is a clear tendency for shops and new commercial undertakings to be opened in the townships as restrictions on these enterprises in the 'white' commercial area of Durban are increased. While it may be argued that this is a logical move as far as the majority of the Black population who live in the African townships is concerned, it has resulted, as we shall see, in severe problems for those who remain in the 'white' areas of the city.

In contrast, the problem for Black township dwellers is to get to work. Although there is a tendency for new industries to be located near to township areas, the vast majority of Africans face long journeys from the townships to work and back each day. Those employed in the Durban central business district in commerce, in the public services, in hotels and offices, and those working as domestic servants in white homes in the suburbs, must expect to travel between 10 and 40 km per day. For the most part these workers bear the cost of commuting themselves. The two largest townships, Umlazi to the south of Durban and KwaMashu to the north-east, are situated at least 9–11 km from the city centre. Chesterville, a small and relatively old township, is only 5 km distant but Clermont, the one area where Blacks can own land rather than merely buy the buildings on plots rented to them by the municipality (as is the case in the other townships), is over 20 km from the Durban central business district. The vast majority of Blacks travel by train or bus. Relatively few can afford private motor vehicles and the cost of taxis is prohibitive for normal commuting and weekend visiting. The number of motor vehicles run by Blacks in the city of Durban is not known but in Umlazi there are only 2600 registered vehicles – a small number to service the population, which in 1973 was estimated to be in the region of 250 000 persons (Maasdorp & Humphreys 1975, p. 91).

Money and time spent by township Blacks on commuting to and from work, and by those living in the 'white' city in the pursuance of leisure activities in the townships, varies. It is, however, safe to say that in both fields most individuals feel pressure and strain. The minimum bus fare from either Umlazi or KwaMashu to central Durban is 30 cents single (there is no cheap return). A monthly season ticket on the railway, at R6.60, is considerably less per journey but the trip by train is often inconvenient for workers who want to disembark in outlying 'white' areas. Most employees have to catch feeder buses either in the townships or in the 'white' residential and commercial areas and the costs of travel average out at 50–60 cents per day. The length of time spent commuting is affected not only by the frequency and efficiency of the transport system but also by the hours of work fixed by employers. Many Blacks are involved in shift work and in services which are performed during the night or early morning when public transport is unavailable. It is largely for this reason that the compound and hostel system in 'white' areas has remained. For workers not accommodated by their employers, and for those wishing to visit the townships in their free time, irregular hours of work may increase their travelling time by as much as one to one and a half hours per journey. This is certainly the case for domestic servants, whose hours of work are perhaps the longest and most erratic of all Black workers in Durban.

The nature of domestic service

The employment of domestic servants is an ubiquitous feature of South African life. Employees work anything from seven to 12 hours per day and many 'live in', that is, they are accommodated on the premises of their employers. In most industrialized societies full-time domestic service is on the decrease and, where it does occur, it is the preserve of the wealthy. In South Africa, in contrast, the vast majority of whites, both rich and poor, and many blacks also, employ servants to clean their homes, do the washing and ironing, care for their often extensive gardens, act as nursemaids, cook and even housekeep. The usual pattern amongst house owners, as opposed to flatdwellers, is for the servant to be engaged on a full-time residential basis. The employee comes on duty at about 6.30 or 7 a.m. and works through the day until 7.30 or 8 p.m., when the evening meal has been served and cleared away. Short breaks are given for breakfast at about 10.30 and lunch from about 2 to 3 in the afternoon. These long working hours are made possible by housing the servant on the premises. Most properties in Durban have servants' quarters, referred to as the *kia* (from the Zulu word for 'home'), attached to either the main building, or to the garage or other out-houses. The quarters vary greatly in quality and repair but most provide besides a room, a shower and a latrine.

In contrast to full-time resident employment, is the growing trend towards non-resident domestic service. In this case the servant comes on duty at about 7 or 7.30 a.m. and leaves the employer's premises by 4 or 4.30 p.m. The work done is, by and large, the same as that done by resident servants – cleaning, laundry, possibly some cooking and child-care. The difference lies perhaps in the intensity of the work demands in each situation; in non-resident service the allotted work must be completed in a relatively short time. Many non-resident servants prepare and even cook the evening meal before they depart in the afternoon and the washing-up may be left for them to do in the morning when they come on duty. This type of work is prevalent in blocks of flats where accommodation for Blacks is seldom sufficient to house servants for all flatdwellers. Some blocks of flats are serviced by a gang of African male cleaners who do live on the premises and who clean the communal corridors and steps and spend about an hour clean-ing individual flats each or every second day. The flatdwellers may employ, in addition, one or more non-resident servants, often women, to do the more demanding domestic work such as laundry, polishing silver, cooking, or caring for small children. Some resident employees do only laundry and remain in their employers' houses for a few hours in the mornings.

One of the major differences between resident and non-resident domestic service is that in the former, employees, though given a 'day off' (or rather an afternoon or two off per week), work over weekends and on Sundays. Non-resident employees may work only from three to six days a week and usually do not come on duty on a Sunday. In this respect non-resident domestic service may be closer in nature to a system of impersonal 'charring' than to full-time resident service which, because of the accommodation factor, puts employer and employee in close and even intimate contact for most of the day and over weekends as well. Both Blacks and whites comment on this difference and profess to prefer non-resident service because it does not entail close and continuous contact. The cost, however, lies in the time, energy and money which the non-resident employee must expend in getting to and from work.

The wages paid for both resident and non-resident service are low. In the 1970s R45 per month was considered by employers to be a high wage and relatively few servants were paid over R35 per month, the more usual figure ranging from R20 to R30 per month. By 1980 wages had risen by about R15 to R20 and in a few cases skilled female servants now receive a wage of between R80 and R100 per month. Though employers consider current wages to be good, these are still inadequate given the increased cost of living including high transport costs to and from the Black townships. Employers point to the fact that both resident and non-resident employees are provided with food and uniforms and non-residents may be given their bus fare in lieu of accommodation. There is no legislative control of wages paid to domestic workers employed by private individuals, no compulsory leave require- ments, and no medical and pension schemes. Wages and benefits are decided privately between employer and employee and any side benefits are made solely through the goodwill of the employer.

The long hours, low wages and few side benefits make domestic service unattractive to many Blacks; the unavailability of alternative employment and lack of any particular skill, however, forces many people into this field particularly women, for whom few other jobs are available. Resident service does, however, have one great benefit for workers – accommodation. In Durban it is extremely difficult for Blacks to find single accommodation, so that both male and female migrants are frequently forced into this form of employment, as the alternative is to be endorsed out of town if they can find no legally acceptable place to live in the Black townships (Preston-Whyte 1968).

There lies, thus, a paradox at the heart of domestic employment in white South African homes. Servants are invariably, and indeed in white ideology are by definition, drawn from the black racial groups. Black servant and white employer must associate together in white homes situated in 'white' residential areas. Many Blacks must, furthermore, live in 'white' residential areas in order to fulfil the demands of their employment and because they cannot find legal accommodation in Black areas. They are expected, however, to seek their recreation and social intercourse in the townships. Occupational imperatives and the harsh realities of scarce accommodation and the politico-administrative policy run counter to the precepts of racial ideology and the spatial separation of the race groups. The casualties of this conflict are, as might be expected, the Blacks who must accept domestic jobs in white homes and whose lives are, as we shall see, dominated by compromises and adaptations which will allow them to live or at least to spend most of their working lives in 'white' areas. However, they may not benefit from any of the facilities or freedoms enjoyed by the residents of these areas and indeed cannot look to the whites who live around them for either companionship or neighbourly social interaction.

Two case studies, one of a resident and the other of a non-resident domestic servant, illustrate graphically the nature of the paradox. In both cases Black employment in 'white' areas imposes constraints and gives rise to imperatives which must be accommodated and met in the structuring of social relations.

Case one: a resident domestic servant Nomusa B. is a single 34-year-old African woman who has been employed as a domestic servant in City North, a 'white' suburb situated some 12 km from the centre of Durban, for about three years (Fig. 8.1). City North is an upper middle class area, the whites are well off and most breadwinners are employed in the business or professional sphere. The three to four-bedroomed bungalows are surrounded by spacious gardens, the house furnishings are of good quality and the properties are well cared for and prosperous in appearance. The elegance of white living in the suburb is due, in no small measure, to the employment of servants who, like Nomusa, are full-time resident employees putting in about 60 hours of work per week. Many of the female servants are expected, in addition, to baby-sit one or two nights a week.

Nomusa's free time is limited, but it is not only her long hours of work which dominate her personal life. The distance of City North from Durban and from the townships, and the paucity of local public transport for Blacks serve to confine her social activities very largely to City North and other parts of 'white' Durban. Feeder buses for Blacks run on the suburb's bus routes at infrequent intervals – at about 7 a.m., 2 p.m., 6 p.m. and sometimes at about 9.30 p.m. The journey into Durban takes 45 minutes. A connecting bus or train to the townships may take anything from another one to one and a half hours. Should Nomusa not be able to catch the City North feeder bus to town she must embark on a 50-minute walk to the nearest bus route serving

KwaMashu. The trip either to town or to the township takes from a half to three-quarters of an hour. It is therefore impossible for Nomusa to leave the immediate vicinity of her employment unless she has at least four hours free. This occurs only on her weekly 'day off' when she may leave the premises at 11.30 a.m. (but there is no local bus until 2 p.m.) and on Sundays when she goes off duty at 1.30 p.m. On both these days Nomusa is fortunate in that she does not have to return to work until the following morning. Many servants are expected to return at about 6 p.m. in order to wash the dishes.

On her day off, which falls on a Thursday, Nomusa usually goes to town. On the way she often calls on her brother who is working at a nearby factory, and later meets a friend or relative who is also free at this time. They may 'window shop' or at the beginning of the month, when they have been paid, make the purchases which they have earmarked on previous trips. Nomusa usually returns to City North by the 6 p.m. bus even though she is not on duty, since there is no other means of getting there safely. The walk from the local bus stop and particularly from the KwaMashu bus route is dangerous after dark as Blacks in City North are terrorized by gangs of male domestic servants who attack lone pedestrians. Sundays may be spent with her lover either in City North or central Durban where the latter works as a policeman, or in visiting Nesta B., Nomusa's father's brother's daughter who works as a domestic servant in Seaview, a 'white' suburb some 15 km away from City North (see Fig. 9.1). Nomusa catches the feeder bus into town at 2 p.m. If she is going to Seaview, she then boards a bus to one of the westerly townships, which passes nearby Seaview. The journey takes 15 minutes and the buses run fairly frequently. It is because of its accessibility that Nesta's room has come to be used as a meeting place for the B. close kin in Durban. Nomusa, her two brothers Elias and Anthony B., another cousin Phyllis B. who is also a resident servant, are all regular visitors and other relatives or friends from their home area often drop in. Nomusa thus spends Sunday afternoon in the 'white' city, although her companions are Black. If she has been to Seaview, she may also spend the night with Nesta, rising at about 5 a.m. on Monday morning in order to find her way to town and so catch the City North morning bus to work.

As Figure 9.1 shows, Nomusa's free time during a typical month was spent completely within the 'white' areas of Durban. In eight months she visited KwaMashu only twice. On the first occasion, she went to look at a room her brother was considering renting in the township. On the return walk to the premises from the KwaMashu bus stop just after dark, she was accosted by three men who threatened her life. This convinced her and her kin that Nesta's *kia* was the most convenient and safe meeting place. On the second occasion, Nomusa went to a football match in KwaMashu with her lover, who later accompanied her home. The couple felt compelled to hurry their walk from the bus stop and even ran part of the way to avoid attack.

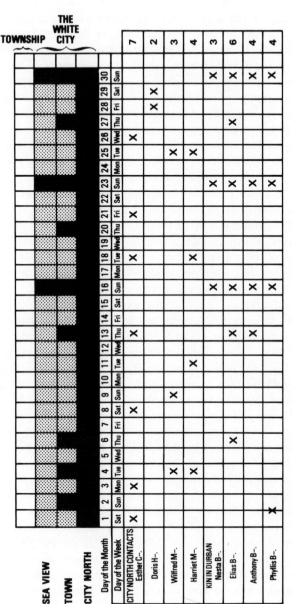

Figure 9.1 Case one:: a resident domestic servant. The spacial and social distribution of Nomusa B.'s leisure time activities during one month. (Notes: black shading indicates daily presence in areas; stippled shading indicates parts of the day; no shading indicates daily absence from areas; no shading indicates parts of Durban (other than place of employment) not visited on the day indicated. The right-hand column shows the number of days of contact with each individual. Both the women discussed in this chapter kept diaries for about eight months. They noted whom they met and what they did in their leisure time. For the present purposes only one month has been chosen to illustrate the nature of their personal activities and relationships. The survey was undertaken in the mid-1970s.)

Given these circumstances, which are by no means unique to City North, it is hardly surprising that Nomusa and indeed many resident domestic servants in all the 'white' areas of Durban confine their activities largely to the 'white' areas of the city and their travelling to the townships to daylight hours. An additional factor in their relative lack of mobility is money. Commuting even to town and to visit friends in other parts of the city may diminish as the month end approaches. In many instances, furthermore, the men and women who are employed as resident servants have little call to visit the townships regularly. Many are migrants to Durban whose social relations centre on other migrants living and working in white suburbs rather than upon townspeople. The exact patterning of social ties and personal interests varies widely but there is a definite tendency for resident servants to look to their immediate surroundings for recreation, companionship and help in times of crises. It is suggested that this has two general results. It tends to limit the number of people with whom individuals interact in any meaningful manner and it tends to the development of a rich Black sub-culture, which operates in 'white' suburbs largely unknown to the white residents of these areas. We may analyse the situation in City North and Nomusa's free time activities, particularly during the month chosen as exemplar, in order to demonstrate these claims (see Fig. 9.1).

Blacks cannot make use of any of the white recreational facilities in City North. Although some white churches have now opened their halls to Blacks, most local clubs, playing fields, libraries, hotels and cinemas are restricted to whites. When Blacks congregate in parks or open spaces they are 'moved off' by the police. The size of any formal or informal group is conditioned by the number of people who can collect in a *kia* at one time or gather on a street corner without drawing adverse attention from whites. What Blacks do in their free time is further limited by the noise they are likely to make. Singing, playing musical instruments and loud talking soon create a 'public disturbance'. Blacks who live in the 'white' city have learned to be largely silent and inconspicuous. During the day, visitors to the premises come single and stealthily so as not to raise comment. Women who collect in the parks in the afternoon do so under the cover of taking white children to play there. At night, Black surburban life begins after whites have retired to their lounges and bedrooms. From 8 or 8.30 p.m. Blacks, who are then off duty, emerge from their rooms and move about the streets. They disappear before 5.30 or 6 a.m. when the white residents again take over the streets and parks of the suburb. Black social relations are predominantly unstructured and informal and where groups such as prayer circles, gangs or drinking cliques do develop, their size is limited and their membership as fluid as the Black population, many of whose members remain in their jobs for less than a year.

Much of Nomusa's free time is spent in sewing, reading and listening to the radio in her room, in visiting and being visited by other women working as servants in nearby white homes. In the afternoon after her lunch, she may call on a friend and they may wander up to the local shops where they windowshop, and make small purchases such as cool drinks, sweets or cosmetics. It is here that Nomusa meets a range of other Blacks working in the area, shop cleaners, delivery men, as well as servants and, in passing the time of day with them, collects and passes on local gossip. On the way back to the premises she may call on other servants or simply chat over garden walls. While these activities appear aimless and unimportant they serve to integrate her into the community life of Blacks in the neighbourhood. She hears of vacant jobs, of illnesses and of any local crises, and passes this information on to other servants who are kept too busy to visit the shopping area. In the evenings when she is not baby-sitting she may visit or be visited by her lover or by a neighbouring woman servant. Many women spend the nights in each other's rooms to avoid being harassed by the gangs in the area, and after dark they usually go round in twos or threes. The amount of visiting and personal movement within the area is high and it is around personal friendship and unstructured and unplanned interactions that much of Black social life in City North revolves.

Personal compatibility and common interests are naturally important in the formation of local friendships. On the whole, resident servants tend to form friendships with other servants of their own sex. Friendships with servants of the opposite sex are rare and both men and women choose sexual partners of a different social type and standing from their co-workers. Women despise male servants as uneducated and look to delivery men, shop assistants and clerks for their lovers and husbands. Male servants are usually involved in marriage negotiations with country women. Where sexual liaisons do occur between male and female servants, they are usually short-lived. Men are drawn together by having come from the same rural area, by interests in music, soccer or gang participation. Women associate largely on the basis of common outlook as well as interest. Nomusa, for instance, is not drawn to women who are very religious nor to those who spend their time drinking in local shebeens. She is a skilled needlewoman and has been taught by her employer to use paper patterns in dressmaking. Esther (see Fig. 9.1), one of the women who worked near her for some time, was a good knitter and she and Nomusa spent two or three evenings weekly working on their garments together. Both turned their skill to good purpose by making garments for neighbours who pay approximately R2 per plain garment.

Making money over and above their monthly earnings is a feature of the leisure time activities of many servants. While brewing illicit liquor is the most lucrative source of income, it is also the most dangerous as brewers risk losing their jobs and also public prosecution. Sewing, knitting and embroidery bring in a small but steady flow of money which can be used for small purchases and day-to-day expenses. It is not only money making but money saving that is a recurrent theme in the life of resident domestic servants.

Though use is made of banks and building societies, women frequently save by joining or forming an informal savings club or association referred to as a *Stokfel* (Kuper & Kaplan 1944). This consists of about three to five friends who agree to put a proportion of their salary, for instance R5–R7, into a common pool each month. The total amount is given to members in rotation and the person receiving the kitty holds a party to which other friends and neighbours are invited on the understanding that they will make a small monetary contribution. By means of this form of 'enforced' saving, individuals amass a fairly large amount in one month. This may enable them to make a substantial purchase such as a sewing machine or furniture or to pay school fees or to finance a trip home. The conviviality of the monthly parties and the feeling of solidarity between members are highly valued. The high labour turnover in domestic service mitigates against long-lasting local friendships. Nomusa, like all resident servants, is very aware of this problem and commented that by joining a *Stokfel* she would immediately have 'good' friends upon whom to rely. Membership of a *Stokfel*, like common church attendance or even kinship and the link of common home area, gives an extra dimension to friendships. This contrasts with the fleeting and transitory nature of many of the social interactions in which resident servants are involved. Against the background of isolated 'white' areas, 'good' friends are extremely important, for it is they upon whom individuals must rely, not only for companionship but also for help in times of need.

Resident servants have little choice of their Black neighbours unless they manage to put a friend or kinswoman into a nearby job, and it is but seldom that they get on well enough with all or even a few of the women working near to them to regard them as 'good' friends. In the month dealt with in Figure 9.1, Nomusa could point to only three women in the neighbourhood whom she really liked. One was Esther, the knitter referred to above, with whom she spent a good deal of time in the early part of the week before Esther left with her employer to live elsewhere in Durban. The other was Doris H., who came to City North to work for the white family which moved into the house vacated by Esther's employers. The third was Mrs Harriet M., a woman from Umlazi who visited the premises each Tuesday to do the ironing. Nomusa was relieved that she got on well with Mrs M., as she had not liked the woman who had been employed previously.

Nomusa is, of course, not completely dependent on local contacts for companionship. She can and does rely on her kin who live in Durban for both friendships and help. Though she meets them on the average only once a week, she telephones Nesta and Phyllis regularly. Blacks living and working in 'white' areas are fortunate in having access to this form of communication, which does not exist in the townships. Though by no means all white employers allow their employees access to their telephones, there are public call boxes and times when employers are out and the employee can use the telephone. The phone mitigates against much of the isolation of 'white' areas and allows individuals to keep up contacts with both kin and friends despite distance and lack of free time.

Nomusa differs from many resident servants in that she does not belong to any clubs or even cliques of women who share the same interests and which meet regularly in City North or elsewhere in Durban. Women who do belong to these groups spend much of their free time in a relatively organized manner with a specific group of people. Moves by whites involved in a national literacy campaign have resulted in the establishment of local literacy groups for blacks in 'white' areas. Resident domestic servants are trained and then financed to run their own classes. Most clubs and cliques have a religious base (Brandel-Syrier 1962). On Thursday afternoon, a popular 'day off' amongst servants, scores of women in distinctive uniforms can be seen going to the *Manyano* or mothers' union meetings. Members of some denominations gather in the rooms of members in the evenings. Though different in organization, very similar in character are prayer circles which consist of ardent churchgoers who find it difficult to visit their own denominations during the week but feel the need for regular common prayer. It is not unusual to find members of different denominations gathered together for scripture reading or healing in each other's rooms. Each woman wears her church uniform but is joined to her fellows in common Christian faith. An important aspect of the activities of these groups is praying for the sick and in many cases one or two of the members may be believed to have special powers of healing. Healing is highly developed also in separatist sects which abound in the urban area (Sundkler 1948). At one time a woman belonging to one of these sects moved into a job in the neighbourhood where Nomusa worked. The woman soon gathered around her at least four of the nearby servants who then met regularly in her room for prayer. As the main services of the sect were held in KwaMashu, this local healing group served to introduce its members to the township to which they travelled as a group on Saturday nights. In such a way local involvements in the 'white' city may spill over into township contacts.

Local prayer and healing groups serve important functions within the local Black community in 'white' suburbs. When members are ill or in trouble the group visits them in order to pray but at the same time brings moral and emotional support to the sufferer. Members may also bring food and clothing if the patient is confined to his or her room. Messages are taken to kin and other friends and the group may also hold a collection if there are expenses involved which the needy person cannot meet. Persons who do not belong to prayer groups often summon them when they are ill and so benefit also from their practical assistance. Crises such as the death of a close relative invariably set in motion visits from these Christian associations, for the news spreads quickly on the local grapevine. Prayer group members also visit newcomers to the neighbourhood and try to draw them into their circle. For a person who has no previous contacts in the area, this is one way of becoming integrated into the community. These groups serve thus as informal welfare and mutual assistance agencies and combat potential Black isolation in 'white' areas (Preston-Whyte 1968). The fact that their membership is fluid, for individuals come and go with the vicissitudes of employment and personal needs and crises, may appear to militate against their effectiveness. These groups do, however, exist over time and in most cases are held together by one or two of the older Black residents, who provide some continuity and who come to fill pivotal positions in the fluid sub-cultural milieu of the local Black community.

Yet another type of clique is typical of City North. This consists of the people Nomusa refers to as 'drinkers' – both men and women who regularly visit the rooms of women known to brew and sell intoxicating beverages. It is important to realize that clients gain a good deal more than mere liquor from their visits to the shebeen. Conviviality characterizes the atmosphere and attracts many people who would otherwise remain alone in their rooms. The problem of loneliness is a major one for many Blacks living in 'white' areas. Nomusa's diary had in it entries such as 'I returned lonely to my room', or 'I remained alone in my room as Esther's husband was visiting her. It was lonely'.

Prayer groups, drinking cliques and even the gangs of young male domestic servants, though very different in nature, have in common the fact that they serve a local community for which no formal facilities exist for meeting other people, relaxing in company, communal worship or recreation, and one which is largely isolated by distance and lack of transport from the centres of Black social life. Though the gangs prey upon the law-abiding and the shebeens often turn into rough-houses, they must be seen as informal attempts at communal life. The young men who join the gangs are often intimidated into doing so, but once members, they are amongst friends; they have something to do with their evenings and when in dire need may be helped by other gang members. Ganglife is also a way of making money. Dagga running and stealing prove lucrative in the face of low wages. Newcomers to the neighbourhood are integrated into the community by gang membership and soon develop local *esprit de corps*. Another factor common to prayer circles and gangs is their small size. Though both may form part of wider institutional structures, the number of people who are together at any one time is small – say three to four as a rule, and five at the outside. As was suggested above, groups larger than this tend to draw the attention of whites. Their restricted size means that even within associations, local social relations are intimate and small scale. Members get to know each other well and rely essentially on personal face-to-face contacts to fulfil their social needs.

A general feature of the interaction between the Black servants living in a white neighbourhood is the sense of sympathy and comradeship. Though age and sex differences impose restraints between individuals, and men and women filling positions of leadership in associations or cliques may be accorded respect and deference, most social relations are those appropriate between equals, or at least between people in the same social category. This is thrown into relief when inter-Black relations in the area are compared with those between Black and white, which are invariably characterized by inequality and social distance. Despite the fact that servants work long hours in white homes and are in potentially close and intimate contact with whites, the framework of the master–servant relationship prevents complete sympathy and freedom of interaction. In the South African situation the employer is always the dominant figure in the relationship by virtue not only of his or her position as employer, but also of colour. Thus even where actual day-to-day interaction appears informal and close, it is clearly between superior and inferior (Preston-Whyte 1976). Friendliness and help offered to servants is indicative of a paternalistic relationship and not one of comradeship and equality.

Resident servants are frequently assisted in the material sense by their employers. Whites teach their servants skills, they lend them money on occasion, and may pay doctors' bills and other medical expenses. Some employers intercede with municipal authorities on their employees' behalf, helping them, for instance, to be allocated houses in the townships. In some cases servants are given extended leave to attend to personal affairs and crises. On the whole, however, help is extended so long as the employers' personal interests are not jeopardized or domestic efficiency disrupted for too long. Since there is no formal domestic service contract, employers often expect gratitude for help and leave which workers in other fields would be able to take for granted. Many servants are reluctant to ask for this help because they do not like to feel beholden to their employers. They choose rather to rely on kin and friends, or even to leave their employment and seek a new job when they have dealt with the crisis. Employees who are dependent on their jobs for the right to remain in town are afraid to take their employers into their confidence over crises, lest the whites dismiss them rather than extend help to them. Because neither employer nor employee is provided with fixed guidelines for behaviour in domestic service uncertainty, misconceptions, confusions and misunderstandings abound. Employers complain of the 'fecklessness', 'lack of gratitude' and 'unreliability' of servants and the employees speak of the harsh and unsympathetic decisions of white employers. These stereotypes in themselves militate against sympathetic interaction.

It is the paternalism of resident service that is most disliked by many Blacks. This is emphasized by the accommodation in often inferior outhouses, their uniform of overalls and, for women, a matching *doek* (Afrikaans for a scarf tied around the neck), and by the fact that the children of their employers not only call them by their first names, but, regardless of their age, refer to them and their friends as 'boy' and 'girl'. Much of the help

and sympathy offered, therefore, by whites to their Black servants, is
assessed by the recipients within a relationship of superiority and inferiority.
Because it is given in a spirit of charity and paternalism rather than as a
formal right, this help is often interpreted as underlining the inequality of
Black and white in South Africa.

Racial and employment factors overlap and, therefore, emphasize the difference between Blacks and whites living in 'white' residential areas. Whites
who see and meet Blacks on the streets immediately think of and treat them
as servants. They call them by their first names and consider them interlopers
if they are making a noise or creating a disturbance. Two distinct communities, one white and one Black, exist side by side in areas such as City
North. Black and white meet in the employment situation and though
Blacks get to know a great deal about the white community from working in
white homes, whites know little or nothing about the black community
which lives around them. Nomusa underlined this fact by pointing out that
her employers had no knowledge of the existence of the gangs which harass
Blacks in City North. Though individual employers may know a fair
amount about their own employees, few see them as part of a community
which shares their immediate social environment. Like most white South
Africans, employers of resident servants think of Blacks as residentially
separate and socially and culturally different to themselves and, despite the
realities of their own domestic situation, subscribe to, and indeed live by and
propagate, the myth of apartheid.

We turn now to consider the problems which residential separation imposes on servants who do not live on the premises of their employers.

Case two: a non-resident servant   Mrs Augustah M. is a widow of about
50 years of age. She lives in a welfare house at KwaMashu with her two
school-going sons and an elder unmarried daughter who is at present working as a resident servant in Durban. Mrs M. has a non-resident domestic job
in one of the central Durban suburbs where she works from 7.30 a.m. to
4.30 p.m. for an elderly white couple. She has been in the same employment
for some 12–15 years and was at one time living on the premises while her
children stayed with her parents in the country. After her father's death some
five years previously she was forced to bring her children to Durban. Mrs M.
was fortunate in being granted a temporary house in the township and also in
that her employers were willing for her to begin living out. When she had
worked for her employers for 10 years she was granted permanent urban
residential rights.

The day begins for the M. family at about 5 a.m. when Mrs M. rises,
makes tea and leaves the house in time to walk to the station and join the long
queues waiting for the morning trains for Durban. She reaches the city about
6.45 a.m. and then takes the 7 a.m. feeder bus to her employer's premises,
arriving just before 7.30 a.m. Her sons, meanwhile, get themselves dressed

and leave for their township school at about 7 a.m. They must get their own food when they return from school, as Mrs M. is seldom home before 6 p.m., despite the fact that she leaves her employment at 4.30 p.m. Five o'clock in the evening is one of the busiest times of the day, for most people are returning to the townships and delays on the train lines are frequent. On occasions Mrs M. visits a neighbour, or her sister who lives in another part of KwaMashu, on her way home, and in these cases may not reach her own house before 7 or 8 p.m. Since there are no telephones in the townships, personal visits must be made whenever township dwellers have matters of common interest to discuss or plans to make.

Thus, though Mrs M. does not work as long hours as Nomusa she has, on the whole, even less 'free time' during the week. Commuting to and from work takes about four hours per day. It is only on Saturdays, when she works a half day and on Sundays, when she does not go to work, that she has time to devote to her own family and friends. On Sunday morning she attends church services, the Sect to which she belongs meeting on alternate Sundays in KwaMashu and Umlazi. Though she always attends the KwaMashu meeting she is less regular in travelling to the other township for, as she says, 'the journey is long and I get so tired of travelling'. Sect meetings are held in KwaMashu during weekday evenings, but Mrs M. invariably feels unable to attend these, as they continue until 11 p.m. or 12 midnight and she has to be up early each morning.

One facet of Mrs M.'s activities which cannot be ignored is her attempts to earn money over and above her wage of R20 per month. When asked what she did in her free time she replied 'I go to church and I make money!' One of her ways of doing the latter is to make suet porridge each day on her employer's stove and sell it to workmen and builders employed on construction sites in the vicinity of her employment. Another is to purchase fruit, vegetables and meat at the Durban market on her way to work and to sell these to her township neighbours on her return in the evening. Over weekends her children help in money making by hawking small cakes and oranges, which Mrs M. has bought in town, round soccer matches and other large gatherings in the townships. In all these ways Mrs M. estimates that she makes about R15 per month. Her success in this field is related to the lack of organized catering facilities for Blacks, both in Durban and in the townships. Many township women amass large incomes from illegal sources such as brewing, or the black market trade in stolen goods, but Mrs M. feels that her responsibility as sole supporter and guardian of her children make these undertakings risky.

The long hours which Mrs M. spends in commuting during the week are not, from a personal point of view, completely wasted. When discussing her personal relations she mentioned with enthusiasm meetings she had with other passengers on the trains. She has regular 'train-friends' who meet each morning and, if possible, each evening at the station and sit together in the same coach. They chat, knit or sew while the journey is in progress and walk together part of the way home from the station. Train-friends get to know a good deal about each other and about their respective families and problems. They assist each other in preparing food for parties and celebrations, which always strain both the time and pocket of domestic servants. When Mrs M. was preparing a visit to her rural home, her three train-friends each gave her a small gift of money to help her meet her expenses. Train-friends also provide something of a protection on the daily journey to and from Durban. The trains are not only crowded, but are filled with people unknown to travellers, some of whom may be pickpockets. Women who travel together regularly can trust each other and so relax. Company on the walk home through the dark township streets is an invaluable guard against attacks and muggings. Should a train-friend not appear on time at the station, her companions will keep her a seat and if she misses one or two journeys, will investigate by visiting her home; if she is ill or in need, they may provide the spearhead of help and succour. In this we have yet another example of an informal association which provides companionship, potential help and security and one, furthermore, which has arisen from the otherwise negative aspect of long daily commuter trips between Black and white residential areas.

Commuting means that non-resident employees like Mrs M. bridge the Black and white sectors of Durban. Figure 9.2, which plots Mrs M,'s movements during one month, presents a strikingly different picture to the one of isolation in the 'white' city given in the case of Nomusa, the resident servant in Figure 9.1. Corresponding with the wider geographical and social spread of the commuting pattern was a wider field of significant social contacts. Mrs M. notes meeting 16 persons during the month whom she regarded as important members of her social circle or social network (Bott 1957). Nomusa noted only eight. Another difference in the patterning of the social relations of the two women lies in the separation within Mrs M.'s network of distinct subsections, her KwaMashu contacts and neighbours, her train-friends, church-friends, and kin. Nomusa distinguishes only her City North contacts and her kin and in her case there was some overlap between the two subgroups, for her kin got to know her good neighbourhood friends when they visited her on her premises. In Mrs M.'s case her interactions with each 'set' were kept largely separate, the only overlap occurring between KwaMashu neighbours and church-friends. This is, of course, characteristic of the pattern of social relations which surrounds people who are highly mobile, who are drawn into various separate ambits of experience and who themselves form the dominant and possibly the only link between the different areas of social life. Resident domestic servants, because they live in 'white' areas, are often more limited in their social field.

Women who come into the white home each day and who leave the premises at night for townships are in a very different category from resident

THE WHITE CITY / KWAMASHU TOWNSHIP																															
Day of the Month	1	2	3	4	5	6	7	8	9	10	11	12	13	14	15	16	17	18	19	20	21	22	23	24	25	26	27	28	29	30	31
Day of the Week	Sun	Mon	Tue	Wed	Thu	Fri	Sat	Sun	Mon	Tue	Wed	Thu	Fri	Sat	Sun	Mon	Tue	Wed	Thu	Fri	Sat	Sun	Mon	Tue	Wed	Thu	Fri	Sat	Sun	Mon	Tue	
KWAMASHU CONTACTS Mr.N–	X										Moved into house as lodger →																					
Mrs.P–		X	X			X					X						X					X				X			X			10
Mr.M–				X	X																											2
Mr.Mn–					X																											1
Isaac P–								X																								1
Mrs.Mg–																	X															1
Mr.Mg–																		X														1
TRAIN FRIENDS Mrs.Ng–			X	X	X	X		X		X	X		X	X	X		X	X		X	X	X		X	X		X	X		X		20
Mrs.Ma–			X	X	X	X	X	X		X	X	X	X	X	X		X	X	X				X	X	X	X	X	X		X	X	23
Mrs.Mo–			X		X	X	X	X		X	X	X	X	X		X	X	X	X	X	X		X	X		X	X	X		X	X	23
CHURCH FRIENDS Mrs.Md–	X							X											X			X										4
Mrs.Mh–	X							X							X							X							X			5
Rev.N–								X							X							X							X			4
KIN IN DURBAN Esther M–.(sister)								X																								1
Mr.D–.(clansman)												X																				1
Elijah M–. (brothers son)																									X							1
KIN VISITING FROM FARM Mrs. Martha T–. (sister)												X																				1

Figure 9.2 Case two: a non-resident domestic servant. Spatial and social distribution of Mrs M.'s leisure time during one month (see note to Fig. 9.1).

employees. Their township base assures them of an independence denied to women who have no home in the city other than a succession of employers' premises. Mrs M. regards herself as a resident of Durban in the legal and emotional sense and her right to be in the city reduces the paternalistic aspect of her employment as a servant. She could at any time stop working and yet remain in Durban. Their residential independence affects the way in which many non-resident servants treat their employers and is at the base of comment by whites that township 'girls' are 'cheeky' and 'don't care how they behave'. In addition, township women often come to the premises dressed in smart up-to-date western clothes. Though they may don the overall or apron while working, their personae as ordinary citizens of Durban are marked by the clothing which their employers cannot help noticing and often openly ridicule and criticize. Resident servants who come on duty in their uniforms are less often seen by whites in their own clothing.

Most whites are unaware of any real difference between relationships with resident and non-resident servants. To them non-resident servants seem less demanding in that they come and go speedily and seldom involve their employers in protracted personal problems. On the other hand their demeanour may provide a subtle threat to the *status quo* of superior and inferior. From the servants' point of view the job is merely an exercise in money making which, apart from the time it demands, does not dominate their life and social relations. It is resident domestic service which encompasses and envelops the employee in the essentially paternalistic role of a non-person in a 'white' area.

Conclusions

The case of Black domestic servants who work and live in the 'white' suburbs of Durban highlights some of the conflicts and problems inherent in the South African system of residential separation. It has drawn attention, however, to the ingenuity of Black social and cultural responses to living in areas set aside for race groups other than their own. Of major importance is the finding that because Blacks reject the paternalism inherent in the situation of resident domestic service many workers prefer, despite the many inconveniences involved, to live in the townships and commute to work in the 'white' areas each day. Paradoxically it is the implementation of residential segregation which has provided non-resident employees with the independence and personal freedom denied to Black servants who live on the premises of their white employers.

Acknowledgements

This chapter is a revised version of a paper which originally appeared in Akeroyd, A. V. and C. R. Hill (eds) 1979. *Southern African research in progress: collected papers*, 4. York: University of York, Centre for Southern African Studies. The study on which this chapter is based was financed by a grant from the South African National Council for Social Research. The author is, however, solely responsible for all ideas expressed in the text.

10 Council housing for low-income Indian families in Durban: objectives, strategies and effects

PETER CORBETT

Housing is vital to man in its more fundamental aspects, and important as a consumer good to the more affluent. Housing being essentially non–homogeneous, consisting of several attributes (space, quality, location, etc.), it is difficult for a family to maximise satisfaction if a sufficient range of choice is not available (see Evans 1973, Muth 1969, and King 1976 for a comprehensive exposition of housing choice theory). Because of the importance of housing, government often becomes involved, either to compensate for externalities or as a welfare measure to improve living standards for low-income families. The extent of government intervention varies according to the political structure and wealth of each country.

In many countries, government assistance is given to enable low-income families to obtain better housing which meets some minimum standards. These standards vary from, for example, one person per room in wealthy countries to a three per room maximum as suggested by the United Nations (nd). The strategies to achieve these minimum standards also differ considerably, as regards ownership or renting, using market forces or direct intervention, and so on. The objective is normally to improve the standard of living of low-income families.

South Africa has a fundamentally capitalist economy. Nevertheless central and local government have for many years intervened in the housing market, presumably having believed that market forces produce the wrong results. As a consequence, they have instituted a complex system of rent controls, subsidies on certain housing and detailed building and planning regulations. They have also attempted to achieve complete residential segregation of the various race groups by legislative means. At the same time the authorities have become involved in large-scale housing projects for low–income families, with rentals subsidized, sometimes substantially, by the state.

The objectives of housing policy in South Africa are of great interest, including as they do, economic, social and political aspects. Strategies are complex too, and cannot be understood without reference to the objectives.

In this chapter the subject matter is housing policies as they affect low-income Indian families in Durban and, in particular, mass housing schemes by the local authority, the Durban City Council. For over 20 years Indian housing in Durban has been controversial, with currently the signs of a mass revolt against the existing level of rentals in housing schemes. The seemingly strange phenomenon of families rejecting policies which should have been aimed at helping them can only be understood by examining the historical objectives of housing policy in Durban, together with the strategies adopted and the effects on the families concerned.

Policy objectives for Indian housing in Durban

The formulation of housing objectives requires, first, the specification of minimum standards, and secondly, the identification of families needing assistance to achieve those standards. The assumption is made here that in capitalist countries, benevolence is the principle motive in providing housing for the poor. The view that it is a capitalist ploy to ensure an adequate and docile labour force is, in the author's view, cynical and misconceives the nature of democratic governments. It is, therefore, important to ensure that the net effect of the policies is to improve the general level of welfare of the families concerned. Where families are free to choose to accept state-providing housing, then welfare must be improved, but where there is compulsion through rezoning, urban renewal schemes, or other causes, the possibility arises that net welfare improvements will not arise. The argument developed in this section is that in Durban the objectives of housing policy have not been entirely, or even predominantly, to create a net welfare benefit for low-income families. Rather, the achieving of total residential segregation for the benefit of prejudiced whites has been a major policy influence. Whether or not a net benefit has, incidentally, been created for the Indian families affected is, therefore, something to consider.

Two facts are important in examining the history of Indian housing policy in Durban. First, political power has always effectively been monopolized by whites, with the franchise denied to Indians at any level. Thus, a group of predominantly low-income families, equal in size to the white group, has been denied the opportunity to show disagreement with housing policies through the ballot box. Secondly, the bulk of rehousing which has taken place has not been by choice. Principally, this compulsory factor was dominated by moves to segregate geographically Indian from white housing, with town planning considerations such as rezoning or highway development also sometimes important.

In Durban the question of residential segregation of whites and Indians was contentious long before central government introduced the Group Areas Act in 1950 (see Maasdorp & Pillay 1977 for a detailed history of this issue). From the late 19th century, pressure was brought on central government to legislate against property acquisition by Indians. Following Union in 1910, anti-Indian sentiments increased: there were abortive attempts to introduce legislation to enforce residential segregation in the 1920s, restrictive clauses were introduced into sales of land by the town council to prevent sales to Indians, and finally, following 'penetration' by Indians into hitherto white areas, the 'Pegging Act' was passed in 1943 freezing the position for three years. In 1946 the 'Ghetto Act' effectively prevented any further integration of residential areas between Indians and whites. At the time the National Party came to power in 1948, Durban had a few central suburbs racially mixed and the city as a whole was a patchwork quilt of Indian areas intermingled with predominantly white areas. The Group Areas Act set out to reverse such integration of residential areas as had taken place, and to 'plan' urban areas so as to achieve the greatest degree of racial separation possible. In Durban this policy required wholesale removals of Indian families from centrally situated locations to the periphery and, since Indians were generally low-income earners, this reversed the pattern predicted by residential location theory and observed elsewhere. Removals on a large scale took place mainly between the early 1960s and the mid-1970s. When examining housing programmes in Durban, therefore, it is important to see them in relation to attitudes and policies concerning residential separation of Indians and whites at different times. The Indian and white populations during the periods concerned were roughly the same, so the size of the housing programmes for each group can be directly compared.

The Housing Act places the responsibility for providing housing for low-income families on the local authority. Between the early 1930s and the early 1960s the Durban City Council provided 2449 dwellings for whites and 3943 dwellings for Indians. Considering that average incomes of whites were some three times those of Indians who, generally speaking, had lower level jobs and lower incomes than whites, these figures are an indication that housing objectives were more concerned with assisting low-income whites than lower-income Indians.

A comparison of housing conditions between the two race groups also displays large differences. The number of occupants per room, which is a commonly used indicator of housing conditions, was calculated in 1943 to be 2.5 for Indians and 1.0 for whites (Department of Economics 1952, p. 87). Many Indian families lived in make-shift dwellings but for whites this was the exception. Clearly an ordering of priorities which aimed to improve conditions for the worst housed would have caused the municipality to concentrate on accommodating Indian families in much greater numbers before building houses and flats for relatively well off whites.

In 1962 work was commenced on the construction of Chatsworth, a suburb on the southwestern periphery of Durban (Fig. 8.1, p. 145). By the mid-1970s just over 20 000 dwellings had been constructed there for Indians, while during the same period only about 2000 dwellings had been added to the council housing stock for whites. However, when consideration is given to the parallel loss of dwellings owned by Indians disqualified from living in them by the Group Areas Act, a change of heart by the authorities seems unlikely. Accurate data on the number of dwellings lost in this way is not available but it is likely to have cancelled out a large proportion of the new housing at Chatsworth. The argument in defence is usually that those moved were living in unacceptable slums, and that rehousing them at Chatsworth was necessary and commendable. However, many disqualified dwellings were substantial and certainly not slums. Others were certainly less substantial but no worse or better than similar dwellings in areas not affected by the Group Areas Act which were not touched. Finally, no effort was made to redevelop those existing Indian areas so as to maintain housing locations, as chosen, near to job opportunities.

The finance for the construction of Chatsworth came, as do virtually all funds for local authority housing, from central government and had never before been available in such amounts. The National Housing Fund obtains its funds from Parliament and is administered by the National Housing Commission and the Department of Community Development (DOCD). Loans from the fund require approval of the DOCD and are usually at subsidized interest rates according to individual incomes. All in all, there are reasonable grounds for the hypothesis that Chatsworth is a monument to the Group Areas Act, not to any change of priorities by local government.

The period following the completion of Chatsworth has seen the planning of Phoenix, on the northern periphery of Durban and Newlands West to the north-west (Fig. 8.1, p. 145). Phoenix to date already has some 8000 dwellings and will contain, if completed as planned by 1985, about 28 000 dwellings. Newlands West will commence in 1982 and, by completion in 1986, will contain about 9000 dwellings. At the same time, the volume of the Group Areas Act removals has slowed to a trickle, although any decision to move Indians out of flats in the Grey Street (CBD) area will give a spurt to the programme. Most housing so far provided at Phoenix has been used for Group Areas Act removals (30 per cent) and priority cases such as slum clearances, rezoning plans, freeway developments, etc. From now on it is likely that the bulk will go to ordinary applicants, most of whom have been on the waiting list for between one and 12 years. Virtually no dwellings for whites have been provided since the mid-1970s. However, until late 1980 the housing situation for whites was of oversupply generally with many council flats standing empty in the less popular schemes. By early 1981 the shortage of low-cost accommodation for whites had led to calls for a suitable housing programme to be implemented. In March 1981 the Indian waiting list contained just over 17 000 names. That for whites contained 75 names.

It appears as if the objectives of one or both of central government and the Durban City Council have changed since the completion of Chatsworth.

With the virtual completion of Group Areas Act removals, the objective which created Chatsworth has fallen away. Logically it seems that concern for low-income Indian housing is now the priority and the possible reasons for this warrant discussion. First, the process of economic growth in South Africa has made available more resources for government use. The accompanying growth in incomes of Indian families has also made possible the provision by the authorities of reasonable quality housing at rents which some families can afford (particularly as government subsidization of interest rates has increased for the lowest-income groups). Secondly, the Durban City Council has obtained far greater allocations of capital funds from central government than in the past, except where Chatsworth was concerned. This probably indicates the allocation of a higher priority by central government to Indian housing. Thirdly, a momentum has been achieved and a 'housing machine' created at local government level which is easier to maintain than to stop or change direction. It is interesting to note the determination with which civic officials fight to preserve 'the building programme'. Finally, political attitudes of the Durban City Council, together with those of most public representatives in South Africa, have changed subtly to one where moral responsibility to uplift the non-white populations in all areas, including housing, is broadly accepted. The majority are still essentially paternalistic, although probably close to half of the current city council would approve of direct and equal representation by non-whites on the council if permitted by central government.

In conclusion then, it has been suggested in the above discussion that objectives behind the provision of housing schemes for Indians today are similar to those of governments anywhere, in other words motivated by considerations of equity, whereas in the recent past they have been primarily concerned with racial separation.

Policy strategies for Indian housing in Durban

Strategies adopted   During the period between 1932, when the borough was expanded to include for the first time extensive areas occupied by Indians, and 1962 when Chatsworth was started, three surveys of Indian housing were undertaken. These were the censuses of 1936 and 1960 and a study by the University of Natal in 1942–43 (Department of Economics 1952). Housing conditions generally were found to be poor, with the majority of the population living in small shacks often without adequate water supply, sanitation or lighting. Density of occupancy was high. The university study estimated that only 24.8 per cent of the Indian population lived in 'reasonably satisfactory dwellings'. Incomes were, as could be expected, low and explained the inability of the Indian population to house themselves adequately relative to white standards. No significant improvement was observed between 1936 and 1960. Recent developments in housing theory question the accepted wisdom of then and (in the minds of many decision and policy makers) now that such dwellings are in fact 'slums' (see Maasdorp 1977). A more realistic judgement is that they perform adequately in a warm climate the primary functions of housing, which is protection and family privacy. As with other commodities purchased by poor families, this housing incorporated few elements of luxury or comfort. At the same time there is much evidence that Indian and white housing aspirations are similar. Private sector developments for higher income Indian families and the improvements and extensions to many of the housing scheme dwellings at Chatsworth illustrate this.

Housing strategies formulated according to modern principles would have assisted low-income families to obtain housing of the best kind possible to suit their incomes. Its central elements would have been:

(a) to create conditions where security of tenure is guaranteed;
(b) to ensure that basic facilities such as clean water, refuse and sewage removal and street lighting are provided;
(c) to provide in the initial planning for eventual improvement of each area to take place as the standard of living there rises;
(d) to make available advice and loans to facilitate the upgrading of homes as desired;
(e) to have constructed housing schemes where a demand for such accommodation existed.

Even with implementation of the Group Areas Act (which the author totally opposes) the appropriate policy would have been to provide conditions whereby relocated families could have been rehoused according to choice with a wide range of options to suit individual circumstances. Choice of location was necessarily removed by this Act, but choice of housing standards need not have been.

The housing strategies adopted have been very different from the above. For the last 20 years, the city council has mass produced modest but solid and conventional houses and low-rise flats. Some of these have been rented to tenants and others have been sold to the occupants with income-related subsidies from central government on rents and, since 1980, on purchase repayments. They have been sited on adequate sized plots with full services of water-borne sewerage, reticulated water to individual dwellings, bath or shower and toilet to each, electrical lights and power points in each room, paved roads, street lighting, underground stormwater disposal, parks, sportsfields, clinics, libraries, swimming pools and so on. Priority has been given first to Group Areas Act removals, followed by slum and shack clearance cases. All new dwellings elsewhere in Durban and extensions of scheme dwellings have had to comply with the city's building by-laws, which prevent any departure from high quality, conventional materials or methods of construction. Thus, the range of choice has been highly restricted and the existing stock of informal or lower standard dwellings has been reduced by administrative action. Effectively, the choice for Indian families needing housing has been between:

(a) high quality houses or flats built by private builders, similar in type and cost to housing in newer white areas;
(b) council houses or flats in mass housing schemes at lower, but still high, costs relative to incomes;
(c) sharing existing dwellings or renting garages or outbuildings while waiting either for a council dwelling to become available or until family income is higher;
(d) moving to informal housing areas outside the city in the few places where such possibilities exist and where tenure is insecure and services poor.

Two questions need to be answered with regard to what seems a history of policies which have not been based on welfare criteria. What are the effects, short and long term, of adopting these policies? Why were these decisions made and what might prevent changes being made in current and future policies?

Effects of past housing policies   In attempting to analyse the effects of past policies, two problems arise. First, there is the problem of separating the effects of objectives from those of strategies. Resentment and reluctant acceptance of council housing can result from any kind of compulsory move, but particularly where racial discrimination, rather than a policy of housing improvement or normal town planning requirements, is the objective. In addition, strategies which produce housing which is too expensive, unless it is the family's freely made choice, is bound to create antagonism at the ensuing impoverishment. Recently this latent antagonism and resentment has manifested itself in protests against rental increases. Although it is clear that political activists used this particular irritant for broader ends, they could only do so because a problem exists.

The second problem is to distinguish between short- and long-term social and economic effects. Family incomes grow and circumstances change. The real burden of rents or repayments diminishes since the capital charges element does not rise with inflation. Anger is blunted, for many, by time and increasing age, and social structures and community spirit regenerate themselves eventually. In the case of Durban, Chatsworth can be taken to represent the medium- to long-term effects since dwellings there have been occupied for between six and 19 years. Phoenix represents short-term effects since the first dwellings are only some five years old, with most families having been there for about two or three years. Although the evidence is far from complete, it seems useful to decide whether short-term effects differ from the long-term since policy makers actually state that the long-term benefits outweigh short-term costs.

Chatsworth   The author conducted a survey to collect data on housing conditions at Chatsworth in 1977 (Corbett 1980). A random sample of 663 dwellings was surveyed by a team of female Indian fieldworkers. At that time, rentals in Chatsworth were roughly half those charged for equivalent housing at Phoenix. This results from several years of inflation in building costs. Most other costs included in rentals (rates, administration, etc.) would generally be the same for old and new schemes. Nevertheless many households are poor and would be poorer still if they were to pay rentals (or repayments where they are purchasers) at current replacement costs.

Table 10.1 describes the proportion of sample households in poverty

Table 10.1   Poverty in Chatsworth, April 1977: percentages of sample.

Amount by which monthly income differs from PCPI[2]	Total		Subeconomic[1] PCPI			Economic[1] PCPI		
	PCPI (1)	PCPI (adjusted) (2)	actual (3)	current (4)	zero (5)	actual (6)	current (7)	zero (8)
Below −R19	2.3	8.0	1.6	1.6	0.8	2.6	3.2	1.6
−R19 to −R10	3.6	17.3	6.1	10.6	2.4	2.4	4.8	2.0
−R9 to 0	15.3	25.6	27.6	28.5	26.4	9.2	14.6	6.6
sub total	21.2	50.9	35.4	40.7	29.7	14.2	22.6	10.2
R1 to R10	23.2	16.3	26.0	26.0	27.2	21.8	22.4	15.1
R11 to R20	18.2	12.0	16.7	14.2	17.5	19.0	17.0	19.9
R21 to R30	12.9	7.9	11.8	10.2	13.8	13.3	12.4	16.5
R31 to R40	8.5	4.3	4.1	2.8	4.5	10.7	8.3	10.9
over R40	16.0	8.6	6.0	6.1	7.3	21.0	17.3	27.4
total	100.0	100.0	100.0	100.0	100.0	100.0	100.0	100.0

Source: Corbett (1980).

[1] Subeconomic dwellings are of cheaper construction than economic dwellings, are more heavily subsidized, and are occupied by lower-income households. Of the total sample of 663 dwellings, 227 were subeconomic and 436 economic.

[2] PCPI = Per Capita Poverty Indicator, see text for explanation.

according to different definitions and rental levels. Poverty is measured, first, in absolute terms by a Per Capita Poverty Indicator (PCPI), which is calculated by subtracting the minimum amount required for a household to exist from household monthly income and dividing this by the household size. (The basis for this calculation is the Household Subsistence Level (HSL) as published periodically by the Bureau of Market Research at the University of South Africa.) This is shown in column (1). By this criterion 21.2 per cent of households do not have sufficient income to meet minimum living standards and a further 23.2 per cent are not more than R10 per head per month above this level. It has been observed elsewhere that only when income exceeds the theoretical minimum by 50 per cent is sufficient actually spent on the essentials (see Ellison *et al*. 1975 for a comprehensive bibliography and discussion of work in this field in South Africa). Therefore, in column (2), the PCPI is adjusted by taking 150 per cent of minimum expenditure from monthly income. The resulting figures suggest that 50.9 per cent of households in Chatsworth spend less on food and other essentials than is necessary.

In columns (3) to (8) the unadjusted PCPI is used to calculate the degree of poverty at different rental levels. In addition, the sample is divided between subeconomic households who rent dwellings and who are subsidized by central government to some 50 per cent of rentals, and economic households where the residents mainly have purchased the dwellings and are not subsidized. First, the proportion in poverty at actual rentals or repayments is shown in columns (3) and (6), then estimates of rentals at replacement cost levels in columns (4) and (7), and finally, if zero rentals were paid, in columns (5) and (8).

Considering the negligible rentals paid in informal housing, the difference between zero and current rentals or repayments shows the effects of forced removals as they might have been originally, except in the cases where earlier rentals were substantial. It also illustrates the benefit which could be gained were the inhabitants currently allowed the alternative of informal housing. In the economic dwellings, where no subsidies are paid, the proportion in poverty jumps from 10.2 per cent at zero repayment to 22.6 per cent if replacement values are used. Because of inflation the proportion in poverty at actual repayment levels is only 14.2 per cent. For subeconomic dwellings the effect is less striking, probably because of the subsidies given by the government.

The effect of current policies on living standards is clearly illustrated by the above. In addition to the effect of the type of housing and its cost, the distance from workplace also affects living standards, through travel costs. The survey showed that nearly half of the workers in the sample spend more than 90 minutes per day travelling. This follows directly from the peripheral location of Chatsworth, whereas most jobs are in the CBD and adjoining areas (Fig. 8.1, p. 145). Over a third of the sample work in or near the CBD. Residential location theory predicts that low-income families will locate near to the breadwinner's workplace. Where this is not permitted there must be some impact on living standards and housing satisfaction, although measurement and quantification is not possible from the data collected.

The theory of utility maximization, assuming diminishing marginal utility, can be used to predict that if you force a family to 'buy' housing space of a minimum quality and quantity which will cause impoverishment, then some sub-letting will take place. Common sense also tells you that if you force a man to buy more of something than he wants, then he will resell some of it, if possible, in order to buy more of things he would prefer. In housing, reselling is achieved through sub-letting. Also where a severe housing shortage exists, doubling-up will occur. However, the two effects are not easily separable. In Chatsworth two phenomena exist which support either or both of the above hypothesis. First, there is considerable sharing, with 663 sample dwellings housing 752 households or 943 nuclear families. Secondly, some 12 per cent of the purchased dwellings (432 of the sample of 663) have outbuildings added and the majority (90 per cent) of these are partly or fully occupied despite this being illegal. Many other dwellings have outbuildings under construction since the process is often slow, depending as it does on spare cash (loan finance seldom being available or used). For many of these cases, the objective is to let the outbuildings to help pay for the original house. For others, it is to help solve the housing shortage for low-income relatives, e.g. retired parents. If these two factors were not present, then the proportion of families in poverty would be substantially higher.

As could be predicted, the incidence of sharing has led to some over-crowding, though not to the extent commonly believed. Some 26.6 per cent of households live at a density of one person per room or less, and a further 56.7 per cent at between one and two persons per room. Only 3.6 per cent experienced densities of three or more persons per room. For low-income families these densities are not remarkable. A local Slums Act definition of overcrowding states that in rooms used for sleeping, each adult equivalent (child equals half) should have 40 ft^2 (3.7 m^2) of floor area. On this criterion 51.1 per cent of dwellings have at least one room overcrowded, but when account is taken of rooms used purely for living purposes, which could be used to relieve this overcrowding, the percentage drops to a nominal figure. However, it seems that, given the desire of families to retain one or two rooms solely for living in, the size of dwellings is too small relative to the number of people, and thus overcrowding results. If families were allowed freedom of choice to build larger dwellings of lower standards, then less sharing would occur and, thus, there would be less overcrowding.

Finally, the effect on attitudes can be examined. Families were asked for their opinion of living in Chatsworth. Only 18.9 per cent said they dislike it, 40.0 per cent accept it, and the rest, 41.1 per cent, like it. Of course, sim-plistic questions and unqualified answers may hide as much as they reveal, but further questions on various aspects of the township did not reveal widespread dissatisfaction. The recent upsurge in protests and threatened rent boycotts in Coloured and Indian housing schemes also seems to have, so far, left Chatsworth untouched despite a higher proportion of families being there as the result of Group Areas Act removals. To isolate reasons for the apparent acceptance of or satisfaction with Chatsworth, is not attempted. But combinations of time, the growth of a community feeling, and rentals or repayments made less onerous by inflation probably accounts for most of it.

Medium- to long-term effects of past and current policies, therefore, seem small relative to attitudes. The Group Areas Act is still an object of hatred by Chatsworth residents but there seems to be acceptance of housing relative to what is alternatively available. Remaining resentment tends to show itself in criticism of the city council's administration of the scheme and demands for improved facilities, services and amenities. Although less so than originally, socio-economic effects are still detrimental to the families since rentals or purchase repayments are higher than in the informal sector to which most lower-income residents would probably belong by choice.

Phoenix   The survey did not include Phoenix and so family income figures are not available. Thus poverty comparisons cannot be made. There is, however, no reason to suppose that the population of Phoenix differs greatly in structure to that of Chatsworth. Therefore the higher level of rentals there is likely to be causing greater hardship than occurs in Chatsworth. Table 10.2

Table 10.2   Monthly income of applicants for Indian housing, March 1981.

monthly income (R)	0–150	151–250	251–350	351–450	over 450	total
No. of applicants	5856	6345	3402	1816	800	18219
Max. rent[1] affordable (R)	below 37.50	37.51–62.50	62.51–87.50	87.51–112.50	112.51 upwards	—

Source: Corbett (1980); data from City Treasurer's Department.
[1] At 25 per cent of applicants income.

indicates the incomes of applicants for housing at Phoenix who are currently on the waiting list. However, these figures are of limited value, first because in Chatsworth about two-thirds of families have two or more income recipients and this is presumably a representative picture. Secondly, income of the applicant is the basis for subsidization so that there is the possibility of false declarations or, in extended family households, the using of the lowest earner as the applicant. A certificate from each applicant's employer is required each year, but there is some evidence that firms collude with employees to state a low figure. The extent of this is not known but is unlikely to be a major distorting factor. The table also shows the range of maximum rentals affordable for each income category using the criterion of no more than 25 per cent of breadwinners income as rental. This is the criterion laid down by the Housing Code, although it is commonly held that for low-income families, this proportion is too high.

In Table 10.3, a selection of rentals for some of the newest dwellings erected at Phoenix is shown. These are not completely comparable with the Housing Code criterion as they include certain elements such as rates which should be excluded. The rentals in Table 10.3 differ for each income group as a result of the differential impact of subsidization – the highest figure, for

Table 10.3 Monthly rentals[3] for different types of dwelling at Phoenix by income category, March 1981[1].

		Monthly income (R)					
	Monthly rent (R):	0–150	151–250	251–350	351–450	451–650	651 plus
F3B	3 room flat	27.21–32.21[2]	63.04	77.31	89.53	102.74	118.52
F4B	4 room flat	31.94–36.94[2]	76.70	94.42	109.60	126.01	145.60
T5A	5 room terrace house	99.42	99.42	126.15	149.03	173.78	203.33
SD5B	5 room semi-detached house	98.66	98.66	125.40	148.31	173.07	202.64

Source: Corbett (1980); data from City Treasurer's Department.

[1] Latest contract awarded; [2] from R0–R150 the subsidy is on a sliding scale; [3] repayments where the houses are purchased are slightly lower.

incomes over R650 per month, is the full non-subsidized rental. A comparison of these rentals with those affordable shows that for applicants earning up to R450 per month, only flats can be occupied. Houses can only be afforded by those whose income exceeds R450 per month, of whom there are some 800 or 4.4 per cent of all applicants. However, the projected building programme over the next three years envisages the construction of 2968 flats and 15 490 houses. Although wages will rise with inflation, so will contract prices and, it therefore seems probable that, first, family incomes will have to be considerably higher than applicant incomes to take up the dwellings offered and, secondly, hardship will occur. Although inflation eventually reduces the overall real burden of rents, of which a major component is fixed, in the early years many tenants are pushed into poverty by their rental payments.

The short-term effects at Phoenix of current housing policies are, thus, likely to be impoverishment. The current (March 1981) rent boycott campaign is some evidence of this, although broader political objectives also intrude to cloud the issue.

Acceptance of housing at Phoenix seems less complete than at Chatsworth. No specific research has been done into this but the author's contacts with social workers and action group leaders in housing schemes strongly indicate a difference in attitude between Chatsworth and Phoenix. Factors responsible would include, first, resentment by those forced to move by official action, either for Group Areas Act reasons or others. Secondly, there are hardships caused by high rentals coupled with policies denying the appropriate range of housing choice for low-income families. Thirdly, there is the increasing politicization of the Indian community. The wrong policies contain, today, partly wrong objectives but, more important, wrong strategies. To improve matters both will need to change. Since Group Areas removals are largely completed, it seems that strategy changes are all that is left to the local authority to examine.

Policy improvements   Originally the objectives behind housing policies were partly to promote a racist ideology and were thus unacceptable to the Indian community. With Group Areas Act removals largely completed, this would no longer be so. Current housing objectives could reasonably be described as the creation of appropriate housing for low-income groups. Therefore the other element of policy – strategies – must be improved to obtain accept-ability and the intended effect. Strategies in the past have been to constrain low-income housing choice very narrowly. These could have arisen from a desire to justify Group Areas Act removals, or alternatively, from subjective opinions that the strategies were 'best for the Indians'. The description used by many decision-makers, even today, of modest shacks as 'filthy slums' supports this view. A senior Durban Corporation official informed the author that it was a disgrace that an item considering self-help housing should appear on a public agenda, as recently happened.

Policy improvements basically require a change in philosophy, from paternalism to one of recognition of the need for choice and of the fact of low incomes. The only other alternative would be subsidization of housing to a degree which is unlikely in practice. Even this would be second best as con-sumer utility would not be maximized. Doubtless, many poor families would prefer poorer housing but more money to spend on food or other necessities. The philosophy of choice at once leads to recognition that the range of options listed earlier should be extended by several actions:

(a) Densities in existing areas could be increased by permitting more dwellings on existing plots. The land is thus free, services are there, and often, no infrastructural improvements are necessary.
(b) Building standards acceptable for new houses or for extensions might be determined by local community option. If some areas did not collec-tively object to shacks or lower standard dwellings then this should be permitted, subject to minimal public health safeguards.

To implement such a programme would require the solution of numerous major and minor practical problems such as legislative changes at local level, approval of the state if National Housing Fund finance is to be available, the acquisition of suitable land, etc. In the meantime, a government commission is currently collecting evidence on the subject, which would solve many problems if the final report is favourable.

In the long run the major advantage to the makers of housing policy would be the removal of criticism that tenants are being impoverished. Those who chose not to move out to other, cheaper, alternatives could not then legitimately criticize rental policies. The most obvious benefit to the families concerned would be their ability to match housing expenditure to income without interference. A further benefit is rather more tenuous. For generations the Indian community managed to house themselves despite their very low average incomes. Pride of ownership, a desire to improve standards as incomes rose, and acceptance that where repairs, extra rooms or other improvements were needed self-help was the only answer, all made the Indian family ambitious and independent. Past policies have instead turned a substantial proportion of the population into a group who have no pride, no incentive to help themselves and who turn to the local authority for assistance whenever anything goes wrong. It is probably the saddest change brought about by ill conceived housing policies.

Conclusion

Indian housing objectives in the past, and strategies for the last 20 years, have not matched the ideals discussed earlier in this chapter. The results have been impoverishment and resentment. In almost every speech or newspaper article by Indians on socio-economic issues, the Group Areas Act and its relationship to housing matters comes up. Although no scientific research has been conducted, the author has no doubt that resentment there is – and in plenty! These are a direct consequence of attempting to maximize the utility of the controlling white voters. Earlier this involved residential segregation as a goal. Then and now, policy also involved the achievement of a minimum standard of housing.

In fairness the group whose objectives have been pursued should pay, instead of pushing the burden onto the target group. Therefore subsidization should take place, at a level which leaves Indian families no worse off in terms of what they spend on everything except housing than they were previously. This should also take into account increased transport costs. Since the Group Areas Act is a government responsibility, some subsidization should derive from that source. If the city council then adopted ideal policies within the constraints imposed by the Group Areas Act, then no obligation would arise for it to subsidize housing. However, the preceding discussion indicates that city council policies are not ideal, and thus, there are two directions which can be taken. Either policies remain the same and the city council subsidizes affected families, or policies are changed so that Indian families can choose the standard of housing they require.

The best way for both groups to achieve maximum utility would be for the city council to give freedom of choice, but to subsidize the housing which they regard as the minimum acceptable, up to the point where Indian families choose to take it voluntarily.

At present the government, for its part, is subsidizing rentals. The city

council is not voluntarily doing so, although it makes losses on some housing schemes because of the Housing Code regulations regarding rental
adjustments. It will be interesting to observe the direction taken resulting
from pressures currently being applied to the city council.

11 Government dispensation, capitalist imperative or liberal philanthropy? Responses to the Black housing crisis in South Africa

J. P. LEA

Several concessions towards the Black population of the townships were introduced by the South African government in the period following the Soweto uprising of 1976 (Hirsan 1979, Kane–Berman 1979a). Amongst them were relaxations in the controls over housing tenure and the adoption of hitherto forbidden self-help housing strategies for squatters and the homeless. These concessions, or 'dispensations' as they are termed locally, appear to represent a significant departure from well established official attitudes to Black housing in the past, which were noted chiefly for their paternalism and an emphasis on the physical aspects of dwellings. The extent to which the housing dispensations are really a departure from past practice is an important consideration in the assessment of policy responses in the post-Soweto period, and cannot be fully understood unless related to a range of well publicized projects supported by the South African business community.

The point has been made elsewhere that the dilemma facing capital after the Soweto disturbances was that it quickly recognized that an array of urban reforms were necessary to 'guarantee the conditions for continued capital accumulation' but the 'mutually reinforcing nature of its relationship to apartheid and its dependence upon the state's repressive political power . . . imposed severe limitations on both the scope of the reform scheme and on the lengths to which capital was prepared to go in asserting its reform interests' (Davies 1981, pp. 4–5). The picture which has emerged is of a business community which acted rapidly to restore stability in the local economy by identifying the more obvious sources of Black grievances. Among these, Black housing problems stood out as the most visible expression of inequality, although they are not generally regarded as being the prime causes of the 1976 disturbances (see South Africa 1979d, Morris & Van der Horst 1981).

The proposition is advanced in this chapter that the housing dispensations granted by the state are primarily functional to the interests of capital in their underlying purpose and do not present a genuine relaxation of control over Black development or a transfer of power in the realm of urban affairs. This in itself may not be an exceptional conclusion to reach, given the distinctive character of the South African state, but it illustrates the nature of a free enterprise system which only appears capable of responding belatedly to serious community tensions. Many of the latter are a direct result of conditions which have made South Africa an ideal environment for commercial profitability. As far as housing is concerned, the dispensations adopt only the trappings of policies which, if adopted in their entirety, might be expected to undermine white capitalist interests in the long term. The hallmark of this approach is an acceptance of certain parts of a self-help strategy of the sites-and-services variety, which do not threaten existing power relationships. Thus, according to this schema, South African self-help projects will embody little or no real autonomy over decision-making and evaluation by Black residents and will be chiefly concerned with the physical process of self-build. Similarly, actions designed to promote greater security of tenure in the Black townships via 99-year leaseholds are limited to assisting those middle- and upper-income groups who are most likely to support and gain benefits from the local variant of the free enterprise system.

Before examining the responses by both capital and the state in detail, it is necessary, first, to give some idea of the scale of the Black housing crisis in South Africa and its historical origins on the Witwatersrand; secondly, to assess the operation of the public housing delivery system for Blacks; and thirdly, to gain an appreciation of how the dictates of 'separate development' has led to a huge increase in squatting close to main centres of population in 'white' South Africa. The last of these is a development which provides the backcloth for the adoption of self-help housing solutions on a wide scale.

The Black housing question

In gross quantitative terms the scale of the Black housing problem in the cities is closely linked to the imperative of the population projections. Some idea of what is involved can be gauged from a comprehensive review by Dewar and Ellis (1979, p. 23), which states that by the year 2000 there is likely to be an increase in the urban population from a present level of 12 million to 40 million of which some 34 million will be Black. Government estimates give a demand figure of over 4 million houses for Blacks by the year 2000, together with a current backlog of at least 200 000 dwellings. In Soweto itself the official housing waiting list had reached 22 000 families by 1977 and the output of the formal public housing programme could manage the construction of no more than 970 dwellings in that year (Dewar & Ellis 1979, p. 149). It is tempting to suggest that the housing crisis alone played a significant role in the disturbances of 1976, but this would be to ignore the complexity of the protest movement and the fact that Black housing had been one of the most serious and intractable problems in urban areas such as the Witwatersrand since World War II. Indeed, the emergence in the post-war period of many squatter movements in greater Johannesburg was in part due to the great pressure on housing resulting from immigration from the rural areas and below subsistence wages. However, Stadler (1979) has demonstrated, in common with a theme of this chapter, that the post-war housing crisis was much more than a physical problem of shelter alone:

> Certainly there was a critical housing shortage in Johannesburg, exacerbated during the war, and the pressure on housing must un-doubtedly have counted as a factor contributing towards squatting. But this shortage had endured for as long as blacks had been settling in the city. The roots of the crisis lay in the same general conditions which gave rise to squatting: the abysmal poverty of blacks in the city, their political disabilities, and the restrictions imposed on their access to accommodation in the city, particularly the inner city.

Thus it may be established at the outset that a policy or set of policies which seeks to solve the housing crisis in South Africa must be sensitive to those causal factors which underly the physical manifestations of poor and sub-standard shelter.

The Black housing delivery system   The incapacity of the present delivery system to provide sufficient numbers of dwellings appears as an obvious and open reason for the recent change in the direction of government housing policy. But it also appears likely that the government deliberately slowed down the rate at which houses for Blacks were being constructed in the 'white' areas during the early 1970s (Kane-Berman 1979a, p. 51). This situation had led to a considerable shortage of dwellings by 1975 which, in turn, resulted in overcrowding levels in 10 urban areas of 17 persons per dwelling in 1975 (Assoc. Chambers of Commerce of South Africa 1976). Only 2734 houses were constructed by the West Rand Administration Board (the authority which administers Soweto) during the five year period 1973–8, which could have done little to reduce the official backlog (Urban Foundation 1978).

The majority of public funds for financing Black housing flow from the treasury by way of loans to the National Housing Fund (NHF) and then, in turn, to the administration boards or community councils at subsidized interest rates. However, one of the reasons why the administration boards or community councils have built few new dwellings in townships such as Soweto in recent years is that they have little financial incentive to do so. Boaden (1979a) has shown that the construction of new houses under the present financing system does not increase the tax base but imposes an additional administrative burden. This is because the boards have no control over house rentals (which go to redeem the NHF loan) and rely on a site rental to cover their operating costs. A typical tenant in Soweto would pay a rent of R20 a month made up of R6 house rental and R14 site rental (1980 figures), the latter amount being subject to periodic increases by the West Rand Administration Board. Thus a prerequisite for a more efficient housing delivery system is an overhaul of existing public finance in this sector, let alone a recognition of the wider difficulties which arise out of the existence of fundamental problems of equity in housing imposed by the discriminatory race legislation.

A further and contributing cause of the housing shortage concerns the peculiar nature of apartheid, which ensures that the filtering process, which normally operates in a free housing market, does not operate in the closed system of the Black townships. Many families well able to own and improve their own properties have been forbidden to do so, and occupy scarce public housing at the expense of those who are in greater need. Yet strangely enough, as Nash (1979) points out, the concept of 'filtering' is now being used by government in the Western Cape to underline the benefits which will flow to low-income households in this region resulting from the creation of the large new Coloured townships of Mitchells Plain and Atlantis (see Ch. 2). The better-off families will supposedly buy housing in the new townships leaving the poor to fill their vacated council flats which will eventually enable the authorities to demolish the squatter camps close to the city. Unfortunately this solution is unlikely to work because of the mismatch between current incomes and the increased housing costs imposed by the move to Mitchells Plain. Indeed, the only way in which such a 'market' solution could work is by the removal of discrimination in employment and the raising of Coloured incomes to the levels enjoyed in the white community. Thus it can be argued that substantial additions to the stock of modern housing such as the construction of Atlantis and Mitchells Plain is as likely to fuel increasing demands to end economic discrimination in the Cape as it is to relieve the pressure on the Coloured housing market and thus a reduction in social unrest. This provides another example of the close inter-relationship between physical improvements to low-income housing stock in South Africa and the overall politico-economic environment, where it is obviously impossible to limit the outcome of policy interventions to a few chosen end products.

Squatting and the locational determinants of separate development   Just as the 1976 unrest in the townships drew attention to major inadequacies in the public housing delivery system in the cities, the enormous increase in squatting close to some urban centres focused national and international concern about the effects of forced removal of urban Blacks living in 'white' areas (Baldwin

1975, Belcher 1979). In addition, the sheer scale of the housing problem thus caused, and the fact that its solution was in several cases now the responsibility of Black homeland governments, led to the active consideration of self-help strategies. These were seen to be cheap and rapid responses to a problem which had got out of hand and which could not be tackled in a similar fashion to the huge public housing programmes for Blacks on the Witwatersrand in the 1950s.

A particularly good example of this peri-urban squatting crisis took place in the Winterveld district within the new Bophuthatswana homeland and in close proximity to Pretoria, the heart of Afrikaner nationalism (the case of Winterveld is considered in another context in Ch. 2).

In the late 1960s the South African government planned the new township of Mabopane some 30 km to the north of Pretoria as a suitable location for the Black residents of the city who were to be displaced by the 'white by night' policy. In 1969, before the new town or sufficient housing was constructed, the resettlement process began. The area adjacent to the township had been sub-divided into 1600 smallholdings and sold, in previous years, to Black families from several tribal groups. This provided the site for a huge influx of squatters. One of the smallholders interviewed in *The Sunday Times* (20 Jan. 1980) is reported as saying: 'One day a Government truck driven by a white official arrived at my smallholding, piled high with the possessions and children of a slum family removed from Lady Selbourne, a Pretoria township then being demolished. The official said I should house them temporarily until they had built enough houses at Mabopane.' Within a month the truck had delivered 25 families and, in subsequent years, the number of tenant families on her smallholding had grown to 40. In a survey conducted in 1972 one plot was found to be housing 431 families, and by 1979 it was estimated that some 200 000 people were settled in the Winterveld (*Sunday Times* 20 Jan. 1980).

A new city had emerged which did not officially exist, a city with no services, formal educational facilities or administration. In 1970 the problem was formally 'solved' when the South African government declared that the Winterveld was part of the new Bophuthatswana homeland, but, of course, it was a problem that did not go away and became additionally complicated through the expression of tribal loyalties. Very few of the original smallholders or the new squatters were Tswanas (Baldwin 1975, p. 223, put the proportion of non-Tswana at 80 per cent), and thus the new homeland government was presented with a physical and financial problem which had no organic connections to its own 'national' circumstances and a political problem which should not, by definition, exist within its territorial boundaries. To its credit the Tswana government took over the corrugated iron and board schools and provided some teachers, but together with this recognition came the requirement that lessons be taught in Tswana which was a language that the majority did not understand. In one of the primary schools surveyed in early 1980, some 1800 pupils were found to be taught by only nine teachers and it was estimated that a further 6000 children in the Winterveld were being taught in their parent tongue of Zulu or Sotho in 'illegal' schools (*Sunday Times* 20 Jan. 1980).

Not surprisingly, few of the non-Tswana settlers are willing to take out citizenship of the homeland for fear of being cut off from jobs in 'white' South Africa and their future is unclear. In a recent development an 18-man landowner committee was set up by the homeland government to investigate ways of solving the squatter problem and the advice and assistance of South African government agencies is being sought. It should be obvious, however, that the solution of a major settlement problem, such as the Winterveld, is only capable within the context of the economic region of which it comprises such an essential part. The fact that a large proportion of Pretoria's Black workforce happens to be classified for political purposes as living in a separate administrative region does not change the economic facts of this or many similar cases, and it is difficult to see how any equitable solution can relieve Pretoria municipality and manufacturing industry of its responsibilities to house its low-income workforce. In this, as in so many other development issues in South Africa, the question of housing problems is soon transcended by more fundamental considerations.

Although the original removals can be interpreted as benefiting the state by freeing urban land for eventual white occupation, and remaining functional to capital by the retention of a large Black workforce within reach of established industry, the loss of control over the Winterveld settlements eventually threatened the stable development of the whole region. Current attempts by the South African and homeland governments to ease the crisis are likely to result in aided self-help housing projects as a means of reasserting control over a situation which had begun to exhibit remarkable levels of local autonomy (Matsetela 1979). This raises an important issue (to be explored later in this chapter): that little community support is forthcoming in self-help projects which incorporate extensive outside control. Response is directly related to responsibility and 'it will only come when there is an intimate spirit of trust between the people and the authorities, so that the people know they will get out what they put in' (Martin 1977, p. 247).

The post-Soweto reforms

Responses by the state Several of the official responses to the unrest in the Black townships after the Soweto riots were hailed in the government media as new and important relaxations in the controls over Black living conditions in the urban areas. They were certainly welcome relaxations as far as white liberal opinion was concerned but an examination of the historical evolution of the controls suggests that in almost every instance the post-Soweto dispensations were a return or partial return to conditions which had been enjoyed by urban Blacks in previous years. This point is well illustrated by the two chief dispensations introduced in the housing arena. The first is the re-introduction of some tenurial security for the occupants of provided public housing via the 99-year leasehold legislation incorporated in the Blacks (Urban Areas) Amendment Act of 1978, which was brought into force in April 1979. This Act re-established the principle of home ownership for Blacks living in the townships which had been embodied in the 30-year leasehold legislation of 1951, and which had led, at that time, to the substantial owner-built properties in the Soweto suburb of Dube (Davenport & Hunt 1974). The second dispensation was the tentative acceptance by government of self-help housing solutions in those situations where squatting had become endemic. A committee of inquiry into such 'unconventional' housing forms was appointed by Cabinet towards the end of 1980 to investigate 'such alternative housing schemes as core, site-and-service and other self-build projects in the country's "white" areas' (Schneider 1980). However, evidence exists to show that self- or owner-build had been officially accepted in the late 1950s as an effective means of increasing the supply of dwellings (Davenport & Hunt 1974), although, by contrast with the post-Soweto situation, it was supposed that such strategies were a temporary necessity in this earlier period to be replaced in due course by standard public housing.

Thus it is possible to demonstrate that in the two chief post-Soweto dispensations the South African government has done little more than return to the development climate which had been standard practice 30 years before. Unfortunately both of the initiatives discussed here – tenurial security and the use of self-help – are subject to more serious criticism. The tenurial security offered to urban Blacks by the new legislation does suggest a substantial improvement over earlier conditions of tenancy at first sight, until it is realized that in order to qualify for leasehold rights, the applicants must be persons qualified to reside in 'white' urban areas in terms of Section 10 (1) (a) and (b) of the Blacks (Urban Areas) Consolidation Act. The barriers to qualification are formidable and are exacerbated by the individual rules for mortgage finance imposed by building societies.

Further restrictions were also responsible for raising early doubts about whether or not township superintendents are able to terminate the Section 10 rights of a leaseholder at short notice (under Regulation 15 of the R 1036 regulations). This set of conditions requires the applicant to be employed and to fulfil certain obligations of tenancy and, if such conditions apply to the *legal* residents of Black townships, the difficulties faced by illegal residents who apply for tenancy rights is 'easy to imagine' (Boaden 1979a, p. 18). Space does not permit a full discussion of the institutional difficulties in creating a housing market under the 99-year leasehold scheme, but this and other considerations can be pursued in Boaden (1978, 1979b). Several problems with the new legislation have been identified and the Urban Foundation (1980a) states that negotiations are proceeding with government for changes to be made. In the first year of implementation of the legislation (April 1979 – February 1980) only 155 individual leasehold titles had been registered and 129 mortgages granted.

The point should also be made that it is the opinion of some Soweto residents that the introduction of 99-year leaseholds had more to do with pressure that was put on the government by building societies seeking greater security for their loans than it had to do with the welfare of urban Blacks *per se*. (Personal communication from a former Soweto family who emigrated to Australia in 1980.) Families with rights under the old 30-year lease arrangements had found it impossible to obtain loans for upgrading and extending their houses but were informed that such funding would be available under the terms of the new leases. Such evidence lends further support to the proposition advanced earlier in this chapter that the housing dispensations are primarily functional to the interests of capital in their underlying purpose.

There are identifiable and significant differences between the approaches of government ministries towards the adoption of self-help housing solutions. Major changes in Cabinet responsibilities in mid-1980 and the presence of some new faces have made earlier assessments subject to revision, but the generalization can still be made that *verligte* (enlightened) civil servants in the Ministry of Co-operation and Development were more prepared than those in any other department to adopt the necessary relaxations for self-build operations to begin.

Senior civil servants of the Department of Co-operation and Development interviewed by the author in January 1980 appeared to support the relaxation in controls necessary to allow a sites-and-services scheme to accommodate the residents of Crossroads. This approach was not in evidence in the Department of Community Development, the other ministry chiefly concerned with Black affairs, where the advocacy of self-help was seen as but a step towards planned slums. It would appear, however, that the inability of 'provided' housing to keep pace with demand, together with the extreme overcrowding experienced in many townships, will force a change in even the most conservative government circles before long. Boaden (1979a, p. 10) has stressed that this insistence on rigid standards makes the resulting housing irrelevant for the majority of low-income earners who are forced into multi-occupancy with the few who have been allocated such a dwelling and can afford to pay for it. In Soweto, for example, severe overcrowding has resulted in occupancy levels of 10–15 persons per dwelling. The same intransigent attitude is noted by Nash (1979, p. 4) in her review of housing conditions in the Cape: 'What hope does this offer to the majority needing to be rehoused or better housed, who have a head-of-household ratio of 92:100 compared with 60:100 for whites? What of the hundreds, if not thousands of families who due to factors like illegitimacy, redundancy, physical or mental disability or alcoholism, have no full-time breadwinner, therefore no reliable source of income?'

Perhaps the most revealing insight into government attitudes towards the more obvious instances of break-down in housing provision for Blacks in the post-Soweto period is contained in a speech by the Deputy Minister of Co-operation and Development to the Cape Nationalist Party Congress in September 1980. In a reference to squatting, the minister is quoted (Schneider 1980, p. 6) as saying: 'Without condoning the phenomenon, we shall have to learn to live with a certain amount of it. We are therefore obliged to plan for a controlled amount of squatting in certain areas while seeking for its control.' Thus the emphasis on direction and control remains and self-help without autonomy is advocated as an appropriate and acceptable solution.

Plus ça change . . .: the response by capital   In the aftermath of the Soweto riots of 1976 a Businessmen's Conference was held on the subject of the 'Quality of Life in Urban Communities'. Out of it arose the establishment of the Urban Foundation of South Africa in November 1976, with the objective of improving the quality of life of urban communities on a non-racial basis. The foundation soon attracted some R19 million in the form of cash contributions or pledges from the private sector together with a Swiss Franc loan of R8 million for investment in Black housing projects (Urban Foundation 1978). The list of donors to the foundation includes much of the blue-chip stock quoted on the Johannesburg Stock Exchange and pride of place among the chief donors at the end of 1978 are the various companies of the Anglo-American Corporation (Table 11.1). Between them, the 14 major donors contributed almost 70 per cent of a total which was subscribed to by 79 companies.

Although it is often couched in liberal and philanthropic terms, the involvement of capital in Black affairs in South Africa has usually more to do with the imperatives of the accumulation process than it has to do with welfare. The establishment of the Urban Foundation in late 1976 was no departure from this rule and should be regarded as a direct and rapid response by capital to the urban unrest. As Davies (1981, p. 15) points out, there is a considerable discrepancy between the motives ascribed to the founding fathers of the organization (Harry Oppenheimer and Anton Rupert) in a speech made by the Executive Director, Justice Steyn, in 1981, and earlier comments made by Steyn shortly after the Soweto riots. The more recent speech indicated that it was the intention that the organization should serve as a 'catalyst for change towards the establishment of a just society' (*Star*, Int. edn 7 Mar. 1981), whereas in an earlier speech made on his appointment, Steyn referred to 'the gravity and urgency of our situation not only so far as the maintenance of the free enterprise system is concerned, but in regard to

Table 11.1 Chief donors to the Urban Foundation of South Africa, October 1978.

Name of company	Donation (R)
Anglo-American, Oppenheimer Group Companies	
AE & CI Ltd	1 000 000
Anglo-American Corporation of South Africa Ltd	2 000 000
De Beers Consolidated Mines Ltd	2 000 000
E. Oppenheimer & Son (Pty) Ltd	1 000 000
Other major donors	
Barclays National Bank Ltd	1 000 000
Ford Motor Co. of South Africa (Pty) Ltd	500 000
General Mining & Finance Corporation	500 000
Goldfields of South Africa Ltd	500 000
Metal Box SA Ltd	500 000
Nedbank Group	500 000
Pick 'n Pay Stores	500 000
Premier Milling Co. Ltd	500 000
Rembrandt Group	1 000 000
Standard Bank Investment Corporation Ltd	1 000 000
total	12 500 000
total donations received as at 31 October 1978	18 672 000

Source: Urban Foundation (1978, p. 12).

the survival of everything we hold dear' (*Financial Mail* 11 Mar. 1977).

The declared objective of the foundation is 'to promote and co-ordinate involvement by the private sector in the improvement of the quality of urban communities within the Republic of South Africa on a *non-political* non-racial basis' [my italics]. One of the fullest statements of the foundation's principles is contained in the report of the Executive Director (Urban Foundation 1980a, p. 6) in which he states: 'These would certainly include a system in which discrimination based on role or colour has been eliminated, in which equal opportunity is available to all population groups and in which the advantages of the free enterprise system are accessible to all.' However, as we have already observed, the real or hidden purposes of the Urban Foundation may indeed be highly political and ideological in the way in which they are directed at securing stability in a social system subject to great stress. Davies (1981, p. 16), in one of the very few analytical examinations of the role of the foundation, identifies three real purposes: first, an organizational role designed to mobilize large-scale capital in defence of its interests at a time of apparent crisis; secondly, an ideological purpose aimed at encouraging the adoption of free enterprise values within the urban Black communities as a counter to the growth of socialism; and thirdly, an attempt to create an urban Black middle class which will act as a buffer between capital and the Black working class and, additionally, give concrete expression to the ideology of free enterprise.

Housing is identified in Foundation literature as the major recipient of project capital and must thus be regarded as the chief means of implementing the purposes listed above, together with investment in education, health and community services.

The assertion has been advanced here that the well publicized interventions by capital in township affairs is a predictable response to unrest which threatened the stability of the economy. But does this rather deterministic viewpoint suggest that philanthropy and liberal concern for Black welfare has not played a part in the century of capitalist investment in Southern Africa? The development record of South Africa's largest and most successful business empire, the Anglo-American Corporation, provides some valuable insights into a question which extends beyond the limited consideration of housing policy alone.

It is not surprising to note that the conference which established the Urban Foundation in 1976 was chaired by the present head of the corporation or to discover that companies controlled by the group contributed R6 million of the initial donations to the establishment fund (Table 11.1). It was this enormous conglomerate corporation (which now produces 40 per cent of South Africa's gold, 80 per cent of world diamonds, together with a large percentage of Africa's copper, coal and platinum) which was the first of the mining finance houses to be founded with the prime objective to invest in *Southern Africa* rather than the central economies (Bienefeld & Innes 1976, Lanning & Mueller 1979). Thus, from its establishment in 1917, the Anglo-American Corporation was closely identified with the local economy and the future of the South African state.

After the Sharpeville disturbances in 1960 it was the same company which invested heavily in manufacturing industry, '. . . to stave off the impending chaos as other international capital fled the country', and the value of its holdings in such interests are said to have risen from £30 million in 1960 to £143 million in 1969 (Bienefeld & Innes 1976, pp. 44–5). There were additional reasons for this diversification in the Anglo-American corporate empire and Clarke (1978) suggests that the emphasis in manufacturing industry investment in the 1960s was the result of government measures to make such investment more attractive. The group as a whole is now the single largest force in the South African economy and has become the largest taxpayer and employer of labour besides the government itself. The amount of this tax in relation to the profits made by the corporation however has been shown to be disproportionately small (Lanning & Mueller 1979, p. 447).

The belated move to marshall the financial resources of the business community in 1976 was led by the Anglo-American Corporation, which acted rapidly and, on past evidence, consistently to safeguard its essential interests in the South African economy. The gravity of the situation clearly demanded a tangible attempt to redress some of the more obvious grounds for Black unrest such as housing. In the opinion of some observers the corporation's record in the past appeared to be largely confined to the role of vocal critic: 'if

Anglo could be seen to be a highly visible and vocal critic of the worst aspects of apartheid and the low wages paid to black workers in South Africa, then any criticism would be more easily defused, and make the company more acceptable in black Africa and indeed throughout the world' (Lanning & Mueller 1979, p. 460). Indeed, it is difficult to accord any sense of altruism or liberal philanthropy to the corporation or to the other large commercial groups which established the Urban Foundation when their powerful position in the economy is considered. An extract from an open letter by Lanning (1980) to Harry Oppenheimer which received wide circulation in *The Guardian Weekly* summarizes this conviction:

I would like to see some international action by you and your group companies . . . Pay black workers a decent wage. Abolish discriminatory labour practices. Remove the appalling hostels for migrant labourers in your mines. Recognize independent black unions. Don't tell me again in next year's report what the government or the white trade unions should do . . . After all, what can the government really do? Neither South Africa nor the Western World can do without your gold, uranium, platinum, coal or vanadium . . . You are unlikely to be detained under the Suppression of Communism Act, or the Prevention of Terrorism Act.

Some idea of the size of the current investment boom in the South African economy underlines the realization that the business community is playing for high stakes, and is unwilling to accept artificial constraints on economic growth. A recent assessment (*Afr. Res. Bull.* 1980, p. 5437) suggests that capital of the order of R29 billion (10^{12}) is already committed for investment up to the year 1995; this includes R3 billion for mining, R19 billion for energy, R1 billion for import substitution industries, and R5 billion in other industries. Although relaxations in the race laws on the part of government in the post-Soweto period are likely to promote confidence in the business community, there is considerable frustration with doctrinaire apartheid. In the words of Lanning and Mueller (1979, p. 465), 'The argument between Anglo-American and the government is about *which* economic and political priorities shall take precedence, economic growth or separate development.' There is increasing evidence to show that in certain important areas, such as the controls over Black housing, the interests of the former are gaining at the expense of the latter.

At a more detailed level of consideration, actions by capital can be shown to have materially affected the housing situation in the cities. At least part of the blame for the appalling neglect of Black housing in Johannesburg before the 1950s lay in the refusal of industry and commerce to pay higher wages or to directly subsidize their employees. This is a problem with a long history in Southern Africa and was not limited in the early years to the exploitation of

Black labour alone. As long ago as 1906 Lionel Phillips, then Chairman of the Central Mining Investment Corporation, wrote in correspondence to the British High Commissioner of the time that poor housing was preventing the recruitment and retention of white mine employees (Fraser & Jeeves 1977, pp. 147–50).

Johannesburg Municipality had built no public housing for Blacks prior to 1934 and, as Stadler (1979) points out, failed to do so because such housing was not allowed as a cost against general revenue and because the municipality's tax base was extremely limited. The large mining houses contributed relatively little to municipal finances because mine land, in particular, was not taxed (Stadler 1979, pp. 116–17):

> In Johannesburg, municipal parsimony should be understood in terms of the limited financial base for revenues; in broader terms, it reflected the power of the great interests, particularly mining, over the city. City finances were drawn from two main sources: rates on the capital value of land and revenue derived from services. Except *qua* property owners in the city, the great interests centred in Johannesburg did not contribute directly to the city's finances. Mining land was not, and still is not, subject to rates.

It was not until the 1950s that 'the great interests' appeared to realize that the slums of Soweto presented a serious and visible threat to the orderly development of the city. In 1956 Sir Ernest Oppenheimer, founding Chairman of the Anglo-American Corporation, arranged a R3 million loan from a group of mining houses to be placed at the disposal of Johannesburg Municipality for slum clearance in Soweto. The municipal council was surprisingly grateful and erected the Oppenheimer Memorial Tower and, later, a tourist tea room in Soweto to commemorate the occasion. In the view of a local white politician of the period this public spirited act was wholly philanthropic: 'In this letter I must pay tribute to your whole humanitarian approach to the problem of living and, although I have said it in public before, I believe that this was the motive which inspired you to go to your mining finance colleagues and ask them to undertake the task with you' (quoted in Gregory 1962, pp. 580–1). Twenty years later, in Johannesburg, the call went out again and a new group of business colleagues set a target of R25 million to invest in the improvement of Black housing, education and welfare services.

It is interesting to note that the housing objectives of the Urban Foundation place particular emphasis on the employment of self-help or, more accurately, self-build strategies, in the provision of dwellings. An illustrative pilot project is the *Ikhaya–Lethu* housing scheme in the Khutsong township, near the Transvaal mining town of Carletonville, which is more important for its 'demonstration effect' impact on the state employees of the local administration board than in the solution of low-income housing problems in the township itself. The scheme does not cater for the lowest-income groups and does not incorporate much autonomy in decision-making outside the physical realm of house layout and building, but it is a good example of an Urban Foundation policy which is designed to demonstrate that considerable relaxation in the existing battery of formal controls over township development are possible without a retreat into chaos. Examples such as this demonstrate the ability of capitalist interests to convince the state that a range of cosmetic changes are possible in the townships, some of which bring considerable relief from the untenable conditions, but which are unlikely to threaten the underlying structure of control and separate development.

A further example of co-operation between capital and the state in self-help housing is the joint collaboration of the National Building Research Institute located in Pretoria and a mining processing company in the eastern Transvaal town of Nelspruit (National Building Research Institute 1980). The KaNyamazane Black housing project was established in 1978 for the employees of the company and was primarily a provided housing scheme which incorporated some opportunity for communal self-help. The project offered home ownership of one of several alternative basic house types, together with some individual responsibility to finish the dwelling with assistance from the company. In addition, various semi-public and public land uses were left to be developed by communal initiative. The declared objectives of the exercise on the part of the state agency were the important aim of securing the co-operation of capital in providing housing in a direct way and, at the same time, to utilize the industry and enthusiasm of residents in creating a more livable environment. Although some success was achieved in fulfilling the primary objective by early 1980, and a considerable number of families were now in occupation, little or no communal activity was in evidence. The reasons for this situation strike at the basic limitations of housing schemes which seek to employ self-help as a major input but which stop far short of any real autonomy in the many decisions and circumstances which affect the living environment. Many Blacks have grown accustomed to the paternalistic handouts of big government and are not willing to work actively to make good the shortcomings which are considered to be attributable to government policy.

The emphasis on control which is evidently so important a part of government policy in the townships is also, unfortunately, just as prevalent a trait in organizations supported by capital such as the Urban Foundation. By early 1980 there was not a single member of the national executive staff of the Foundation who was Black, and the response given to questions about this anomaly was that no African with the necessary financial or administrative skills was yet available for appointment although a number were being trained. Herein lies one of the most intractable dilemmas of the South African situation. The very policies which are seen to have been responsible for high levels of community tension and which are now subject to adaptation and removal, are also responsible for preventing the acquisition of essential skills by the Black population.

Responses by the universities and other institutions   It is only possible to comment briefly on some of the published research into Black housing in the post-1976 period and this must, inevitably, do injustice to those whose work is not readily available. Some representative works are Boaden (1981), Ellis *et al*. (1977), Finlayson (1977), Maasdorp (1977, 1980b), Mashile and Pirie (1977) and National Building Research Institute (1975). Certain generalizations are made here which no more than reflect the 'state of the art' but which do nevertheless indicate a significant difference between the nature of the local debate as compared to recent international contributions to housing theory and practice (see Murison & Lea 1979, Swan 1980, Drakakis-Smith 1981).

Most visible of the university research is the series of publications originating from the Urban Problems Research Unit of the University of Cape Town.* The unit was established in 1975 with the aid of a grant from the Anglo-American Corporation to examine housing problems in the Cape Peninsula but has subsequently broadened its terms of reference considerably. The early works are characterized by a particular emphasis on physical design considerations, but two recent publications by Andrew and Japha (1978) and Dewar and Ellis (1979) are of much wider relevance to the housing question. However, both these publications do not suggest that the authors are aware of the serious contemporary critique of widely promoted housing policies such as sites-and-services, and of the fact that any interventions in the Black housing market must involve considerations which far transcend the debate on housing itself. The same applies to the series of interim reports from the Low-Cost Housing Research Project of the Departments of Economics and Architecture at the University of Natal which have been published since 1978†, to the monographs on informal housing in Durban published by the Centre for Applied Social Sciences at the University of Natal, published from 1978–80, and to reports on selected informal and housing scheme areas in metropolitan Durban published by the Institute of Social and Economic Research at the University of Durban–Westville between 1978–80. There appears to be a ready acceptance of the 'Turner School' of self-help, bottom-up, squatter regeneration (e.g. Turner 1976), without any serious discussion of the wider implications of such activity. Perhaps the best illustration of this perspective can be found in the introduction to Dewar and Ellis (1979, p. 6):

Since the focus of concern here is housing, issues are discussed to the

---

* Some of the work emanating from this unit is the subject of Chapter 7 in the present volume [Ed.].

† See Chapter 8 of this book [Ed.].

point where they are no longer directly relevant to this focus. For example certain developmental issues which are central to housing have political or economic implications. If no cut-off is imposed and these implications are fully explored, a point is reached where the focus is no longer housing, but rather politics or economics and their inter-relationship with other issues. The cut-off is made at the point where the switch in emphasis occurs.

Although it must be admitted that there are real constraints on the freedom of academic expression in South Africa, the difficult and arbitrary nature of the cut-off points which have been self-imposed in the above example raise serious doubts about the usefulness of such a debate. It might, indeed, be asked what is there left to discuss about low-income housing policy in South Africa when the serious political and economic issues are left unexplored? One of the real weaknesses of many housing studies is that a failure to recognize important political, economic and social interrelationships has resulted in a discussion of symptoms, with little prior focus on the structural causes of the problem. Although it is obviously much easier to make such a judgement from the isolated standpoint of an overseas observer, it is a fact that unless research is prepared to include some of these structural issues, the results are unlikely to do more than scratch the surface of a problem which is demon-strably related to basic inequalities in South African society.

Limitations of the self-help debate in South Africa   The debate about the advan-tages and disadvantages of promoting self-help housing strategies and the consequent acceptance of unconventional dwellings in the Black townships and squatter camps appears to have passed through two stages in South Africa and has yet, belatedly, to enter a third. The stages may be identified from comparative Third World experience as: first, a formal opposition to spontaneous settlement and the active promotion by government of squatter removal and the supply of limited numbers of high standard finished dwellings; secondly, a widespread support for locally appropriate or 'incre-mental' housing solutions which utilize self-help as a means of upgrading *in situ*, together with the provision of new sites-and-services schemes (as exemplified in World Bank 1974); and thirdly, a recognition that although such 'incremental' strategies may offer the only financially feasible and politically expedient choice, they do not overcome basic structural deter-minants of housing inequality and therefore act to preserve the *status quo* (Burgess 1978, Harms 1976). Although this schema is a highly simplified summary of what is a continuing debate, it serves to highlight some of the shortcomings of the South African housing literature.

In the pre-Soweto period all government agencies were firmly in stage one, though there were some calls from university sources to promote stage two strategies (Lea 1975). Since 1976 it has become clear that one, at least, of the government ministries concerned with Black housing (the Department of Co-operation and Development) has moved to stage two, together with the National Building Research Institute and several university-related researchers. In addition, the advocacy of secure tenure via long leaseholds for township Blacks in provided housing can also be related to a stage two approach because such dispensations will promote considerable self-help adaptation and improvement of standard dwellings, a development which was forbidden hitherto. Most of the advocacy of self-help by the Urban Foundation can similarly be located in stage two. However, the important reservations raised elsewhere in the stage three debates about the long-term validity of self-help strategies have not yet arisen in the South African consideration of housing options, where the motives of the government–capital alliance might be expected to be the subject of much closer scrutiny. The reasons for this are hard to explain because it must be clear to many observers of the urban scene that the post-1976 dispensations have offered little more than some economic participation in self-build together with a measure of tenurial security for middle- and upper-income blacks, and serious attempts to introduce effective political participation in urban affairs have scarcely begun. Indeed, the record to date may be interpreted as attempts to institutionalize poverty in cleaner shanty towns (McGee 1979b), or helping the poor without any major threat to the rich (Bromley 1978a).

A source of confusion in the current debate about stage three issues is the lack of precision in the use and definition of the term 'participation'. Until recently there have been few attempts in the international literature to distinguish between the characteristics of a 'development' participation and the narrower and more traditional focus on 'political' and 'economic' participation. Cohen and Uphoff (1980, see also Lea 1980) have shown that it is possible to identify at least four essential kinds of participatory activity in a development project: (a) in decision-making; (b) in implementation; (c) in benefits; and (d) in evaluation. The first two of these categories concern inputs to the programme and the last two deal with outputs. The participation in the housing process thus far offered to Black South Africans represents some involvement in (b) and (c) but has scarcely touched the important issues of decision-making (in the widest sense of the term) and evaluation. It is not particularly productive to guess at the changes which might follow full participatory activity of the kind described here even if it were permissible. Housing, however, would probably lag far behind basic human rights issues for most urban Blacks. These issues are the achievement of enfranchisement, free access to employment, and equal rights to ownership of and access to land. It is open to question whether self-help housing in South Africa (or elsewhere) will achieve the broader objectives of societal advancement which have been claimed by some urban specialists, but the proposition advanced here is that the South African brand of self-help, thus far displayed, cannot do more than impinge on certain physical dimensions of the housing crisis

(Hallen 1977). Full autonomy in the housing arena is the necessary precondition which is claimed by the theorists for meaningful structural change to occur (Turner 1978), and it is obvious that this has not taken place. Self-help housing of the type presently on offer will be viewed by many as a cynical device to reduce the financial burden of providing shelter for the urban poor.

Conclusion

It is difficult to avoid the conclusion that recent changes in attitude towards Black housing in South Africa on the part of capital and the state suffer from the belief that it is possible to isolate the housing question from other basic problems of societal inequality and, having done so, to pursue policies of a variety which are designed to leave untouched the basic elements of the *status quo*. Unfortunately the point is now reached which presents most critics with a serious moral dilemma. Is it justified to support or to initiate policies which may bring some immediate relief to a situation where so little freedom of expression has been possible, or will this very support do little more than delay some more fundamental solutions? The dilemma was posed succinctly by King (1974, p. 10) in his work on the informal sector in Kenya:

> No sooner had the informal economy and non-formal education been identified as productive objects of policy than it became commonplace to stress that activities subsumed under informal economy and education were not so much alternatives to the prevailing system as symptoms of its malaise. You could not exalt into national policy a sector that was the yellow underbelly of the beast you wished to transform ... Intellectuals appear to have discovered the plight of the working poor, only to decide rather rapidly that unfortunately nothing can be done about it.

Although this appears to be a serious dilemma, there are reasons for suggesting that it may not contain the mutual contradictions which at first seem so apparent as far as housing for Black South Africans is concerned. It has been stressed that the prime emphasis of the post-Soweto dispensations has been on the small and emerging middle class in the Black townships and there is evidence, already presented, that few residents appear able to benefit from the new leasehold legislation. If this is the case, the great majority of urban Blacks will receive little advantage from the changes. Furthermore, the supposition by some Marxist scholars that self-help initiatives are counter-revolutionary is open to debate, as there is evidence from other parts of the world to show that possession of material benefits and education (i.e. a self-built house) is more likely to radicalize the owners than if they were left with nothing at all (Lea 1979). Thus the morality of supporting or opposing urban policy changes of the type described here is not a question which can be easily answered on the basis of available evidence, and depends on the extent to which it is possible to achieve the amelioration of poverty within an existing political system.

An interesting though equally unresolved question which was raised in the introduction to this chapter is the extent to which the post-Soweto dispensations, and other changes which appear to relax some of the strict controls over Blacks in South African society, will actually hasten fundamental changes of an irreversible kind. In other words, although the theme of this chapter has been to stress the way in which the post-Soweto changes are functional to capital, the possibility exists that they may lead, via a revolution in rising expectations, to concessions which may undermine these same interests eventually. This progression of events lies outside the scope of the present discussion but leads to at least one distinctly possible outcome. Governments in some countries may have encouraged self-help projects of a limited variety – such as Kenya's *Harambee* schools – in preference to participation in competitive politics expressed electorally (Bienen 1974). However, 'even activity that is purposely designed to be non-political cannot remain isolated from politics for very long' (Huntington & Nelson 1976, p. 39). Thus calls of this kind for limited economic participation may well lead to extensive political claims on governments in the future (see Lea & Wu 1980 for further discussion).

The likelihood that the post-Soweto dispensations will achieve anything other than limited and short-term success in removing an important cause of unrest in the townships rests on two characteristics of current policy which have been underlined in this analysis. In spite of increased government spending on housing and basic services – said to be a R400 million programme in Soweto (South Africa 1981) – concessions regarding housing tenure are directed at the small Black middle class and do not affect the large majority who cannot afford to finance a mortgage. Furthermore, self-help, the part of the policy which is directed at the very poor, will not flourish under the constraints of tight administrative control. There is plenty of evidence from other parts of Africa to demonstrate that considerable autonomy over a wide range of decisions is a pre-requisite for community support (Norwood 1975). The solution to Black housing problems in South Africa lies primarily outside the technological arena of shelter itself and, until this is officially recognized, it is difficult to discuss the merits of existing programmes for they are not designed to tackle the causes of the present housing crisis.

12 The geography of urban social control: Group Areas and the 1976 and 1980 civil unrest in Cape Town

JOHN WESTERN

In 1976 large-scale civil unrest occurred in Cape Town. There can be no exact casualty count, but of the 128 people reported killed, at least 108 were shot by the police during the months of August and September. This was the first time that so-called 'Cape Coloured' people, who in general terms occupy an intermediate position in the South African racial hierarchy between the ruling whites and the subordinated Black Africans, had rioted on such a large scale. At the end of that year, in Cape Town's segregated Black African townships, further rioting occurred. Official figures listed 36 deaths, 13 as a result of police action, the rest from internecine Black African conflict (Gordon *et al.* 1978, p. 109). In June 1980 another bout of rioting occurred in Cape Town, centred on the Coloureds-only suburb of Elsies River; about 40 people were killed.

The relationship between such unrest and the general concerns of this volume – urbanization, housing and employment – is not capable of precise dissection. It is evident, however, that there *are* links from poor housing, overcrowding and unemployment to certain social dysfunctions. These may be manifest in elevated crime rates – Cape Town has the highest violent crime rate of any city in South Africa, and perhaps therefore one of the highest in the world – and also manifest, indeed, in civil unrest (Slabbert 1980). The focus in this chapter is upon the link between civil unrest and a particular facet of urbanization: the ghettoization of Cape Town over the past 30 years by *de jure* residential apartheid. This topic is approached by way of three questions: (a) how has the present government been planning – especially via space – to deal with unrest; (b) what were the patterns – similarities and dissimilarities – of the 1976 and 1980 unrest; and (c) how did prior government plans affect these patterns, and how will such plans condition the unrest which undoubtedly lies in the near future?

Spatial planning for social control: theory

Of metropolitan Cape Town's present population of about 1 150 000, some-thing under 30 per cent is comprised of whites, 60 per cent disfranchised 'mixed-blood' Coloureds, and something over 10 per cent voteless Black Africans. There are also, in terms of the apartheid racial classification, about 15 000 Indians comprising a little over 1 per cent of the metropolis' popu-lation. The whites' proportion is steadily falling, as it is in the country as a whole. In this situation the present white government is looking for means of maintaining and improving its domination, and of perfecting its ability to neutralize unrest. For example, its Cillié Commission of Inquiry into the 1976 riots, reporting in February 1980, found that the joint causes of the unrest were the application of the compulsory use of Afrikaans as a medium of instruction in Black African secondary schools, and the inability of edu-cation and police officials to anticipate unrest and to take counter-measures (Gordon 1981, pp. 234–6). It is evident that the first conclusion is a superficial one, which does not address the root of it all: the oppressive racial domination and economic exploitation imposed by a fearful minority. It is also evident that the second conclusion is not in the least aimed at amelior-ating the situation, but merely *containing* it – no wonder Black South Africans boycotted the commission's inquiries. (Many were also fearful of appearing publicly before the commission: if they criticized the conduct of the police, they could anticipate subsequent problems and harassment from that source in one way or another; if they did not criticize the police, but rather provided information, they could expect subsequent trouble from fellow blacks – see South African Institute of Race Relations 1978, pp. 129–34.)

There are many ways of containing potential unrest, such as the parading or the exercise of armed might; or the use of secret police power; or the care-ful control of education; or of the content of the communications media; or the gradual permitting of access to consumer goods to a selected portion of Black African urban workers in return for political docility. There is also a particularly *geographical* way of containing potential unrest, and this takes us to one of the major foci of apartheid legislation: urban racial residential segre-gation, by the laws titled the Natives (Urban Areas) Acts, the Group Areas Act, and the Community Development Act. The white minority has been trying to maintain its rule by segregating its darker, outnumbering, and poorer fellow-citizens. The social geography of South African cities is a product of witting intent; the hand is not hidden here.

In endeavouring to achieve the desired apartheid or Group Areas city – whites-only at the centre and holding those sectors with strategic signifi-cance (such as routeways or commanding topography), non-whites-only on a distanced periphery (very few whites have been displaced, whereas Black Africans and Coloureds have continually been moved around), government spokesmen frequently choose to present this spatial manipulation as a well intentioned attempt to erase health hazards or slum conditions, under which the poorer (mainly darker) citizens have lived. However, as Mrs Helen Suzman alleged in Parliament in 1961: 'You do not need a Group Areas Act to clear slums; there is a Slum Clearance Act under which one can quite readily clear slums; and . . . to put up great housing schemes [in which those removed have been resettled] . . . also has nothing whatever to do with the operation of the Group Areas Act.' The point is indeed not the establishment of great schemes, but rather *where* they have been established: at the periphery of the now whites-only central cities. The *location* of resettlement reveals an intent quite different from that of government pronouncements: it is one of social distancing and not concern for health hazards. Herein lies a strategic motive. The outnumbering of whites by non-whites in the country as a whole and in the cities in particular continues to grow more marked. A parallel here may be drawn with the fears of the upper, ruling classes of 19th-century Britain when confronted with that totally novel and therefore unpredictable phenomenon, the great industrial city epitomized by Manchester. Of this city a contemporary observer (Cooke Taylor 1842, p. 6) wrote:

> [One] cannot contemplate those 'crowded hives' without feelings of anxiety and apprehension almost amounting to dismay. The population is hourly increasing in breadth and strength. It is an aggregate of masses, our conceptions of which clothe themselves in terms that express something portentous and fearful. We speak of them . . . as of the slow rising and gradual swelling of an ocean which must, at some future and no distant time, bear all the elements of society aloft upon its bosom, and float them – Heaven knows whither. There are mighty energies slumbering in those masses.

As a description of a widespread white South African fear of the urban *swart gevaar* ('black peril'), this passage can hardly be bettered.

How might this 'problem' be dealt with? In 20th-century South Africa, Van den Berghe (1966, p. 411) shows us that Baron Haussmann's 19th-century planning methods may yet be of relevance:

> The older non-white shanty towns with their maze of narrow, tortuous alleys were often located close to White residential or business districts; they are now systematically being razed as a major military hazard . . . The new ghettos are typically situated several miles from the White towns, with a buffer zone between.

And Adam (1971, p. 111) also subsequently opined that,

> Since the widespread unrest of the early sixties, white rule is efficiently

prepared for internal conflicts. The design and location of the African townships has been planned on the basis of strategic considerations. Within a short time such a location could be cordoned off, and in its open streets any resistance could be easily smashed.

Such statements are not searching for ideological-conspiratorial or Machiavellian motives where none exist. Slum clearance and (usually) improved non-white segregated housing is not, to reiterate, merely the result of a managerial and meliorative planning concern for health hazards. Surely no more striking proof of this could be found than the expressed opinions of the government minister who was in charge of the security system within South Africa. Mr Jimmy Kruger, Minister of Justice, interviewed by *The Financial Gazette* (*SA Digest* 2 Sept. 1977) on the possibilities of urban guerrilla warfare,

> said he did not think an organised campaign would get off the ground. One of the big advantages of South Africa was that the residential areas were segregated. Overseas, urban terrorism was largely sparked off by a mixture of mutually antagonistic groups within a limited geographical area, and this was often accentuated by overcrowding. 'We have fortunately managed to avoid this here,' said Mr. Kruger.

Whether or not we agree with his analysis of the causes of urban guerrilla warfare which predictably leans on the so-called 'friction theory', which asserts that *any* interracial contact is liable to engender inter-racial conflict and therefore that all 'unnecessary' contact should be suppressed (see Kuper *et al.* 1958), the strategic motive for Group Areas segregation has been made crystal-clear. It is in this light that we may understand the wholesale clearance of, for example, Cape Town's District Six. The government's justification for this is that it simply constitutes 'slum clearance'. Certainly there were sections of deteriorated housing, but equally important was its status as a 95 per cent Coloured area immediately adjacent to the 'white' city centre. Generations of Coloured occupancy had made it a symbolic focus for the Coloured people; but with its proclamation as a Group Area for whites-only, the Coloured homes were demolished. We should note that when legally imposed residential segregation against Coloureds was being first mooted in 1939, a night-long riot in District Six occurred after police attacked spectators at a political rally over the issue outside Parliament, right next to the Mother City's central precincts: District Six was too close. An observer who saw the situation in such a light was Arthur Keppel-Jones, in his astonishingly prescient tour de force *When Smuts goes*, published in 1947. He imagines in 1972 an abortive Black uprising: 'there were two other theatres of rebellion [in addition to the Zulu and Xhosa homelands] which, though small, were dangerous because of their proximity to the nerve-centers of the

Republic. One lay on the western fringe of Johannesburg [i.e. Orlando and Western Native Township, soon to become the core of Soweto]; the other, stretching from District Six to Maitland and Langa, isolated central Cape-town . . .' (Keppel-Jones 1947, p. 121).

The importance of the strategic motive was underlined again during the urban unrest in 1976. After a number of weeks of rioting in the Black African and Coloured ghetto townships outside the city on the Cape Flats, violence eventually flared in the city centre itself. An editorial in the city's Afrikaans daily newspaper (*Die Burger* 3 Sept. 1976) is illuminating:

> This is the work of cunning people . . . It was also a cunning, calcu-lated move to get [school] children to come to the center of the city and make it the scene of their rioting. Obviously it was intended to involve the general public [an interesting euphemism for whites] in what had up till then been confined to Black and Brown residential areas, helping to create a crisis psychosis and thereby ensuring much more publicity.

Clearly, according to *Die Burger*, violence and riot in the non–white town-ships is not as intolerable, nor is it deserving of as much publicity, as that which occurs in the 'white' central city.

Patterns of riot, spatial and aspatial

This in fact has brought us directly to the second question: what were the patterns of the 1976 as opposed to the 1980 unrest? The very idea of 'civil unrest' as some aberration that occasionally breaks out in the republic within certain discrete time-periods, is to a degree misleading. It is occurring *continually*, as Figure 12.1 shows. The news media presently document such incidents of unrest in ongoing fashion; a report in *The Christian Science Moni-tor* (Boston) on 4 September 1981 states there had been 37 bomb and gun attacks by the outlawed African National Congress since January of that year. Also, a report in *The Manchester Guardian Weekly* (4 Oct. 1981) tells of a South African Defence Force memorandum to newspaper editors in South Africa on how such incidents may be reported: 'the stage has been reached *in the escalating war* when everyone, including the public, must be made aware of the vital need for security' [my italics].

Furthermore, all manner of unreported, minor incidents (taken singly) portend popular disaffection. Examples are Black labour's widespread unconcerned wastage or petty larceny of raw materials in white-owned industry, lack of caring maintenance of machinery, wilful misconstruction of instructions, or general resentful dissimulation, which all add up to lower productivity. This is the kind of situation so frequently seen elsewhere under unpopular imposed régimes, as for example was widely reported of

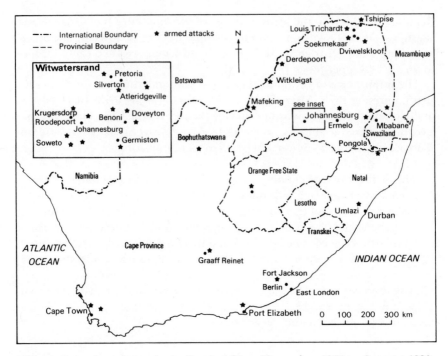

Figure 12.1 Armed attacks in South Africa, November 1976 to January 1980. (Source: compiled from information in the Johannesburg *Sunday Express* 10 February 1980.)

Czechoslovak industry after the Soviet invasion of 1968. Larger-scale examples of South African disaffection are found in the continuing climate of Black labour strikes in the republic, running at a level pointedly higher than in the forever-departed era of apparent docility prior to the 1973 Durban strikes.

So, in both 1976 and 1980 civil unrest did not suddenly burst upon the scene. Rather there had been a gradual swelling of tension toward it. From February 1976 onwards there was a current of discontent in Black African schools in Soweto which eventually surfaced in a student strike beginning 17 May. After a further month, on 16 June police fired on these school children, killing some, and setting in motion the unrest of the next three months in which hundreds were to die. On 11 August the unrest spread to Cape Town and continued for a month there. Four years later in Cape Town, the lead-time was longer: a boycott of classes, which began in February, at two Coloured high schools, eventually spread widely, but it was not until 28 May that there were any casualties, when two Coloured children in Elsies River, Cape Town, were shot dead by police as they stoned white vehicles. As opposed to 1976, both students and police had until then – for four months – acted with relative restraint: 'Rights not riots' was a typical student placard. The Elsies River shootings served to polarize sentiment, however, and two weeks later at the emotion-laden fourth anniversary of 'Soweto' (16 June), there was an almost total stay-away from work by non-white Capetonians. That night large-scale civil unrest broke out, and continued for a week.

A second parallel between 1976 and 1980 was that in both years active protest began by school students over specific issues, but as the protest mushroomed, so did the breadth of the demands (for a more detailed report, e.g. see Charney 1980, p. 128). In 1976 the focus of early complaints against Afrikaans' use in teaching broadened to an attack on segregated Bantu education, and then upon white domination. In 1980 protests started against the lack of material provision – no textbooks, broken windows, no electricity – and the summary removal of three teachers; they broadened into an attack on Coloured education, and then on the apartheid system.

A contrast between 1976 and 1980 is that in 1976 unrest *began* with Black Africans on the Rand and then spread to the rest of the country, first to Black Africans in Cape Town, then to Coloureds there. In 1980 passive protest began among Coloureds in Cape Town and spread through the country non-violently, but the degree of participation by Black Africans in the rest of South Africa was limited – despite the fact that the apogee of protest in Coloured Cape Town, finally waxing violent, occurred at the anniversary of what some might have chosen to think of as a Black African trauma (the Soweto riots). Whatever else this may or may not indicate, it does show an increasing politicization of Coloureds. Until 1976 whites had generally paternalistically viewed Coloureds as an ignorable, unfortunate, not-quite-white minority group (whites outnumber Coloureds in the ratio 5:3, Black Africans outnumber Coloureds by more than 6:1). Coloureds were 'in between' whites and Black Africans in status, but in the crunch they could surely, whites supposed, be expected to side with 'us' against 'them'. As Adam Small, a well known Coloured poet and playwright, almost caricatured the situation in 1971: 'We Coloureds, we have been on the side of the Whites for so long. I remember one history book which says, "At the time of Sharpeville, the casualties on the side of the Blacks were so many, I don't know how many [67 shot dead, 186 wounded], and on the side of the Whites it was one Coloured". This was true' (Small 1971, p. 24). If this *was* once true, it is less so now.

Intimations of such a shifting politico-social alignment of Coloureds can be sensed in a report at the time of the 1976 unrest from *The Cape Herald* (31 Aug. 1976), a newspaper which circulates on the Cape Flats, i.e. Coloured and Black African Cape Town. Making allowances for its customary sensational style, we read '*They said it could never happen*' by Maruwan Gasant (a Coloured Muslim reporter):

BONTEHEUWEL, Wednesday August 25 1976 – a day to remember.

A day people said would never happen. Soweto, yes. Guguletu, Langa, Nyanga, yes. But never a Coloured township. But then it happened. And when the dust and teargas had cleared, a 15-year-old pupil lay critically injured among the spent shotgun cartridges, stones, broken glass and gas canisters in the no-man's land between angry rioters and hard-pressed regular and riot police.

. . . Then the feelings that had built up in the crowd were unleashed. They stoned cars occupied by Whites. They ran in droves along the pavements as teargas was fired from passing trucks and vans.'

At such a juncture, the only safe space for whites in Cape Town is 'race' space. Even in times of civil calm, most whites feel an unease about the Cape Flats, stemming from ignorance born of separation. Such unease becomes active fear in times of tension. At such times, reliable information is scarce and people are prepared to believe far-fetched rumours which under other circumstances would be liable to be 'laughed out of court'. Thus *The Argus* announced, after much arson, looting, violence, and death in the metropolis, that (16 Sept. 1976) it had set up a 'Fact not rumour' service, which was

constantly busy with calls from anxious Cape Town people . . . Rumours are dangerous. They make matters seem worse than they really are . . .,

and (18 Sept. 1976):

The vast majority of calls came from worried people who wanted to know the best routes in getting from A to B, or whether it was safe to send staff home [therefore clearly these callers were almost all Whites] . . . many called about the activities of a totally fictitious mob that spent two entire days marching along De Waal Drive.

This last quote is most interesting, for in the Langa unrest in 1960 in Cape Town (at the time of Sharpeville) a procession of over 30 000 Black Africans marched on the main Caledon Square police station and on Parliament, along De Waal Drive, one of the two main freeways down into the city centre, and caused great alarm. A Cape Muslim acquaintance told me he watched them go by 'silently, there were so many, they stretched for miles; I was scared I think'. A visible embodiment of the *swart gevaar*, whose image is still so strongly etched in Capetonian memory that it surfaced, *wholly a hallucination*, in the next civil unrest 16 years later.

Figure 12.2 shows, probably somewhat imperfectly, the location of civil unrest in metropolitan Cape Town in August and September 1976, in which about 120 persons died. Most casualties occurred in the non-white residential areas.

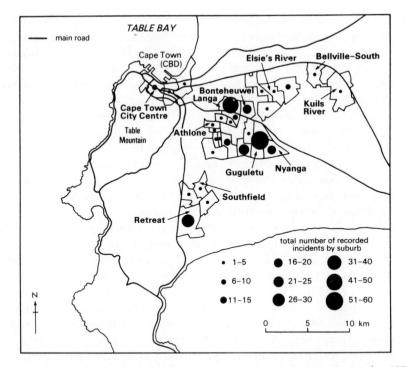

Figure 12.2 Consequences of civil unrest in Cape Town, August–September 1976. The following were treated as individual incidents: persons killed (113); damage to houses (7); motor vehicles stoned (23); shops and factories damaged (27); protest marches (10); hospitals, clinics and post offices damaged (6); liquor outlets damaged (25); civic halls, community centres and libraries damaged (15); municipal buildings damaged (9); damage to educational institutions (28). (Source: information derived from reports in main Cape Town daily newspapers. Map based on Putterill & Bloch 1978, redrawn in Western 1981, p. 267.)

It is difficult to evaluate the *precise* meaning of the rioting. There seem to have been anti-white overflowings of frustration and resentment, fuelled particularly by bitter anger at police heavy handedness. Even as sober a source as *The Economist* (19 Sept. 1981) was prepared to refer, in the context of Soweto, to 'what have in effect been white police riots'. (Simon Jenkins, political ed. in The survival ethic. South Africa: A survey, 11.) Particular targets for riot and arson (by both Black Africans and Coloureds) were the symbols of the apartheid system such as Bantu Administration offices, Black African beer halls ('Drink keeps us down', 'The scourge of the Black man'), government schools, housing offices, civic centres, police stations, houses of policemen and of suspected informers, and even the public library in Kewtown (a Coloured housing project area). Such unrest is basically spontaneous, as is its exploitation by *skollie* [ruffian] elements to loot, to assault fellow township dwellers, and to behave generally in an anti-social manner.

Skollies were, naturally, blamed by the Minister of Coloured Relations, Mr H. Smit, on 8 September 1976: 'I ask you not to judge the mass of Coloured people by the actions of a few people in the Cape Peninsula – people who have certainly run amuck under the incitement of certain elements – because then you will be making a mistake.' Mr Smit was addressing the Orange Free State National Party congress.

However, we have seen that *Die Burger* expressed a degree of concern over 'the work of cunning people'. In addition to spontaneity, a measure of organization *was* detectable, as seen perhaps in the selectivity as to which buildings were attacked, but particularly concerning both the widespread loci of the demonstrations by Coloured high school students, and the burden of what they were demonstrating about. This was even more true of the organization of the 1980 boycotts and demonstrations.

In 1980, indeed, we see a locational spread generally similar to that of 1976 (see map in Western 1981, p. 330). Again, unrest is largely confined to non-white residential areas. *The Daily Dispatch* in East London (18 June 1980) reported that:

> A large portion of the Cape Flats was in a virtual state of siege last night with crowds of rioters stoning cars, looting and burning shops and blocking roads with barricades of flaming motor-tyres . . . By sunset yesterday, traffic policemen had sealed off the Cape Flats from Retreat to Ravensmead and Matroosfontein in an attempt to end the chaos.

One could also note that Cape Town's civilian airport is, for whites, in a bad position: it is on the city's periphery and, because of the city's topography, it cannot be reached except by passing *through* Coloured areas. White airline passengers were asking for police escort on the freeway into town, or simply confusedly milling about at the airport itself. Nevertheless the general picture so far is of containment of civil unrest, more or less, to the peripheral ghettos. Is this then a 'success' for white spatial manipulative planning? At first sight 'yes', the answer becomes 'no' in longer perspective. This is thus where we address the third and last question: the past, present, and future effects of government spatial plans upon patterns of unrest.

The effectiveness of spatial planning in practice

The city's racial geography has been redrawn in bold manner (see Ch. 2). The various apartheid laws, especially the Group Areas Act, have by fiat removed Coloureds and Black Africans to the city's periphery. Group Areas were introduced by the whites for the whites. It is clear that the whites have benefited in various ways, as in business and in real estate. They have also gained a measure of perceived security in the sense that the non-whites and their problems, many of which (such as higher violent crime rates and lower health standards) are those of the poor in other societies, have been put at a distance. This distancing is also supposed to have lessened the potential for 'friction' and thereby to have 'improved race relations', which means that the subordination of non-whites is proceeding without as yet too much overt resistance or dysfunction such as sabotage or urban guerrilla warfare. However, it may be easier to argue the converse, i.e. that Group Areas have *worsened* race-relations, and have exacerbated inter-racial tensions. The government's Theron Report (Van der Horst 1976, p. 62) strongly implies this, Maasdorp and Pillay (1977, p. 165) state it flatly to be the case, and so has the Cape Town City Council on numerous occasions (e.g. see Gordon 1979, p. 393). The author too, from his own researches, considers this to be so. In the longest term, then, it would seem that such exacerbation of intra-societal tension by Group Areas may in fact be going to make daily life less tolerable for white (and indeed, all) South Africans, and may be undermining the security of that shrinking minority of the inhabitants of South Africa who are white. We therefore encounter here a broader question than just the relationship of patterns of civil unrest to spatial planning. It is the question of the role of Group Areas in maintaining apartheid: are Group Areas *functional*, or do they of themselves engender stresses that will be *dysfunctional* for apartheid?

In seeking an answer, consider that for the majority of Capetonians who are Coloured people, the Group Areas Act has been a bane. Again, the official Theron Report observes as much in its ninth chapter. The politically liberal South African Institute of Race Relations, in addressing the government's Cillié Commission on the causes of the 1976 unrest, declared, 'No single Government measure has created greater coloured resentment, sacrifice and sense of injustice' (South African Institute of Race Relations 1978, p. 111). Studies by Dewar (1978), Slabbert (1980), Whisson (1972), and the author (Western 1981), amply document such a contention. The Cillié Commission itself concluded that decisions in terms of the Group Areas Act contributed to the 1976 rioting in Stellenbosch and Mossel Bay. Even Professor Erika Theron, who once served on Group Areas planning boards and who chaired the government commission which reported in 1976, now concurs (Theron 1981). In innumerable ways, by moving Coloureds out of their previous Cape Town homes to a sand-dune periphery, both tangible and intangible increased costs have been imposed: higher crime rates, loss of sense of community, longer and more expensive journeys to work and to other elements of social life, less time with the family therefore less parental supervision . . . the list can go on and on. The people affected by this Act are not unaware of how it has changed their lives in so many ways for the worse, and they are bitter about it.

How does such anti-white bitterness bear upon one of the main goals of Group Areas: the strategic goal of clearly demarcating in both society and space the Coloured people from, on the one hand, the whites, and on the other hand, the Black Africans? Has the Group Areas conception succeeded in defining such a buffering, intercalary, separate group? If we are looking for some enhanced Coloureds-specific solidarity, some enhanced self-consciousness of 'a-nation-in-the-making', the answer, certainly in Greater Cape Town, is *no*. But if we are trying to discern whether the Group Areas Act has enhanced the separation in affect, the lack of empathy, between Coloured and whites, then the answer is in general *yes*. As Whisson (1971, p. 75) expressed it: 'The policy of apartheid has been successful in creating self-sustaining barriers which make group attitudes of suspicion more likely and individual non-racist attitudes less likely.'

Does this evaluation also apply to the affective relations between Coloureds and Black Africans? Here we have a paradox. The Coloureds and Black Africans have been spatially segregated from each other, on purpose, by government Group Areas planners. Prior to the mid-1950s perhaps three-quarters of Black Africans lived in mainly Coloured areas such as Windermere, District Six, Athlone, and Lansdowne. Separating them out spatially, as then was done through the Group Areas Act, would presumably be anticipated to lead to less empathy between them: divide and rule. Any reasonably objective observer of South African society must report that there *is* a general lack of solidarity between Coloureds and Black Africans. And yet this lack of solidarity is now starting to erode, especially among the educated youth. Already in 1968, O'Toole (1973, p. 144) reported concerning Group Areas:

> Although all the Coloureds consider this human removal humiliating at best and robbery at worst, there are some young militants who foresee that the government's plan will backfire. 'In Cape Town we thought of ourselves as Capetonians,' a young man told me. 'Whites lived in District Six and Woodstock, and Coloureds were scattered throughout the White neighbourhoods. Now only Coloureds will be in one horrible slum. This will prove to my dense people once and for all where we stand in this country. The Sand Flats are natural breeding grounds for a revolution.'

This I believe to be a premature evaluation, but it does seem that the manipulation of Cape Town space by the government is not proceeding totally as planned. For in 1976 and 1980 young Coloureds demonstrated for solidarity, and redefined themselves as blacks to some degree. In 1976, for example, Coloured schoolchildren from Heideveld tried to march into Guguletu and Nyanga to show solidarity with the Black Africans there, and were forcibly turned back by police at the one road bridge in to these townships. The like of this had never been seen before in Cape Town.

Group Areas may be credited with decreasing what empathy there ever was between white and Black African Capetonians, but especially what there certainly was between white and Coloured Capetonians. After the Coloured schools boycott had by April 1980 rapidly gained full momentum (but before any violent incidents of civil unrest), the pro-government newspaper *The Citizen* (22 Apr. 1980) editorialized:

> Education, however, is only one area in which we are running into trouble with our Coloured folk . . .
>
> They have become more radical.
>
> Far too many Coloured people have thrown in their lot with the Black militants, instead of regarding the Whites as friends and natural allies, as people with whom they can link hands to ensure a peaceful and prosperous future for all.
>
> The fact that there is a new militancy among Coloured students, a linking up of Coloured youth and Black school radicals, is warning enough . . .
>
> We stress: the alienation of the Coloureds must not be allowed to continue unchecked.

The Citizen can be seen here to be directing its attention to two issues. The first is concerned with the effects of government policies on white–Coloured relationships; these effects have clearly been negative. Group Areas segregation has indubitably played a major role in this, and one can only predict further civil unrest as a result. The second issue proves to be more intractable. It concerns the evaluation of the effects of government policies on Black African–Coloured relationships. In the particular context of this chapter, then, we should ask whether spatial manipulation by Group Areas, having evidently 'put distance' between Coloureds and whites, is having the same divisive effect between Coloureds and Black Africans. I do not know the answer to that, and neither, I suspect, does a concerned white government.

Acknowledgements

Earlier versions of this chapter were given as papers at the annual meeting of the Association of American Geographers in Los Angeles, 20 April 1981, and of the African Studies Association in Bloomington, Indiana, 22 October 1981. Parts of the chapter are based on Western (1981).

Conclusion

DAVID M. SMITH

The purpose of this collection of papers has been to present results of some current research into various aspects of life under apartheid. The integrating theme of urbanization and social change was explained briefly in the Introduction, along with some indication of the continuity of the collection. However, welding the individual papers into a coherent whole has been precluded by the diversity of perspectives among the individual contributors; in any event the findings of many of the papers must be regarded as preliminary, for research into such matters as spontaneous settlement and informal economic activity is still in its infancy in South Africa. In these circumstances a lengthy and weighty conclusion would not be appropriate, so all that is offered is a few general observations relating to the central issue of social change under the distinctive conditions of apartheid. The intention is not to make predictions as to South Africa's future but to outline some of the dynamics of the process whereby South Africa's future will arise.

Two particularly influential themes have emerged in recent years as features of the analysis of social change in geography and other disciplines concerned with development. The first is what is sometimes referred to as the 'dialectic' between social structure and spatial form. Until recently, geographers placed extreme emphasis on the role of spatial organization in human affairs, while other social scientists tended to consider spatial form as a trivial outcome of (non-spatial) economic, social or political processes. The essence of the emerging contemporary view is that both social structure and spatial form are active and mutually interactive features of a process which can be comprehended only by a holistic perspective transcending disciplinary boundaries and in which the traditional geographical 'fetishism' of space is as misguided as the neglect of space characteristic of economics, for example. Thus society is seen as creating spatial form, which promotes or constrains subsequent social change.

The second major theme is that of the relationship between what are generally referred to as 'structure' and 'agency'. That human affairs are determined by some underlying structure is a common feature of attempts to understand the nature of our existence on Earth. Geography has moved from a teleological view of the world, through the era of environmental determinism, to the adoption in some quarters of the economic determinism implicit in more dogmatic forms of Marxism, in which the prevailing mode of production generates the superstructure of institutional, social and cultural forms. The various kinds of determinism stand in contradiction to the view that free will or individual volition proceed independent of or unconstrained by wider structural forces, whether natural or supernatural. The contemporary challenge is seen as understanding the role of human agency within societal–structural constraints, recognizing their mutural interdependence.

A third theme might be regarded as implicit in the two identified here, and has special significance to the practice of planning. It is that any change in human affairs has the capacity to set in motion other changes, which may be unanticipated and even contradictory with respect to the initial change. This view may be little more than a statement of the obvious – something both evident from everyday experience and integral to the systems approach with its so-called negative feedback effects. It does, however, serve to highlight the dynamics of the relationships between social structure and spatial form on the one hand, and between structure and agency on the other, in circumstances where planning plays an important part in human affairs. This can be illustrated by South African experience.

As was indicated in the Introduction, apartheid is a bold exercise in applied geography, involving the planned spatial reorganization of society, economy and polity. Its purpose is the perpetuation of a distinctive social formation characterized by a dominant capitalist mode of production and a racist ideology, which facilitates and legitimizes a particularly effective form of exploitation. The country is divided up on racial grounds, and the rights of Blacks (Africans) to live in 'white' areas are severely restricted. The outcome is what Fair and Davies (1976) have termed 'constrained urbanization', effected by various influx control measures. The grand design keeps Blacks neatly in their place (literally as well as figuratively) within the peripheral homelands unless their labour is required in 'white' South Africa, in which case they must reside in segregated townships. A particular spatial form is thus planned and implemented, in the interests of the reproduction of a white-controlled capitalist economy.

However, this constrained form of urbanization itself entails a series of consequences, which rebound back onto the capacity of the state to maintain its grand design. Exclusion of Blacks from the cities is associated with what Rogerson (Ch. 3) described as 'exclusionary' industrialization. Those Blacks who are able to participate in the 'modern' sector of the economy can enjoy living conditions which, if harsh by white South African standards, are probably superior to those of wage labourers elsewhere in (Black) Africa. The excluded have to endure severe poverty in peripheral reserves, as part of a growing population surplus to South Africa's need for labour, under prevailing economic conditions. Recent labour legislation, involving more freedom of movement for Blacks once inside the 'white' cities, coupled with greater powers of influx control implicit in the concept of 'independence' for the homelands, reinforces the distinction between spatial inclusion and exclusion. But such a rigid system of control of labour supply frustrates short-term interests of employers, as well as the desire of the excluded Blacks for access to areas of economic opportunity. The limits of effectiveness of influx control measures are clearly revealed by spreading of spontaneous settlement, as well as by the less conspicuous illegal residents who swell the populations of the townships. Consistency with general apartheid policy requires the elimination of the squatter camps and the 'repatriation' of illegals to their peripheral homelands. Yet this practice conflicts with the evident functionality of spontaneous urbanization, which brings part of the cheap labour reserve to the metropolitan market (see Ch. 2). There is also strong and vocal opposition in liberal political and academic circles to the destruction of these settlements. The ambivalence of the authorities, reflected in the survival of Crossroads and similar settlements, encourages the process of informal urbanization, which further weakens the state's powers of influx control.

Spontaneous settlement has now reached a scale at which it is itself an important element in the spatial form of urbanization, with major implications for social change. Paradoxically, the very illegality of the spontaneous settlements provides a freedom to create homes, work and a family or community life that is limited for township dwellers and virtually denied in the case of the inhabitants of hostels. The informal sector has not yet developed in South Africa on the scale of major Third World cities of a more conventional kind, but it is likely to become a steadily more important feature of the country's economy. The authorities will not welcome this, but their inclination to destroy it will be tempered by recognition of its economic functionality and its contribution to social stability. In a land of widespread poverty it is hard to sustain policies which actively prevent people from creating their own shelter and opportunities for work, thus relieving the 'burden' on the state, especially where strongly held ethics of free-enterprise prevail.

Thus, two distinct groups of Blacks are now consolidating their position as *de facto* if not *de jure* permanent residents of the 'white' cities. Most numerous are the township dwellers, with the security of employment on which their residence rights depend, with rising living standards and aspirations, and perhaps dreaming of home ownership. They may still be 'temporary sojourners' in apartheid ideology and even in a formal sense citizens of some distant homeland. But the reality is that they are of necessity part of the permanent urban population, with urban attitudes and values. The migrant labour system promises capital and state the best of both worlds – the labour of Blacks but without their permanent residence. But the improved quality of Black labour required by an increasingly sophisticated economy is leading to longer and more secure migrant contracts, as Lemon pointed out (Ch. 4).

The contemporary compromise of frontier commuters externalizes part of the reproduction costs of labour as well as residence and political rights, but at the expense of large and permanent Black urban conglomerations separated from the 'white' cities by 'international' boundaries, which are more illusion than reality. However much the growth of KwaMashu, Umlazi and so on may be portrayed as 'urbanization in the homelands' (Ch. 5), the reality is that they add substantially to the Black population of the wider metropolitan areas incorporating what are supposedly white South African cities. Their inhabitants help to make these cities what they are, and inevitably contribute to what they will become.

The second group of Blacks now living permanently in the 'white' cities is the million and more inhabitants of spontaneous settlements. They are less secure in employment than the township dwellers, but in some respects less constrained in the kind of lives they can live. Quite how the spontaneous settlements will develop (assuming that the bulldozer is kept at bay) remains to be seen. If left largely to themselves, they could become fairly stable areas of upwardly mobile 'improvers', after the fashion of Lima's *barriadas* for example. Alternatively, they could turn into the stereotype frequently, if erroneously, attributed to them by state authorities – congregations of unemployed, angry and politicized people subject to less control than in the townships and with more capacity and inclination to change their own conditions of existence. While violent opposition to the established order has thus far been very largely confined to the township dwellers (e.g. the Soweto Blacks and Cape Flats Coloured), the propensity for resistance among an increasingly organized spontaneous settlement population must be considerable. Those who live in these areas are already testing apartheid in the realm of housing and employment policy. They could well become agents of more fundamental change, if they can see beyond the satisfaction of immediate needs for shelter and work and begin to articulate broader demands.

Squalid though they may appear by conventional standards, the spontaneous settlements around South Africa's cities provide an eloquent expression of the power of the oppressed to transcend the controls of apartheid – to make their own lives in conditions not necessarily of their own choosing but rejecting the place assigned to them by the state. The superficial chaos of these settlements contrasts with the ordered regularity of the townships – the landscape of rigid social control in which human freedom and creativity is so severely constrained. Straight streets are easier to shoot down, it is said. Less cynically, the form of the townships and the spatial arrangement of Group Areas do serve to keep people in their place. Industrial areas, roads and railways act as inter-racial buffers, preventing social mixing, miscegenation and trans-racial or tribal solidarity. Divide and rule is part of spatial planning strategy locally, as well as nationally. And, just as the whites control the national heartland with its metropolitan cores, so the Blacks (Africans), Indians and Coloureds are forced out to the periphery of the cities, so that even their occasional riots will be contained without undue discomfort to the whites (as in Cape Town – see Ch. 12).

But again, there are limits to how far even the most carefully contrived spatial form can determine human existence and contain or mould change. Political control of the mass of the Black population is largely effective, yet the reality of day-to-day living provides scope for expression of human individuality. Even in the 'white' residential areas there is a richness and diversity of social activity on the part of Blacks; for example, domestic servants establish their own social networks quite independent of their white employers. Coming to terms with the necessities of life under apartheid may even have a positive side. A case in point is the 'train-friends', described by Preston-Whyte (Ch. 9), who travel to and from work together for mutual protection and then become sources of support back in the township. It is out of this kind of solidarity that some of the strength to endure apartheid comes – a strength that might eventually be mobilized to promote fundamental change.

This leads to a final question of policy and tactics with respect to social change in South Africa. State policy seeks to protect the *status quo*, or at least to control very closely a gradual process of change well short of conceding real political power to blacks. But such policy inevitably incorporates concessions to blacks. This is illustrated by the relaxation of what is usually referred to as petty apartheid, e.g. the segregation of transportation and cultural facilities, which is a source of day-to-day irritation and indignity for blacks. More fundamentally, concessions in the realm of residence rights and property ownership are being made (see Chs 2 & 11), to satisfy the aspirations of the upwardly mobile elements within the Indian, Coloured and (to a lesser extent) African population. On the one hand, such concessions may be seen as a form of co-option which is instrumental in ensuring compliance with the broader structure of racial domination and thus promoting social stability. On the other hand, they do represent significant improvements in the life of some blacks.

Herein lies the dilemma, highlighted by Lea (Ch. 11), for those seeking fundamental change – that reforms which are welcomed by blacks may in fact facilitate the perpetuation of apartheid. Something of this dilemma is reflected in different attitudes to the spontaneous settlement and to the informal sector. These phenomena exemplify the 'coping' strategies developed by blacks in the struggle to house themselves and to make a living, and there are those who argue for the all-out use of this kind of informal activity to combat unemployment and poverty (e.g. Maasdorp, Ch. 8 and Corbett, Ch. 10). Others would argue that such a strategy implicitly accepts the structural conditions that generate affluence for the few and poverty for the masses. Dewar and Watson (Ch. 7) attempt a compromise, arguing for selective assistance in the stimulation of small-scale economic activity to help the poorest, while at the same time working for fundamental structural change.

The dilemma still survives however, for anything which makes life more tolerable for the poor may be construed as relieving the pressure that could eventually promote revolutionary change – the only thing likely to eliminate apartheid altogether.

To advocate particular kinds of change as being in the interests of the oppressed thus requires sound knowledge of the society concerned – of its present form and its on-going dynamics. This collection of papers should have revealed something of the complexity of action and reaction, not only with respect to the dialectics of social structure and spatial form but also in terms of how individuals and groups may find some freedom of response within the most rigid of constraints and thus force some change in the broader structure itself. As they take a more positive role in the process of South Africa's urbanization, the blacks are helping to mould their own future in a manner more significant than is generally appreciated. That these trends are taking place both because of and in spite of apartheid highlights the paradox of contemporary South Africa.

Bibliography

Adam, H. 1971. *Modernizing racial domination.* Berkeley: California University Press.

Andrew, P. and D. Japha 1978. *Low income housing alternatives for the Western Cape.* Cape Town: Urban Problems Res. Unit, Univ. Cape Town.

Andrew, P. and J. Western 1978. *Crossroads: Black shantytown and white government in Cape Town.* Mimeo.

Arrighi, G. and J. S. Saul 1973. Nationalism and revolution in sub-Saharan Africa. In *Essays on the political economy of Africa*, G. Arrighi and J. S. Saul (eds), 44–102. New York: Monthly Review Press.

Association of Chamber of Commerce of South Africa 1976. *Submission to the Commission of Inquiry into the Riots at Soweto and other Places in the Republic during June 1976.* Johannesburg.

Baldwin, A. 1975. Mass removals and separate development. *J. Sthn Afr. Stud.* **1**, 215–27.

Beavon, K. S. O. 1979. Unpublished paper. Delivered at seminar, Dept Geog., Univ. Cape Town.

Beavon, K. S. O. 1981. *From hypermarkets to hawkers: changing foci of concern for human geography.* Johannesburg: Univ. Witwatersrand, Dept Geog. Environ. Stud., Occ. Pap. no. 23.

Beavon, K. S. O. and C. M. Rogerson 1980. The persistence of the casual poor in Johannesburg. *Contree* **7**, 15–21.

Beavon, K. S. O. and C. M. Rogerson 1981. Trekking on: recent trends in the human geography of Southern Africa. *Prog. Hum. Geog.* **5**, 159–89.

Becker, C. J. 1878. *Guide to the Transvaal.* Dublin: Dollard.

Bekker, S. B. and J. H. Coetzee 1980. *Black urban employment and coloured labour preference.* Grahamstown: Rhodes Univ. Inst. Social Econ. Res., Dev. Stud. Work. Pap. 1.

Belcher, T. 1979. Industrial decentralization and the dynamics of freed labour in South Africa. *J. Mod. Afr. Stud.* **17**, 677–86.

Bell, R. T. 1973. *Industrial decentralization in South Africa.* Cape Town: Oxford University Press.

BENSO (Bureau for Economic Research: Co-operation and Development) 1980. *Statistical survey of black development 1979.* Pretoria: BENSO.

Bienefeld, M. and D. Innes 1976. Capital accumulation and South Africa. *Rev. Afr. Pol. Econ.* **7**, 31–55.

Bienen, H. 1974. *Kenya: the politics of participation and control.* Princetown: Princetown University Press.

Biesheuvel, S. 1979. *Planning for the informal sector: hawking in Johannesburg.* Unpublished MSc dissertation, Univ. Witwatersrand.

Black, P. A. 1980. Consumer potential in Mdantsane. In Cook and Opland (1980, pp. 65–72).

Black Sash 1980. Emergency Report. Reprinted in *Race Relations News* January. Johannesburg: South African Institute of Race Relations.

Boaden, B. G. 1978. *The financial aspects of black home ownership in four main urban areas.* Johannesburg: Urban Foundation (unpublished report).

Boaden, B. G. 1979a. *A laissez-faire approach the housing of urban blacks.* Johannesburg: Univ. Witwatersrand, Lab. Res. Prog., Rep. no. 23.

Boaden, B. G. 1979b. *From tenant to homeowner: an analysis of the mutual benefits and pitfalls of the new 99-year leasehold legislation.* Johannesburg: Urban Foundation (unpublished paper).

Boaden, B. G. 1981. *The low-income housing problem: the economic impact of alternative technologies on the community.* Durban: Univ. Natal (inaugural lecture).

Board, C. 1976. The spatial structure of labour migration. In Smith (1976).

Board, C., R. J. Davies and T. J. D. Fair 1970. The South African space economy: an integrated approach. *Reg. Stud.* **4**, 367–92.

Boserup, E. 1965. *The conditions of agricultural growth.* London: George Allen & Unwin.

Bott, E. 1957. *Family and social networks.* London: Tavistock.

Bozzoli, B. 1978. Capital and the state in South Africa. *Rev. Afr. Pol. Econ.* **11**, 40–50.

Brandel-Syrier, M. 1962. *Black women in search of God.* London: Lutterworth Press.

Bromley, R. 1978a. Introduction – the urban informal sector; why is it worth discussing? In *The urban informal sector: critical perspectives,* R. Bromley (ed.). Special issue of *World Dev.* **6** (9–10), 1033–9.

Bromley, R. 1978b. Organization, regulation and exploitation in the so-called 'urban informal sector': the street traders of Cali, Colombia. *World Dev.* **6**, 1161–71.

Bromley, R. 1978c. The locational behaviour of Colombian urban street traders: observations and hypotheses. In *The role of geographical research in Latin America,* W. M. Denevan (ed.), 41–51. Conf. Latin Am. Geogs, Muncie, Indiana, Publn no. 7.

Bromley, R. 1981. Working in the streets: survival strategy, necessity or unavoidable evil? In *Urbanization in contemporary Latin America,* A. Gilbert, J. Hardoy and R. Ramirez (eds). New York: Wiley.

Bromley, R. and C. Gerry (eds) 1979. *Casual work and poverty in Third World cities.* New York: Wiley.

Brookfield, H. C. 1957. Some geographical implications of *apartheid* and partnership policies in Southern Africa. *Trans Paps, Inst. Brit. Geogs* **23**, 225–47.

Browett, J. G. 1975. *The evolution of the South African space economy.* Unpublished PhD thesis, Univ. Witwatersrand.

Bundy, C. 1972. The emergence and decline of a South African peasantry. *Afr. Affs* **71**, 369–88.

Bundy, C. 1978. *The rise and fall of the South African peasantry.* London: Heinemann.

Burger, J. J. 1970. *Transport systems as a basis for the application of a policy of separate development.* Paper delivered to the South African Bureau for Racial Affairs Congress on 'Homeland development – a programme for the Seventies', Port Elizabeth, 6 August.

Burgess, R. 1978. Petty commodity housing or dweller control? A critique of John Turner's views on housing policy. *World Dev.* **6** (9–10) 1105–33.

Chana, T. and H. Morrison 1975. Nairobi's informal sector. *Ekistiks* **257**, August.

Charney, C. 1980. Parallels between 1976 and 1980. *S. Afr. Outlook* **110**, no. 1310, 128.

Clarke, D. G. 1976. *Contract labour from Rhodesia to the South African gold mines: a study in the international division of a labour reserve.* Univ. Cape Town, S. Afr. Lab. Dev. Res. Unit (SALDRU) Work. Pap. 6.

Clarke, D. G. 1977. *The South African Chamber of Mines: policy and strategy with reference to foreign labour supply.* Pietermaritzburg: Univ. Natal, Dept Econs, Dev. Stud. Res. Grp Work. Pap. 2.

Clarke, S. 1978. Review of the book *The future of Southern Africa. J. Sthn Afr. Stud.* **1**, 257–61.

Cohen, D. J. 1974. The people who get in the way: poverty and development in Jakarta. *Politics* **9** (1), 1–9.

Cohen, J. M. and N. T. Uphoff 1980. Participation's place in rural development: seeking clarity through specificity. *World Dev.* **8**, 213–35.

Cohen, R., P. C. W. Gutkind and P. Brazier (eds) 1979. Introduction. In *Peasants and proletarians: the struggles of Third World workers*, 9–23. New York: Monthly Review Press.

Cook, G. P. 1980. Position in an urban hierarchy. In Cook and Opland (1980, pp. 73–88).

Cook, G. P. and J. Opland (eds) 1980. *Mdantsane: transitional city.* Grahamstown: Univ. Rhodes, Inst. Social Econ. Res., Occ. Pap. 25.

Cooke Taylor, W. 1842. *Notes of a tour in the manufacturing districts of Lancashire.* Quoted by Glass, R. 1955. Urban sociology in Great Britain: a trend report. *Curr. Sociol.* **4** (4), 5–19.

Corbett, P. J. 1980. *Housing conditions in Chatsworth, Durban.* Durban: Univ. Durban–Westville. Inst. Social Econ. Res.

Davenport, T. R. H. and K. S. Hunt (eds) 1974. *The right to the land.* Cape Town: David Philip.

Davies, J. 1981. *Capital, state and educational reform in South Africa.* Paper presented to Conf. Afr. Studs Assoc. Australia and Pacific, School Pol. Sci., Univ. New South Wales.

Davies, R. 1978. The informal sector: a solution to unemployment. *From Rhodesia to Zimbabwe*, no. 5. London: Catholic Institute for International Relations.

Davies, R. 1979. Capital restructuring and the modification of the racial division of labour in South Africa. *J. Sthn Afr. Stud.* **5**, 181–98.

Decentralization Consultants of South Africa 1980. *Progress in the government's policy of decentralization and current location trends.* Johannesburg: mimeo.

De Kiewiet, C. W. 1941. *A history of South Africa.* Oxford: Oxford University Press.

de Klerk, M. J. 1979. Structural unemployment in South Africa. *S. Afr. Outlook* **109**, 35–8.

Department of Co-operation and Development 1979. *Report for the period 1 April 1978 to 31 March 1979.* Pretoria: Government Printer.

Department of Economics 1952. *The Durban housing survey: a study of housing in a multi-racial community.* Durban: Univ. Natal, Res. Sect. Dept Econs.

Dewar, D. 1976. Some issues of urbanisation in South Africa. *Proc. Businessmen's Conf. on the quality of life of urban communities.* Johannesburg: Urban Foundation.

Dewar, D. and G. Ellis 1979. *Low income housing policy in South Africa, with particular reference to the Western Cape.* Cape Town: Univ. Cape Town, Urban Problems Res. Unit.

Dewar, D. and V. Watson 1981. *Unemployment and the 'informal sector': some proposals.* Univ. Cape Town, Urban Problems Res. Unit. Cape Town: Citadel Press.

Dewar, N. 1978. *Spatial dimensions of political frustration and resentment in South African cities: the example of metropolitan Cape Town.* Paper presented at Am. Conf., Assoc. Am. Geogs, New Orleans, 12 April 1978.

Dewar, N. 1980. Decentralization in South Africa, prospects and problems. *Dev. Stud. Sthn Afr.* **2**, 321–32.

De Wet, C. J. 1980. Betterment and trust in a rural Ciskei village. *Social Dynamics* **6**, 24–35.

Drakakis-Smith, D. W. 1981. *Urbanization, housing and other development processes.* London: Croom Helm.

Drury, A. 1967. *A very strange society: a journey to the heart of South Africa.* New York: Trident Press.

Du Pisanie, J. A. 1980. *Position paper for the Urban Foundation on political, social and economic trends in South Africa for the period 1980/82.* Pretoria: Univ. Pretoria (unpublished paper).

Du Plessis, D. T. 1980. The creation of job opportunities for the Black labour force of South Africa within the framework of the policy of multi-national development. *Dev. Stud. Sthn Afr.* **2** (4), 436–67.

Ehrensaft, P. 1976. Polarized accumulation and the theory of economic dependence: the implications of South African semi-industrial capitalism. In *The political economy of contemporary Africa,* P. C. W. Gutkind and I. Wallerstein (eds), 58–89. Beverley Hills: Sage.

Eiselen, W. W. M. 1959. Harmonious multi-community development. *Optima* **9**, 1–15.

Ellis, G., D. Hendrie, A. Kooy and J. Maree 1977. *The squatter problems in the Western Cape: some causes and remedies.* Johannesburg: South African Institute of Race Relations.

Ellison, P. A., N. Pillay and G. G. Maasdorp 1975. *The 'poverty datum line' debate in South Africa: an appraisal.* Durban: Univ. Natal, Dept Econs, Occ. Pap. no. 4

Erwin, A. 1978. An essay on structural unemployment in South Africa. *S. Afr. Lab. Bull.* **4** (4), 51–69.

Evans, A. W. 1973. *The economics of residential location.* New York: St Martins Press.

Fair, T. J. D. 1953. *The distributions of populations in Natal.* Unpublished PhD thesis, Univ. Natal.

Fair, T. J. D. 1965. The core–periphery concept and population growth in South Africa, 1911–1960. *S. Afr. Geog. J.* **47**, 59–71.

Fair, T. J. D. 1969. Southern Africa: bonds and barriers in a multi-racial region. In *A geography of Africa,* R. M. Prothero (ed.), 325–79. London: Routledge.

Fair, T. J. D. 1973. Discussion paper. In *Proc. Urban and Reg. Dev. Sem.* S. Afr. Geog. Soc., Johannesburg.

Fair, T. J. D. and J. G. Browett 1979. The urbanization process in South Africa. In *Geography and the urban environment,* D. T. Herbert and R. J. Johnston (eds), vol. 2, 259–94. Chichester: Wiley.

Fair, T. J. D. and R. J. Davies 1976. Constrained urbanization: white South Africa and Black Africa compared. In *Urbanization and counter-urbanization,* B. J. L. Berry (ed.), 145–68. Beverley Hills: Sage.

Fair, T. J. D. and C. F. Schmidt 1974. Contained urbanization: a case study. *S. Afr. Geog. J.* **56** (2), 155–66.

Finlayson, K. A. 1977. *The role of community involvement in low income housing.* Paper presented to the S. Afr. Inst. Housing Manag., Biennial Conf., Durban.

Forbes, D. 1979. *The pedlars of Ujung Pandang.* Monash Univ., Centre for SE Asian Studs, Work. Pap. no. 17.

Forbes, D. 1981. Production, reproduction and underdevelopment: petty commodity producers in Ujung Pandang, Indonesia. *Environ. Plann. A* **13**, 841–56.

Frank, A. G. 1979. Unequal accumulation: intermediate, semi-peripheral and sub-imperialist economies. *Review* **2**, 281–350.

Fraser, M. and A. Jeeves (eds) 1977. Letter to Lord Selbourne, January 1906. In *All that Glittered: selected correspondence of Lionel Phillips, 1890–1924,* 147–50. Cape Town: Oxford University Press.

Friedmann, J. and W. Alonso 1977. *Regional policy: readings in theory and applications.* Cambridge, Mass.: MIT Press.

Fröbel, F., J. Heinrichs and O. Kreye 1980. *The new international division of labour.* Cambridge and Paris: Cambridge University Press and Editions de la Maison des Sciences de l'Homme.

Gerry, C. 1979. *Poverty in Employment: a political economy of petty commodity production in Dakar, Senegal.* Unpublished PhD thesis, Univ. Leeds.
Goodfellow, D. M. 1931. *A modern economic history of South Africa.* London: Routledge.
Gordon, L. (ed.) 1980. *A survey of race relations in South Africa 1979.* Johannesburg: South African Institute of Race Relations.
Gordon, L. (ed.) 1981. *A survey of race relations in South Africa 1980.* Johannesburg: South African Institute of Race Relations.
Gordon, L. et al. 1978. *A survey of race relations in South Africa 1977.* Johannesburg: South African Institute of Race Relations.
Gordon, L. et al. 1979. *A survey of race relations in South Africa 1978.* Johannesburg: South African Institute of Race Relations.
Gottschalk, K. 1977. Industrial decentralization, jobs and wages, *S. Afr. Lab. Bull.* **3** (5), 50–8.
Granelli, R. and R. Levitan 1977. *Urban black housing: a review of existing conditions in the Cape Peninsula with some guidelines for change.* Cape Town: Univ. Cape Town, Urban Problems Res. Unit.
Gregory, T. 1962. *Ernest Oppenheimer and the economic development of Southern Africa.* Cape Town: Oxford University Press.
Grimes, O. F. 1975. *Housing for low-income urban families.* Baltimore: Johns Hopkins University Press.
Grundy, K. W. 1981. On domesticating transnational corporations: South Africa and the automotive industry. *J. Commonwealth Comp. Pol.* **19**, 157–73.

Hallen, H. 1977. The quality of life and urban development. *Optima* **26**, 198–215.
Hart, K. 1971. *Informal income opportunities and the structure of urban employment in Ghana.* Paper presented at a Conf. on urban unemployment in Africa, Inst. Dev. Studs, Univ. Sussex.
Harms, H. 1976. Limitations of self-help. *Archit. Design* **4**, 230–1.
Henning, J. J. 1969. *Dorpstigting in die Bantoetuislande.* Unpublished PhD thesis, Univ. Potchefstroom.
Herbst, D. A. S. 1980. *Southern Africa potential giant.* Johannesburg: Southern African Freedom Foundation.
Heyzer, N. 1981. Towards a framework of analysis. *Bull., Inst. Dev. Stud.* **12** (3), 3–7.
Hindson, D. C. 1980. *The role of the labour bureaux in the South African State's-urban policy, with particular reference to the Riekert Commission's recommendations.* Paper presented to the Univ. Witwatersrand, Afr. Stud. Inst. Sem.
Hirsan, B. 1979. *Year of fire, year of ash, the Soweto Revolt: roots of a revolution?* London: Zed Press.
Horner, D. and A. Kooy 1976. *Conflict on South African mines, 1972–1976.* Univ. Cape Town, SALDRU Work. Pap. 5.
Horrell, M. (ed.) 1964. *A survey of race relations in South Africa 1963.* Johannesburg: South African Institute of Race Relations.
Horrell, M. 1973. *A survey of race relations in South Africa 1972.* Johannesburg: South African Institute of Race Relations.
Horwood, O. 1978. Statement regarding the revaluation of South Africa's official gold reserves. *S. Afr. Reserve Bank Q. Bull.,* no. 128, June, 23–5.

Huntington, S. P. and J. M. Nelson 1976. *No early choice: political participation in developing societies*. Cambridge, Mass.: Harvard University Press.

ILO 1972. *Employment, incomes and equality: a strategy for increasing productive employment in Kenya*. Geneva: International Labour Organization.
ILO 1976a. *Abidjan: urban development and employment in the Ivory Coast Sudan*. Geneva: International Labour Organization.
ILO 1976b. *Growth, employment and equity: a comprehensive strategy for the Sudan*. Geneva: International Labour Organization.

Kane-Berman, J. 1979a. *South Africa: the method in the madness*. London: Pluto Press.
Kane-Berman, J. 1979b. The crisis over the land. *S. Afr. Outlook* **109** (1293), 41–3.
Katzen, M. F. 1969. White settlers and the origin of a new society, 1652–1778. In *The Oxford history of South Africa,* M. Wilson and L. M. Thompson (eds), vol. 1, 183–232. Oxford: Clarendon Press.
Keeble, D. 1977. Industrial geography. *Prog. Hum. Geog.* **1**, 304–12.
Keppel-Jones, A. 1947. *When Smuts goes: a history of South Africa from 1952 to 2010; first published in 2015*. Pietermaritzburg: Shuter and Shooter.
King, A. T. 1976. The demand for housing: a Lancastrian approach. *Sthn Econ. J.* **43**, 1077–87.
King, K. J. 1974. Kenya's informal machine-makers: a study of small-scale industry in Kenya's emergent artisan society. *World Dev.* **2**, 9–28.
King, R. 1976. The evolution of international labour migration movements concerning the EEC. *Tijd. Econ. Sociale Geog.* **67**, 66–82.
Knight, J. 1977. *Labour supply in the South African economy*. Univ. Cape Town, SALDRU Work. Pap. 7.
Koornhof, P. 1981 Statement made at King William's Town, reported in the *Daily Dispatch* (East London), 17 April 1981.
Kuper, H. and S. Kaplan 1944. Voluntary association in an urban township. *Afr. Stud.* **3**, 178–86.
Kuper, L., H. Watts and R. J. Davies 1958. *Durban: a study in racial ecology*. London: Jonathan Cape.
KwaZulu Government Service 1979. A white paper on economic development. Based on the paper: *Towards a plan for KwaZulu – a preliminary development plan* by Thorington-Smith, Rosenberg and McCrystal. Department of the Chief Minister and Minister of Finance, Ulundi.

Lanning, G. 1980. The trouble with Harry, an open letter to Harry Oppenheimer. *Guardian Weekly* **123** (11), 7 September.
Lanning, G. and M. Mueller 1979. *Africa undermined*. London: Penguin.
Lea, J. P. 1975. Housing as a verb: some lessons from the Third World. *Plan 75* (South Africa) **1**.
Lea, J. P. 1979. Self-help and autonomy in housing: theoretical critics and empirical investigators. In Murisan and Lea (1979, pp. 49–53).
Lea, J. P. 1980. The politicization of housing policy in less developed countries. In *Urbanization and its problems in Papua New Guinea,* R. T. Jackson *et al.* (eds), 225–35. Port Moresby: University of Papua New Guinea.
Lea, J. P. and C-T. Wu 1980. Decentralization and devolution: a review of the United Nations Conference on human settlements, Nairobi, 1978. *J. Mod. Afr. Stud.* **18**, 533–40.
Legassick, M. 1974a. South Africa: capital accumulation and violence. *Economy and Society* **3**, 254–91.

Legassick, M. 1974b. Legislation, ideology and economy in post-1948 South Africa. *J. Sthn Afr. Stud.* **1**, 3–35.

Legassick, M. 1975. South Africa, forced labor, industrialization and racial differentiation. In *The political economy of Africa,* R. Harris (ed.) 229–70. Cambridge, Mass.: Schenkman.

Legassick, M. 1977. Gold, agriculture and secondary industry in South Africa 1885–1970: from periphery to sub-metropole as a forced labour system. In *The roots of rural poverty in Central and Southern Africa,* R. Palmer and N. Parsons (eds), 175–200. Berkeley: California University Press.

Legassick, M. and D. Hemson 1976. *Foreign investment and the reproduction of racial capitalism in South Africa.* London: Anti-Apartheid Movement.

Legassick, M. and H. Wolpe 1976. The Bantustans and capital accumulation in South Africa. *Rev. Afr. Pol. Econ.* **7**, 87–107.

Leistner, G. M. E. 1977. Bophuthatswana: economic development – problems and policies. *S. Afr. J. Afr. Affs* **7**, 135–47.

Lemon, A. 1976. *Apartheid: a geography of separation.* Farnborough: Saxon House.

Lemon, A. 1980. Migrant labour in Western Europe and Southern Africa. In *Studies in overseas settlement and population,* A. Lemon and N. C. Pollock, 127–58. London: Longman.

Leys, R. 1975. South African gold mining in 1974: 'the Gold of Migrant Labour'. *Afr. Affs* **74**, 196–208.

Lipton, M. 1980. Men of two worlds: migrant labour in South Africa. *Optima* **29**, 72–202.

Lombard, J. A. 1974. Background to planning the development of Bantu homelands in South Africa. In *Accelerated development in South Africa,* J. Barratt, S. Brand, D. S. Collier and K. Glaser (eds), 460–78. London: Macmillan.

Lombard, J. A. and P. J. Van der Merwe 1972. Central problems of the economic development of Bantu homelands. *Finance and Trade Rev.* (Volkskas) **10**, 1, 1–46.

Louw, L. 1981. *The unrecorded (informal) sector.* Free Market Foundation of Southern Africa, mimeo.

Lukes, S. 1979. Apartheid: visible and invisible. *Spectator* 19 October, 586–7.

Maasdorp, G. 1977. *Alternatives to the bulldozer: an economic approach to squatter housing, with lessons for South Africa.* Durban: Univ. Natal, Dept Econ., Occ. Pap. no. 6.

Maasdorp, G. 1980a. *Problems in the promotion of small enterprises and the informal sector.* Paper delivered at Conf. on work for the future, Durban.

Maasdorp, G. 1980b. *Squatter housing in South Africa: empirical backing for a new approach.* Paper delivered to the S. Afr. Inst. Mgmt Sem. 'Shelter for plural communities', Pretoria.

Maasdorp, G. (ed.) 1981. *Greater Inanda planning area: economic and social report.* Durban: Univ. Natal, Econ. Res. Unit (restricted report).

Maasdorp, G. and E. Haarhoff (eds) 1981. *Alternative strategies for low-income housing in the Durban Metropolitan Region.* Durban: Univ. Natal, Econ. Res. Unit – School of Architecture (restricted report).

Maasdorp, G. and A. S. B. Humphreys (eds) 1975. *From shantytown to township.* Cape Town: Juta.

Maasdorp, G. and N. Pillay 1977. *Urban relocation and racial segregation: the case of Indian South Africans.* Durban: Univ. Natal, Dept Econs.

Maasdorp, G. and N. Pillay 1978. *The informal sector in Clermont.* Durban: Univ. Natal, Dept Econs – School of Architecture and Allied Disciplines, Interim Rep. no. 4

Maasdorp, J. 1981. Analysis of fieldwork and household interviews. In G. Maasdorp (1981, pp. 50–87).

Magubane, B. 1975. The 'Native Reserves' (Bantustans) and the role of the migrant labor system in the political economy of South Africa. In *Migration and development*, H. I. Safa and B. M. du Toit (eds), 225–67. The Hague: Morton.

Magubane, B. 1979. *The political economy of race and class in South Africa*. London: Monthly Review Press.

Mangin, W. and J. F. C. Turner 1969. Benavides and the Barriada Movement. In *Shelter and society*, P. Oliver (ed.), 127–36. London: Barrie and Jenkins.

Mangope, L. M. 1980. The Winterveld is a disaster area. *Housing in South Africa* (Jan.). S. Afr. Inst. Housing Mgmt, Johannesburg.

Maree, J. 1978. The dimensions and causes of unemployment and underemployment in South Africa. *S. Afr. Lab. Bull.* **4** (4) 15–51.

Maree, J. and J. Cornell 1978. *Sample survey of squatters in Crossroads, December 1977*. Univ. Cape Town, SALDRU Work Pap. 17.

Martin, R. 1977. Response and responsibility. In *Housing people*, M. W. Lazenby (ed.), 233–47. Johannesburg: Danker.

Mashile, G. G. and G. H. Pirie 1977. Aspects of housing allocation in Soweto. *S. Afr. Geog. J.* **59**, 139–49.

Massey, D. 1979. In what sense a regional problem? *Reg. Stud.* **13**, 233–44.

Matravers, D. R. 1980. It's all in the day's work. In Cook and Opland (1980, pp. 27–48).

Matsetela, T. 1979. *The informal sector in the political economy of the Winterveld*. Unpublished BA (Hons) dissertation. Univ. Witwatersrand.

McCrystal, L. P. 1969. *City, town or country*. Cape Town: Balkema.

McGee, T. G. 1971. *The urbanization process in the Third World*. London: Bell.

McGee, T. G. 1974a. In praise of tradition: towards a geography of anti-development. *Antipode* **6** (3), 30–47.

McGee, T. G. 1974b. *Hawkers in Hong Kong: a study of policy and planning in the Third World city*. Hong Kong: Univ. Hong Kong, Centre for Asian Stud.

McGee, T. G. 1976. The persistence of the proto-proletariat: occupational structures and planning the future of Third World cities. *Prog. Geog.* **9**, 1–38.

McGee, T. G. 1978. An invitation to the 'ball': dress formal or informal? In *Food, shelter and transport in Southeast Asia and the Pacific*, P. J. Rimmer, D. W. Drakakis-Smith and T. G. McGee (eds), 3–27. Canberra: Australian National University.

McGee, T. G. 1979a. Urbanisation, housing and hawkers: the context for development policy. In *Housing in Third World countries: perspectives on policy and practice*, H. S. Murison and J. P. Lea (eds), 13–21. London: Macmillan.

McGee, T. G. 1979b. Conservation and dissolution in the Third World city: the 'shantytown' as an element of conservation. *Dev. Change* **10**, 1, 1–22.

McGee, T. G. and Y. M. Yeung 1977. *Hawkers in Southeast Asian cities: planning for the bazaar economy*. Ottawa: Int. Dev. Res. Centre.

Milkman, R. 1977–8. Apartheid, economic growth and US foreign policy in South Africa. *Berkeley J. Sociol.* **22**, 45–100.

Milkman, R. 1979. Contradictions of semi-peripheral development: the South African case. In *The world-system of capitalism: past and present*, W. L. Goldfrank (ed.), 261–84. Beverley Hills: Sage.

Moller, V. 1978. *Mobility on the urban fringe*. Durban: Univ. Natal, Centre App. Social Sci.

Moller, V. and P. Stopforth 1980. *Aspirations, experience and needs in informal housing*. Durban: Univ. Natal, Centre App. Social Sci.

Moolman, H. J. 1977. The creation of living space and homeland consolidation with reference to Bophuthatswana. *S. Afr. J. Afr. Affs* **7**, 149–63.

Morris, M. 1977. *Apartheid, agriculture and the state: the farm labour question*. Univ. Cape Town, SALDRU Work. Pap. 8.

Morris, P. 1980. *Soweto: a review of existing conditions and some guidelines for change*. Johannesburg: The Urban Foundation.

Morris, P. and S. Van den Horst 1981. Urban housing. In *A review of race discrimination in South Africa*, S. T. Van den Horst and J. Reid (eds), 90–126. Cape Town: David Philip.

Moser, C. 1977. The dual economy and marginality debate and the contribution of micro analysis: market sellers in Bogota. *Dev. Change* **8**, 465–89.

Moser, C. 1978. Informal sector or petty commodity production: dualism or dependence in urban development? *World Dev.* **6**, 1041–64.

Moser, C. 1981. Surviving in the suburbios. *Bull. Inst. Dev. Stud.* **12** (3), 19–29.

Murison, H. S. and J. P. Lea (eds) 1979. *Housing in Third World countries: perspectives as policy and practice*. London: Macmillan.

Muth, R. F. 1969. *Cities and housing*. Chicago: Chicago University Press.

Nash, M. 1976. *Home? an introduction to the housing crisis in Cape Town*. Cape Town: Board of Social Responsibility, Anglican Diocese of Cape Town and the Cape Flats Committee for Interim Accommodation.

Nash, M. 1979. *Mitchells Plain: alternative to District Six?* Cape Town: South African Council of Churches.

National Building Research Institute 1975. *Urban settlement dynamics*. Pretoria: Council for Scientific and Industrial Research.

National Building Research Institute 1980. *The KaNyamazane project: some salient issues with regard to the physical planning of the neighbourhood*. Pretoria.

Nattrass, J. 1976. Migrant labour and South African economic development. *S. Afr. J. Econs* **44**, 65–83.

Nattrass. J. and R. P. C. Brown 1977. *Capital intensity in South African manufacturing*. Durban: Univ. Natal, Dept Econs, Black/White Income Gap Project, Interim Res. Rep. no. 4

Nelson, J. M. 1976. Sojourners versus new urbanites: causes and consequences of temporary versus permanent cityward migration in developing countries. *Econ. Dev. Cult. Change* **24** (4), 721–57.

Nelson, N. 1979. How women and men get by: the sexual division of labour in the informal sector of a Nairobi squatter settlement. In *Casual work and poverty in Third World cities*, R. Bromley and C. Gerry (eds), 283–302. New York: Wiley.

Niddrie, D. L. 1968. *South Africa: nation or nations?* Princeton, NJ: Van Nostrand.

Norwood, H. 1975. Squatters compared. *Afr. Urban Notes*, *B* **2**, 119–32.

Oberai, S. A. 1977. Migration, unemployment and the urban labour markets: a case study of the Sudan. *Int. Lab. Rev.* **115** (2), 211–23.

Oppenheimer, H. 1973. Black labour: charting the way – (1) the corporation's policies and objectives. *Optima* **23**, 68–70.

O'Toole, J. 1973. *Watts and Woodstock: identity and culture in the United States and South Africa*. New York: Holt, Rinehart, and Winston.

Palmer, P. N. 1980. Industrializing the national states: the Bophuthatswana example. *Dev. Studs Sthn Afr.* **3**, 33–55.

Palmer, R. and N. Parsons (eds) 1977. *The roots of rural poverty in Central and Southern Africa*. Berkeley: California University Press.

Peattie, L. 1979. The organization of the 'marginals'. *Comp. Urban Res.* **7** (2), 5–21.

Perloff, H. S., E. S. Dunn, E. E. Lampard and R. F. Muth 1960. *Regions, resources and economic growth*. Baltimore: Johns Hopkins Press.

Phillips, E. 1974. State regulation and economic initiative: the South African case. *Int. J. Afr. Hist. Studs* **7**, 227–54.

Potgieter, J. F. 1980. *The household subsistence level in the major urban centres of the Republic of South Africa.* Univ. Port Elizabeth, Inst. Plan. Res., Fact Pap. no. 36.

Preston-Whyte, E. 1968. The adaptations of rural-born female domestic servants to townlife. In *Focus on cities.* Proc. Inst. Social Res. Conf., Univ. Natal, Durban.

Preston-Whyte, E. 1976. Racial attitudes and behaviour: the case of domestic employment in white South African homes. *Afr. Stud.* **35** (2), 71–89.

Proctor, A. 1979. Class struggle, segregation and the city: a history of Sophiatown, 1905–40. In *Labour, townships and protest: studies in the social history of the Witwatersrand,* B. Bozzoli (ed.), 49–89. Johannesburg: Ravan Press.

Pulterill, M. and C. Bloch 1978. *Providing for leisure for the city dweller.* Cape Town: Univ. Cape Town, Urban Problems Res. Unit.

Ratcliffe, A. 1979. Industrial development policy: changes during the 1970s. *S. Afr. J. Econs* **47**, 397–421.

Richards, C. S. 1935. Subsidies, quotas, tariffs and the excess cost of agriculture in South Africa. *S. Afr. J. Econs* **3**, 365–403.

Rogerson, C. M. 1975. *Government and the South African industrial space economy.* Environ. Stud. Occ. Pap. no. 14. Johannesburg: Univ. Witwatersrand, Dept of Geog. and Environ. Stud.

Rogerson, C. M. 1978. Corporate strategy, state power and compromise: television manufacture in Southern Africa. *S. Afr. Geog. J.* **60**, 89–102.

Rogerson, C. M. 1980. *Making out in the 'city of gold': the coffee-cart traders of Johannesburg.* Paper presented at the An. Mtg, Assoc. Am. Geogs Conf., Louisville.

Rogerson, C. M. 1981. Industrialization in the shadows of apartheid: a world-systems analysis. In *Spatial analysis, industry and the industrial environment: international industrial systems,* F. E. I. Hamilton and G. J. R. Linge (eds), 395–421. Chichester: Wiley.

Rogerson, C. M. forthcoming. Multinational corporations in Southern Africa: a spatial perspective. In *The geography of multinationals,* M. J. Taylor and N. J. Thrift (eds). London: Croom Helm.

Rogerson, C. M. and K. S. O. Beavon 1980. The awakening of 'informal sector' studies in Southern Africa. *S. Afr. Geog. J.* **62**, 175–90.

Rogerson, C. M. and S. M. Kobben 1982. The locational impact of the Environment Planning Act on the clothing and textiles industry of South Africa. *S. Afr. Geog.* **10**, 19–32.

Rogerson, C. M. and G. H. Pirie 1979. Apartheid, urbanization and regional planning in South Africa. In *Development of urban systems in Africa,* R. A. Obudho and S. El-Shakh (eds), 323–44. New York: Praeger.

Rutman, G. L. 1964. Temporary labour migration: a process of wealth formation in the indigenous economies of Southern Africa. *S. Afr. J. Afr. Aff.* **4**, 24–32.

Sabbagh, M. E. 1968. Some geographical characteristics of a plural society: apartheid in South Africa. *Geog. Rev.* **58**, 1–28.

SAIP 1980. *The road to nowhere: removal and resettlement in South Africa.* London: Southern African Information Programme (SAIP) of the International University Exchange Fund.

Salt, J. and H. Clout (eds) 1976. *Migration in post-war Europe: geographical essays.* Oxford: Oxford University Press.

Samoff, J. 1978. Transnationals, industrialization and black consciousness: change in South Africa. *J. Sthn Afr. Aff.* **3**, 489–520.

Santos, M. 1976. Economic development and urbanization in underdeveloped countries: the two sub-systems of the urban economy. *J. Geog. Assoc. Tanzania* **14**, 6–36.

Santos, M. 1979. *The shared space: the two circuits of the urban economy in underdeveloped countries*. London: Methuen.

Savage, M. 1978. The ownership and control of large South African companies. *S. Afr. Lab. Bull.* **4** (6) 9–43.

Schneider, M. 1980. Government takes a softer line on squatters. *Rand Daily Mail* 2 October 1980, 6.

Schollhammer, H. 1974. *Locational strategies of multinational firms*. Los Angeles: Center for International Business, Pepperdine University.

Seidman, A. 1979. Why US corporations should get out of South Africa. *Issue* **9** (1 & 2), 37–41.

Seidman A. and N. Makgetla 1978. *Activities of transnational corporations in South Africa*. UN Centre Against Apartheid Notes and Documents, 9/78.

Seidman A. and N. Makgetla 1980. *Outposts of monopoly capitalism: Southern Africa in the changing global economy*. Westport, Connecticut: Lawrence Hill.

Seidman, A. and N. Seidman 1977. *US multinationals in Southern Africa*. Dar-es-Salaam: Tanzania Publishing House.

Selvan, D. 1976. *Housing conditions for migrant workers in Cape Town 1976*. Univ. Cape Town, SALDRU Work. Pap. 10.

Sethuraman, S. V. 1976. The urban informal sector: concept, measurement and policy. *Int. Lab. Rev.* **114** (1), 69–81.

Sethuraman, S. V. (ed.) 1981. *The urban informal sector in developing countries: employment, poverty and environment*. Geneva: International Labour Office.

Shafer, D. M. 1979. *The Wiehahn Report and the Industrial Conciliation Amendment Act: a new attack on the trade union movement in South Africa*. UN Centre Against Apartheid Notes and Documents, 25/79.

Simkins, C. 1978. Measuring and predicting unemployment in South Africa 1960–1977. In *Structural unemployment in Southern Africa*, C. Simkins and D. Clarke, 1–49. Pietermaritzburg: Natal University Press.

Simkins, C. 1981a. Agricultural production in the African reserves. *J. Sthn Afr. Stud.* **7**, 256–83.

Simkins, C. 1981b. *The demographic demand for labour and institutional context of African unemployment in South Africa, 1960–1980*. Univ. Cape Town, SALDRU Work Pap. 39.

Slabbert, M. 1980. Soaring crime rate more than mere statistics. *Argus* 14 October.

Small, A. 1971. A brown Afrikaner speaks: a coloured poet and philosopher looks ahead. *Munger Africana Library Notes*, no. 8.

Smit, P. 1976. The Black population. In Smith (1976, pp. 39–62).

Smit, P. 1977. Basic features of the population of Bophuthatswana. *S. Afr. J. Afr. Aff.* **7**, 175–201.

Smit, P. 1979. Urbanisation in Africa: lessons for urbanisation in the homelands. *S. Afr. Geog. J.* **61**, 3–28.

Smit, P. and J. J. Booysen 1977. *Urbanization in the homelands – a new dimension in the urbanization process of the black population of South Africa?* Pretoria: Inst. Plural Socs, Univ. Pretoria.

Smit, P. and J. J. Booysen 1981. *Swart verstedeliking: proses, patroon en strategie*. Cape Town: Tafelberg.

Smith, D. M. (ed.) 1976. *Separation in South Africa. 1: people and policies*. London: Queen Mary College, Dept Geog., Occ. Pap. 6.

Smith, D. M. 1977. *Human geography: a welfare approach*. London: Edward Arnold.

Smuts, J. C. 1942. *The basic of trusteeship*. New African Pamphlet 2. Johannesburg: South African Institute of Race Relations.

South Africa 1941. *Third report of the industrial and agricultural requirements commission*. UG 40. Pretoria: Government Printer.

South Africa 1943. *Report of the interdepartmental committee on the social, health and economic conditions of urban natives.* Annex one, 47.

South Africa 1946. *The native reserves and their place in the economy of the Union of South Africa.* Social and Economic Planning Council, UG 32. Pretoria: Government Printer.

South Africa 1955. *Report of the commission for the socio-economic development of the Bantu areas within the Union of South Africa* (Tomlinson Report). UG 61. Pretoria: Government Printer.

South Africa 1959. *Report of the commission of inquiry into European occupancy of the rural areas.* Pretoria: Government Printer.

South Africa 1970. *Second report of the commission of inquiry into agriculture.* RP 84. Pretoria: Government Printer.

South Africa 1971. *White paper on the report by the interdepartmental committee on the decentralization of industries.* Pretoria: Government Printer.

South Africa 1978. *Census of manufacturing 1976: statistics according to major groups and subgroups.* Rep. no. 10–21–32. Pretoria: Government Printer.

South Africa 1979a. *Report of the commission of inquiry into legislation affecting the utilisation of manpower (excluding the legislation administered by the Departments of Labour and Mines)* (Riekert Report). RP 32. Pretoria: Government Printer.

South Africa 1979b. *White paper on report of the commission of inquiry into legislation affecting the utilization of manpower.* WP T. Pretoria: Government Printer.

South Africa 1979c. *Report of the commission of inquiry into labour legislation* (Wiehahn Report). RP 97. Pretoria: Government Printer.

South Africa 1979d. *Report of the commission of inquiry into rioting in Soweto and elsewhere from 16 June 1976 to 28 February 1977* (Cillié Report), vol. I. Pretoria: Government Printer.

South Africa 1979e. *Ninth economic development programme for the republic of South Africa 1978–1987.* Pretoria: Office of the Economic Advisor to the Prime Minister.

South Africa 1980a. *Interim report.* Commission of inquiry into the constitution, RP 68. Pretoria: Government Printer.

South Africa 1980b. *Census of manufacturing 1976: principal statistics on a regional basis.* Rep. no. 10–21–33. Pretoria: Government Printer.

South Africa 1981. *South Africa 1980–1981.* (Official yearbook.) Pretoria: Government Printer.

South African Institute of Race Relations 1978. *South Africa in travail: the disturbances of 1976–77.* Johannesburg: SAIRR.

South African Labour Bulletin 1979a. Focus on Wiehahn. **5** (2).

South African Labour Bulletin 1979b. Focus on Riekert. **5** (4).

Southall, R. J. 1980. Independence for the Transkei: mystification and diversion in the model Bantustan. In *Southern Africa since the Portuguese coup*, J. Seiler (ed.). London: Westview.

Spandau, A. 1980. A note on Black employment conditions on South African mines. *S. Afr. J. Econs* **42**, 214–17.

Spiegel, A. D. 1980. Changing patterns of migrant labour and rural differentiation in Lesotho. *Social Dynamics* **6**, 1–13.

Stadler, A. W. 1979. Birds in the cornfield: squatter movements in Johannesburg, 1944–1947. *J. Sthn Afr. Studs* **6**, 92–123.

Steel, W. F. 1977. *Small scale employment and production in developing countries: evidence from Ghana.* New York: Praeger.

Steyn, J. H. 1979. The role of the Urban Foundation. In *Urban Blacks in urban space*, J. H. Lange and R. van Wyk (eds), 109–14. Pretoria: Univ. South Africa, School of Business Leadership.

Stopforth, P. 1978. *Profile of the Black population in a spontaneous settlement near Durban*. Durban: Univ. Natal, Centre Appl. Social Sci.

Sundkler, B. 1948. *Bantu prophets in South Africa*. Oxford: Oxford University Press (2nd Edn 1961).

Swan, P. J. (ed.) 1980. *The practice of people's participation: seven Asian experiences of housing the poor*. Bangkok: Asian Institute of Technology.

Swart, C. F. and A. J. G. Oosthuizen 1978. Urbanization. In *South Africa's urban Blacks: problems and challenges*, G. Marais and R. van der Kooy (eds), 19–49. Pretoria: Univ. South Africa, School of Business Leadership.

Taylor, M. and N. Thrift 1981. Some geographical implications of foreign investment in the semiperiphery: the case of Australia. *Tijd. Econ. Sociale Geog.* **72**, 194–213.

Theron, D. H. 1979. Housing in urban Black areas. In *Urban Blacks in urban space*, J. H. Lange and R. van Wyk (eds), 61–79. Pretoria: Univ South Africa, School of Business Leadership.

Theron, E. 1981. Foreword. In Western (1981), Human and Rousseau edn.

Tomaselli, R. E. 1981. Johannesburg Indian flower sellers: a history of people on the street. Unpublished paper read at the History Workshop 1981, Univ. Witwatersrand.

Transvaal 1922. *Report of the Transvaal Local Government Commission*. Transvaal Provincial Government, TP 1. Pretoria: Government Printer.

Turner, J. F. C. 1976. *Housing by people: towards autonomy in building environments*. London: Marian Boyars.

Turner, J. F. C. 1978. Housing in three dimensions: terms of reference for the housing question redefined. *World Dev.* **6** (9–10), 1135–45.

United Nations 1976. *Global review of human settlements*. Conf. on human settlements. Oxford: Pergamon.

United Nations (nd). *Methods of estimating housing needs*. Studies in Methods, Ser. F, no. 12.

Urban Foundation 1978. *First progress report*. Johannesburg.

Urban Foundation 1980a. *Annual report 1979/80*. Johannesburg.

Urban Foundation 1980b. *Soweto*. A study by the Transvaal region of the Urban Foundation, Johannesburg.

Van den Berghe, P. L. 1966. Racial segregation in South Africa: degrees and kinds. *Cah. d'Etudes Afr.* **23**, no. 6.

Van der Merwe, P. J. and J. J. Stadler 1977. *Stedelike Swartes. Fokus op ekonomiese Kernvrae*, no. 19. Johannesburg: Mercabank.

Van der Horst, S. T. (ed.) 1976. *The Theron Commission Report*. Johannesburg: South African Institute of Race Relations.

Van Eeden, F. J. 1980. 'n Kritiese ontleding van die vordering met ontwikkelings-programme in die nasionale state. *Dev. Stud. Southern Afri.* **2**, 416–35.

Van Onselen, C. forthcoming. *New Babylon, new Ninevah: essays on the social and economic history of the Witwatersrand, 1886–1914*. London: Longman.

Venter, A. 1976. *'n Ekonomiese ondersoek na die behoefte aan behuising in Bantoedorpe met besondere verwysing na die rol van selfbouskemas*. Unpublished MA thesis, Univ. Pretoria.

Wallerstein, I. 1979. *The capitalist world-economy*. Cambridge and Paris: Cambridge University Press and Editions de la Maison des Sciences de l'Homme.

Webster, D. 1979a. *The political economy of survival: the unemployment crisis and informal income opportunities in Soweto*. Unpublished working paper, Univ. Witwatersrand.

Webster, D. 1979b. From peasant to proletarian: the development/underdevelopment debate in South Africa. *Africa Perspective* **13**, 1–15.

Wegelin, E. A. 1978 *Urban low-income housing and development*. Leiden: Nijhoff.

Weiss, R. 1975. The role of para-statals in South Africa's politico-economic system. In *The economic factor: foreign investment in South Africa*, J. Suckling, R. Weiss and D. Innes (eds), 55–91. London: Study Projects on External Investment in South Africa and Namibia.

Welsh, D. 1971. The growth of towns. In *The Oxford history of South Africa*, M. Wilson and L. M. Thompson (eds), vol. 2, 172–243. Oxford: Clarendon Press.

Western, J. 1978. Knowing one's place: 'the Coloured people' and the Group Areas Act in Cape Town. In *Humanistic orientations in geography*, D. Ley and M. Samuels (eds).

Western, J. 1981. *Outcast Cape Town*. Cape Town, Johannesburg and Pretoria: Human and Rousseau; London: George Allen & Unwin; Minneapolis: Minnesota University Press.

Whisson, M. G. 1971. The Coloured people. In *South Africa's minorities*, P. Randall (ed.), 46–77. Johannesburg: SPROCAS.

Whisson, M. G. 1972. *The fairest Cape?* Johannesburg: South African Institute of Race Relations.

Williams, J. C. 1971. Lesotho: economic implications of migrant labour. *S. Afr. J. Econ.* **39**, 149–78.

Williams, M. 1975. An analysis of South African capitalism – Neo-Ricardianism or Marxism? *Bull. Conf. Socialist Econ.* **4** (1), 1–38.

Williamson, P. 1977. Is there an urban informal sector or just poverty? *Yagl-Ambu* **4** (1), 5–24.

Wilson, F. 1971. Farming 1866–1966. In *Oxford history of South Africa*. Vol. 2: *South Africa 1870–1966*, M. Wilson and L. Thompson (eds), 104–71. Oxford: Clarendon Press.

Wilson, F. 1972a. *Labour in the South African gold mines 1911–1969*. Cambridge: Cambridge University Press.

Wilson, F. 1972b. *Migrant labour in South Africa*. Johannesburg: South African Council of Churches and SPROCAS.

Wilson, F. 1975a. Unresolved issues in the South African economy: labour. *S. Afr. J. Econ.* **43**, 516–46.

Wilson, F. 1975b. The political implications for Blacks of economic changes now taking place in Southern Africa. In *Change in contemporary South Africa*, L. Thompson and J. Butler (eds), 168–200. Berkeley: California University Press.

Wilson, F. 1976. *International migration in Southern Africa*. Univ. Cape Town, SALDRU Work. Pap. 1.

Wilson, F. 1979. The economics of rising expectations. *Race Relations News* August 1979. Johannesburg: South African Institute of Race Relations.

Wilsworth, M. 1979. Poverty and survival: the dynamics of redistribution and sharing in a Black South African township, *Social Dynamics* **5** (1), 14–25.

Wilsworth, M. 1980. *Strategies for survival: transcending the culture of poverty in a Black South African township*. Grahamstown: Rhodes Univ., Inst. Social Econ. Res., Occ. Pap. no. 24.

Wolpe, H. 1972. Capitalism and cheap labour-power in South Africa: from segregation to apartheid. *Economy and Society* **1**, 425–56.

Wolpe, H. 1974. The theory of internal colonialism: the South African case. *Bull. Conf. Socialist Econ.* **9**, Autumn, 1–12.

World Bank 1974. *Sites and services projects*. Washington DC.

Yap, L. Y. L. 1977. The attraction of the cities. *J. Dev. Econs* **4** (3), 239–63.

Contributors

K. S. O. Beavon. Keith Beavon is Professor of Human Geography and currently Head of the Department of Geography and Environmental Studies at the University of the Witwatersrand, Johannesburg. He has also taught at Rhodes University, the University College of Swansea and the University of Cape Town. His previous publications are mainly in the central place theory, including *Central place theory: a re-interpretation* (London: Longman 1977). Current research interests are in the general field of urban poverty and the informal sector.

J. J. Booysen. Jan J. Booysen is a researcher in the Department of Geography, University of Pretoria. He obtained the BA degree at the University of Stellenbosch in 1972. During 1973–5 he lectured in geography at the University of South Africa. He is currently doing research on labour migration and on the ethnicity of the Black population of South Africa.

John G. Browett. John Browett is Lecturer in the School of Social Studies, The Flinders University of South Australia. After postgraduate studies at Southern Illinois University he became a research fellow in the Urban and Regional Research Unit at the University of the Witwatersrand. His current research interests include theories of development, the restructuring of capital and its implications for regional inequality and public policy, and the process of economic development in South Africa. John Browett was an academic visitor to the Geography Department at Queen Mary College, University of London in autumn 1981.

Peter Corbett. Peter Corbett is Lecturer in Economics, University of Natal. Previously he worked at the University of Durban–Westville and at Rhodes University. He has undertaken a research project on Indian housing at Chatsworth, Durban, and is author of several publications on Indian housing. In 1980 Peter Corbett was elected to the Durban City Council and, as such, is a member of its Health and Housing Committee, Sub-Committee on Housing Policy and Sub-Committee on Self-help Housing. He represents the council on the Southern Durban Indian Local Affairs Committee and on the Steering Committee for a major research project on Indian housing undertaken by the Institute of Social and Economic Research at the University of Durban–Westville, sponsored by the Natal Town and Regional Planning Commission.

D. Dewar. David Dewar is Associate Professor in the Department of Urban and Regional Planning, University of Cape Town, Director of the Urban Problems Research Unit and a planning consultant. Current consulting work includes servicing low-income communities. He was born in Bulawayo, Rhodesia (now Zimbabwe), and attended the University of Cape Town, where he obtained the degrees of BA and Master of Urban and Regional Planning and recently completed a PhD on low-income housing policy in South Africa. He worked as a planner in the public service and private practice before joining the staff of the University of Cape Town in 1973. He has co-authored three books and written over 40 papers on issues of development and underdevelopment in Southern Africa. Professor Dewar was an academic visitor in the Department of Geography, Queen Mary College, London in 1980.

J. P. Lea.   John Lea is Senior Lecturer in the Department of Town and Country Planning at the University of Sydney. He was born in India and educated in the UK at Cambridge University and the Polytechnic of Central London. He is a Council Member of the African Studies Association of Australia and the Pacific and taught at the University of the Witwatersrand, Johannesburg, from 1969 to 1975. He undertook doctoral research in Swaziland in the early 1970s and has since conducted studies in Uganda, Zimbabwe and the Botswana–Lesotho–Swaziland countries. A visit was made to South Africa in 1980 to examine housing policy in the post-Soweto period.

Anthony Lemon.   Dr Lemon has been Fellow and Tutor in Geography at Mansfield College, Oxford University, since 1970. His research interests are in political geography, race relations and the regional geography of Southern Africa. He has held visiting lectureships at the University of Natal (Pietermaritzburg) in 1973 and 1975, the University of Zimbabwe (then Rhodesia) in 1977, and Rhodes University in 1979. In 1981 he was University Research Fellow at the Institute of Social and Economic Research, Rhodes University. His publications include *Apartheid: a geography of separation* (Farnborough: Saxon House 1976) and, with N. C. Pollock, *Studies in overseas settlement and population* (London: Longman 1980).

Gavin Maasdorp.   Professor Maasdorp is Director of the Economic Research Unit, University of Natal, Durban. He has worked extensively on urban problems in South Africa, notably the impact of the Group Areas Act and informal housing, and has a number of publications in these fields. He has also written on industrial decentralization, homeland development and international economic relationships in Southern Africa. He serves on various committees of the South African Institute of Race Relations and the Urban Foundation.

J. J. Olivier.   Jan Olivier is an urban geographer and Senior Lecturer at the University of Pretoria. He studied at the Universities of the Orange Free State and Natal (Durban). From 1969 to 1974 he lectured in geography at the University of Zululand and during 1975 at the University of South Africa. His main research interest is urbanization in the homelands, on which he is currently working for the completion of a PhD.

Eleanor Preston-Whyte.   Eleanor Preston-Whyte is Associate Professor in Social Anthropology in the Department of African Studies at the University of Natal, Durban. Her major research has been on Zulu women in the metropolitan area of Durban and in KwaZulu, where she has studied female migration and the adaptive strategies of Black women drawn to the city in search of employment. Her publications include studies of the nuances of racial interaction in domestic service in the city and also of Black family and kinship structures. Her current research is focused upon trading networks and the informal sector in rural KwaZulu. In addition to various papers on the topic of women in urban and rural areas she is co-author with W. J. Argyle of *Social system and tradition in Southern Africa* (Cape Town: Oxford University Press 1978).

Christian Rogerson.   Christian M. Rogerson is Lecturer in Human Geography at the University of the Witwatersrand, Johannesburg. Formerly, he was a lecturer at the University of Natal, Durban, and visiting lecturer at the University of Adelaide, South Australia. His research interests include industrialization in Southern Africa, studies of the informal sector in Johannesburg and Soweto, and underdevelopment in Namibia.

P. Smit.   Professor P. Smit is Vice-President of the Human Sciences Research Council in South Africa. He was previously in charge of the research programmes of the African Institute of South Africa, and Professor and Chairman of the Departments of Geography at the University of South Africa and the University of Pretoria. His main interests are population geography, development problems in Southern Africa and urbanization of the Black population of South Africa. He is author and co-author of a number of books and articles. Professor Smit held a visiting appointment in the Department of Geography, Queen Mary College, London in 1979.

David M. Smith.   David Smith is Professor and Head of the Department of Geography, Queen Mary College, University of London. He has held appointments in South Africa at the Universities of Natal, the Witwatersrand and Cape Town, as well as in a number of American and Australian universities. His research interests include industrial location, urban and regional development and international-comparative perspectives on inequality. His books include *Human geography: a welfare approach* (London: Edward Arnold 1977), *Where the grass is greener: living in an unequal world* (London: Penguin 1979) and *Industrial location: an economic geographical analysis* (New York: Wiley – 2nd edn 1981); he is also co-editor of *The dictionary of human geography* (Oxford: Blackwell 1981).

V. Watson.   Vanessa Watson works in the Urban Problems Research Unit at the University of Cape Town. She completed the BA in Geography at the University of Natal, Durban, in 1971. She taught in high school until 1974 and then took a Masters degree in Urban and Regional Planning at the University of Cape Town where she became a studio assistant–lecturer in 1977. She took the postgraduate Planning Diploma at the Architectural Association, London, in 1978–9. She then returned to Cape Town where she has been engaged in a major research project with David Dewar on the informal sector as well as producing working papers on planning and related issues.

John Western.   John Western is an Assistant Professor in the Department of Geography, Temple University, Philadelphia. He graduated from Oxford University, took a Masters degree at the University of Western Ontario, and then obtained his PhD at the University of California, Los Angeles. His teaching experience includes two years in Burundi, Central Africa. In 1974–6 he held a research scholarship at the Centre for Intergroup Studies, University of Cape Town. He has a number of publications on the Coloured population in Cape Town, most notably *Outcast Cape Town* (London: George Allen & Unwin 1982).

Index

Note: entries for place names are confined to matters of substance; incidental appearances in the text are omitted from the index.

Act of Union 14
African National Congress 23, 221
Afrikaans 218, 223
Afrikaners 11, 20, 21
agency 231–2
agriculture 13, 15, 17
Anglo-American Corporation 72, 75, 206–10, 212
Anglo-Boer war ('Boer war') 15, 16
apartheid, era of 20–3
applied geography 1, 231
armed attacks 222
Asians 2, 143
   see also Indians
Atlantis 38, 201

Babelegi 40, 55, 57
banning 23
Bantu 2
Bantu Administration Board 130
Bantu Homeland Citizens Act 88
Bantustans 51, 53, 54, 55, 57–9, 62, 121–3
   see also homelands
Black/Coloured relations 228–9
Black Community Development Act 104
Black (Urban Area) Consolidation Act 112–13, 125, 150, 204
black identity 2
Black Labour Act 124
'black spots' 22–3, 79, 97
Bloemfontein 56
Boer Republics 13–14
Boers 17
Bophuthatswana 4, 38–44, 57, 83, 102, 103, 202–3
border areas 31, 40, 54, 63
border industries 83
Botha, D. W., Prime Minister 1, 32
Botswana 71, 76, 79
British colonial government 11–13
British South Africa Company 14
building by-laws 188–9
building societies 204, 205
business community 198
Buthelezi, Chief 102

Cape Flats 36, 103–4, 221, 224
Cape Town 6, 8, 21, 32–8, 76, 127–38, 217–29
   see also Western Cape

capital accumulation 130
capital requirements in informal sector 159–60
capitalism 21, 25, 28–30, 31, 39, 45, 50, 108, 109, 111–12, 199
Cato Manor 147
central/local government relations 187
Central Mining Investment Corporation 210
Centre for Applied Social Sciences, University of Natal 212
Chamber of Mines 71–3, 75
Chatsworth 7, 185–93, 194
cheap black labour 21, 27–30, 36, 39, 41–3, 50–1, 62, 108–9, 232
church attendance 174, 175
Cillié Commission 218, 227
circuit of capital 29
Ciskei 69, 80, 83, 102, 104
class 25, 41, 45
Clermont 6, 147, 148–54, 155, 156–60
clothing industry 60, 61
clubs 174–5
coal mines 71, 74
colonial conquest, era of 10–14
Coloured labour preference area, of Western Cape 21, 26, 32, 67, 88, 92, 94, 124, 125
Coloureds 2, 6, 8, 21, 22, 124, 131–8, 143, 146, 164, 217–29
community councils 95, 104, 200
Community Development Act 218
community life 164, 172–3
commuting
   see frontier commuters, journey to work
compounds 65, 125, 169
consolidation of national territory 14
constellation, of Southern African states 52
constrained urbanization 44, 231
construction costs, in informal settlements 152–3
containment 21–2
crime 217
Crossroads 4, 35–7, 103–4, 128–30, 133–6, 137, 138, 205

De Beers 76
decentralization (of economic activity) 4, 22, 30–1, 47–63, 100–1, 110
defended space 113
dehumanization of labour 30

Department of Co-operation and Development 82, 161, 205, 214
Department of Community Development 161, 186, 205
dependent working 115, 121
diamonds 14–15, 65
disenfranchisement of blacks 23
disguised wage work 115
District Six 37, 220
divide and rule 25, 32, 228, 233
domestic service 6–7, 122, 164–5, 167–82
drinking cliques 176
Du Plessis Commission 78
Durban 6–7, 21, 143–63, 164–82, 183–97
Durban City Council 184, 185, 186–7
Durban–Pinetown region 53, 56, 59, 61
Dutch East India Company 10

economic indicators 27
education 122
Eiselon line 26, 94
Elsies River 217, 222–3
employment in informal sector 132–3, 137, 151–2, 158, 162
employment prospects, for blacks 30–2, 101
Environment Planning Act 47, 56–7, 59–63, 110
European immigrants 15–16
exclusionary industrialization 47–8, 52–3, 231
export subsidization 52–3

farm labour 77–8
filtering process 201
flower selling 115, 116, 117
foreign capital 48–50
foreign technology 49–50, 109
frontier commuters 5, 28, 64, 82–7, 96, 102–3, 232–3

gangs 173, 176, 178
Ga-Rankuwa 39, 41
Ghetto Act 185
Glen Gray Scheme 14
gold 14–15, 65, 72
Gordimer, Nadine 24
Grahamstown 11
Great Trek 12
Group Areas Act 7, 8, 22, 37, 86, 94, 112, 133, 146, 148, 184–5, 192, 194–6, 218–20, 226–9
growth points 55, 63
growth poles 49

hawkers 128, 156
  see also street traders
healing groups/sects 175
Heidereld 131, 133–6

high-technology industries 53
home ownership, for blacks 37–8, 44–5, 94, 95
  see also leasehold system, property rights
homelands 2, 5, 20, 22, 23, 25–6, 28–9, 39–44, 51, 67–8, 72, 79–81, 82–7, 90–105, 125, 152, 202, 232–3
  see also Bantustans
Household Subsistence Level 190
housing 4, 6–8, 32–8, 98–9, 125, 143, 183–97, 198–216
Housing Act 185
Housing Code 193, 197

ideology 8–9
Immigrants Regulation Act 18
immobilization of Black labour 110–11
import controls 48–9
import substitution 48
income, distribution of 27
income, in informal sector 151–2, 158–9, 162
independence, of homelands 39–44, 82
Indians 2, 7, 13, 21, 32–8, 116, 117, 146, 147–8, 152–4, 164, 183–97
Industrial and Commercial Workers Union 18
industrial change 4
industrial colour bar 52, 109–10
industrial reserve army 51
industrial system 46–53
industrialization 46–53, 94
inequality 26–7
influx control 21, 40, 44, 65–6, 90, 93–4, 125, 143, 232
informal housing settlements
  see spontaneous ('squatter') settlements
informal sector of economy 5–7, 35, 106–7, 111–23, 127, 155, 173, 179, 232, 234
  see also hawkers, self-help street traders
Institute of Social and Economic Research, Univ. of Durban–Westville 212
Isipingo Farm 147–8, 152–3

Johannesburg 5–6, 101, 107, 111–23, 200, 209, 221
  see also Pretoria–Witwatersrand–Vereeniging region, Witwatersrand

journey to work 166–7, 178, 179–81, 191

'Kaffir Wars' 11
Kane-Berman, John 2
Kenya 215–16
KeNyamazane 24
Khoi Khoi 11, 12
Khoi San 11
Khutsong 210–11
Kimberley 14, 16, 17, 65, 76

King William's Town 11, 87
Koornhof, Dr Piet (Minister of Co-operation and Development) 35, 130
Kruger, Jimmy 220
KwaMashu 82, 165–6
KwaZulu 42–3, 82, 83, 100, 102, 144, 148, 165

labour aristocracy 17, 20, 52
Labour Bureaux 21, 44, 66, 88, 94, 124
labour-coercive economy 53
labour shortages 11–14
Langa 224
leasehold system, for Blacks 95, 125, 143, 199, 204, 205
Leborva 83
Lesotho 71, 74, 76–7, 79, 80
locational preference matrix 54–5

Mabopane 39, 41, 86–7, 202
Malawi 68–9, 71–2, 79
Malukazi 152, 153
Manchester 219
Mangope, Chief 43, 103
manufacturing 17, 20, 110, 203, 208
    see also industrialization
Maputu 81
marginal occupation 111
'master–servant' relationships 176–8
Mdantsane 86, 102
mechanization, in mining 74–5
middle class, emergence of 4, 31–2, 38, 44–5, 88, 141, 207, 215
migrant labour 5, 16, 18, 28, 30, 51, 64, 67, 77, 78–83, 109, 125, 232
military–industrial complex 52
Mine Workers Union 74–5
mineral discovery, era of 14–17
mining 18–19, 65, 93
mining centres 15
Mitchells Plain 37–8, 131, 133–6, 201
Mossel Bay 227
motor vehicle industry 49
Mozambique 68, 71–2, 79, 81
Mozambique Convention 16, 81
multinational corporations 49, 109
multinationalism 2

Natal 12–13
National Building Research Institute 211, 214
National Housing Commission and Fund 186, 195, 200
National Party (Nationalists) 1, 20, 21, 185, 206
Native Laws Amendment Act 66, 77
Native Laws (Fagan) Commission 20
Native Recruiting Organization 18

Natives (Abolition of Passes and Co-ordination of Documents) Act 66–7, 124
Natives Land Act 18
Natives Trust and Land Act 18, 65, 66
Natives (Urban Areas) Act 19, 93–4, 218
Ndebele 41
Nelspruit 211
Newcastle 83
Newlands West 186
New Farm 147–8, 152–3
Nguni 11

Openheimer, Ernest 210
Oppenheimer, Harry 206, 209
Orange Free State 12, 13
overcrowding 192, 205
overspill 148–50

Pan African Congress 23
parastatal corporations 48
pass system 21–2, 44, 66
paternalism 177–8
peasantization 108–9
Pegging Act 185
Per Capita Poverty Indicator 190
petty-commodity production and trading 127–40
    see also informal sector
Phalaborwa 75
Phoenix 186, 189–90, 193–5
poor whites 17–18
population growth 15–16
population migration 15–16, 126, 146, 148–50
Population Registration Act 67
Port Elizabeth–Uitenhage 53, 56, 60
poverty 190–91
prayer groups 175, 176
pre-capitalist modes of production 19, 28–9, 108, 109
Pretoria 39–40, 42, 202–3
Pretoria–Witwatersrand–Vereeniging (P–W–V) region 21, 53, 57, 60, 101, 110
Prevention of Illegal Squatting Act 32, 66, 126
proletarianization 108–9
Promotion of Black Self-government Act 96
property rights 4, 28, 30–2, 41

racial terminology 2
Reagan, President 1
recreation facilities 172
rentals 152, 193–4, 201
rent boycott 194
research and development 109
reserves 18, 19, 28–9, 109
    see also Bantustans, homelands
resettlement 22–3, 97–8, 100
residential location theory 191

residential segregation 7, 164–82, 184
   see also Group Areas Act
restrictive classes, in sale of land 185
retailing 133
Richard's Bay 83
Riekert Commission 44, 51, 62, 87–8, 102,
   111, 125
riots 217, 221–9
Rosslyn 40
Rupert, Auton 140, 206

savings clubs 174
Section 10 rights, under Black (Urban Areas)
   Consolidation Act 22, 66–7, 87–8, 111,
   125, 150, 204
segregation, era of 17–20
self-help 36, 195, 203–6, 211, 213, 214–15
   see also informal sector, spontaneous settlement
separate development 2
Sharpeville massacre 1, 49, 208, 223
site-and-service schemes 144, 147, 160, 161,
   199, 204, 205
slum clearance 98, 186
Small, Adam 223
Small Business Development Bank and Corporation 6, 127, 139–42
Smuts 20, 66
social control 29, 217
social indicators 27
social networks 180
social stability 30–2
social structure and spatial form 230–1, 235
Sotho 203
South African Republic 13, 14, 15
Soweto 99, 125, 199, 204, 205, 210
Soweto riots 7, 31, 198
spatial division of labour 63
spatial industrial change 57–62
spontaneous ('squatter') settlements 4, 6, 24,
   32–6, 38, 41, 83, 103–4, 130–1, 143,
   147–54, 156, 160–3, 165, 191, 193, 198,
   200, 201, 232–3
   see also Crossroads
Stallard Commission 19
state, role of 25, 48–9, 203–6
Stellenbosch 227
Steyn, Justice 206
street traders 107–23, 133, 159
   see also informal sector, petty commodity
   production and trading
strikes 222
structure and agency 230
subcultures 164
sub-imperial expansion 52
sub-letting 192
sugar industry 77

suppression 23
Suzman, Helen 219
Swaziland 71

Tanzania 71
tenancy-at-will 152
tenure, in informal settlements 152
Theron Report 227
Tomlinson Commission 22, 54
trade unions 209
train friends 179–80, 234
Transkei 67, 69, 104
transportation, of commuters 86–7
Transvaal 12, 13
Trekboers 11
Tswana 39–41, 202
Turner school (of self-help housing) 35, 213

Umlazi 82, 96, 102, 165–6
underdevelopment 109
unemployment 30, 50, 62, 63, 106, 107–8,
   111, 126, 151
United Party 20
urban commitment 150–1
Urban Foundation 8, 31–2, 94–5, 205,
   206–11, 214
urban guerrilla warfare 220
Urban Problems Research Unit, Univ. of
   Cape Town 212

Verwoerd 20
voluntary association 173–6
Voortrekkers 12
Vrygrond 130–1, 133–6, 137, 138

wages 27, 72, 74, 77, 159
wage legislation 57
Western Cape 4, 6, 11, 32–8, 130, 201
   see also Coloured labour preference area
West Rand Administration Board 45, 113,
   200, 201
white-by-might policy 202
Wiehan Commission 44, 51, 62
Winterveld 41, 103, 202–3
Witbank 74
Witwatersrand 14, 15, 16, 19, 28, 60–1, 65,
   199, 200, 202
Witwatersrand Native Association (WINELA)
   16, 18
working class 138–9, 207
Wulpe, Harold 29

Xhosa 11

Zambia 71
Zimbabwe 14, 68–9
Zulu 203